The End of
International Adoption?

Families in Focus

Series Editors

Naomi R. Gerstel, University of Massachusetts, Amherst

Karen V. Hansen, Brandeis University

Rosanna Hertz, Wellesley College

Nazli Kibria, Boston University

Margaret K. Nelson, Middlebury College

The End of International Adoption?

An Unraveling Reproductive Market and the Politics of Healthy Babies

ESTYE FENTON

RUTGERS UNIVERSITY PRESS

NEW BRUNSWICK, CAMDEN, AND NEWARK,
NEW JERSEY, AND LONDON

Library of Congress Cataloging-in-Publication Data

Names: Fenton, Estye, author.
Title: The end of international adoption? : an unraveling reproductive market and the politics of healthy babies / Estye Fenton.
Description: New Brunswick : Rutgers University Press, [2019] | Includes bibliographical references and index.
Identifiers: LCCN 2018032221 | ISBN 9780813599687 (pbk.) | 9780813599694 (hardcover)
Subjects: LCSH: Intercountry adoption—United States.
Classification: LCC HV875.55 .F4625 2019 | DDC 362.734—dc23
LC record available at https://lccn.loc.gov/2018032221

A British Cataloging-in-Publication record for this book is available from the British Library.

∞ The paper used in this publication meets the requirements of the American National Standard for Information Sciences—Permanence of Paper for Printed Library Materials, ANSI Z39.48-1992.

www.rutgersuniversitypress.org

Manufactured in the United States of America

Contents

The End of
International Adoption?

Introduction

It was an idyllic fall afternoon when I pulled my car up outside Catherine's large historic inner-suburban home. Turning off of the main road, I slowed down as a group of boys grabbed their scooters and moved to the side of the street. I smiled and waved, wondering if one of those boys was Catherine's eight-year-old son, Tucker, whom she had adopted from Kazakhstan when he was nine months old. A successful, active, stylish fifty-four-year-old, Catherine had emailed me asking to participate in this project after hearing about it through her informal but close-knit single-mothers' support network. She welcomed me into her immaculate living room and pointed Tucker out to me through the front windows. Catherine had worked for many years in international development, earned a PhD, and more recently, worked at the helm of a series of large charitable organizations. We sat down to talk, and I asked her to tell me how she had made the decision to adopt from Kazakhstan. She told me about a close friend of hers who, as a single woman, had adopted two daughters from China. "She was my inspiration," Catherine explained, relating how she had always wanted to be a parent, even before becoming an "auntie" to her friend's daughters. Following the path her friend had taken, Catherine began the process of adopting from China without a sense of urgency. Soon after, though, her mother died. She told me, "I was really sad that my mom never got to see my child. So I wanted to accelerate the process; I had all my paperwork done, I thought I would be going to China, I thought I would be adopting a little girl. But then China instituted a quota on single women." The year was 2001, and Catherine had found herself enmeshed in the beginnings of the worldwide political and programmatic changes that would redefine international adoption in the United States over the next fifteen years.

Of course, Catherine didn't know that at the time. She explained to me that she simply "started looking into other countries" and heard about the international adoption program in Kazakhstan. "It seemed like a really good option," she said. "They had a very good orphanage system, the children were very well taken care of; I was concerned about having a special needs child," she explained, "being a single parent and working full time." Like so many of the well-resourced and highly educated mothers that I interviewed, Catherine knew the literature, popular and academic, on the negative effects of institutional care on internationally adopted children's physical, behavioral, and emotional health outcomes (for a review, see Fisher 2015; Misca 2014). Of course, Catherine wanted the best possible outcomes for her child. Catherine also knew the circumstances of everyday life that she would face upon her return—the expense and the scarcity of childcare, the demands of her professional life, and overall, the lack of support for mothers' caregiving work, particularly for special needs children.

Seamlessly, Catherine then began to tell me about "all the bumps in the road" that cropped up as she joined the Kazakhstan program. Initially, Catherine received a "referral"—a "match"—with a little girl (she had always thought she would adopt a girl). Following the advice of her adoption agency and the example of her friends who had adopted internationally, Catherine showed the girl's medical records to a pediatrician specializing in international adoption medicine. The pediatrician told Catherine that he suspected the girl had fetal alcohol syndrome and advised her not to accept the match. The advice placed Catherine in emotional limbo as well as in a practical bind; as she explained to me, "It was a weird thing with Kazakhstan, because you were not actually supposed to get a referral before you went; you were supposed to go there and pick from the children there in the orphanage. But the agencies were matching families with children as sort of an under-the-table thing." Nonetheless, Catherine traveled to Kazakhstan—only to find out that the girl initially referred to her was no longer available for adoption.

Once in Kazakhstan, Catherine was introduced to another little girl, a six-month-old infant. Catherine spent two weeks vising the baby multiple times a day, per the adoption program's policy. "You're bonding with them on their territory," which, as Catherine explained, she thought was good for the children and she "really liked." But this match was also troubled. As Catherine related to me, "I spent a week with this little girl, and then I was told that she was not available for adoption. In Kazakhstan, it's a Soviet system, so all the kids are supposed to be on this list that they're available for adoption for six months, but somehow, this little girl had never been put on the list. My agency never checked the list, and then it was probably a glitch at the orphanage. It was really devastating." Catherine spoke to the orphanage director, who told her that while there were no girls available for adoption at that time, there were three young boys. The director told Catherine that she could spend two days meeting the boys, but that at the end of those two days, she would have to select one of them to bring home. Faced with the alternative of leaving Kazakhstan in the hope of receiving a new referral for a baby girl, Catherine quickly accepted. As she explained to me, she was faced not only with emotional uncertainty but with political uncertainty as well. "At the time," she said, "the legislature in Kazakhstan was debating whether to shut down international adoption. The country had really become wealthier, and there was more domestic adoption happening. And of course, it's always the issue of whether you think you should have other people adopting kids from your country, as if it's like a point of pride." By then, the year was 2003, and many nations around the world were beginning to have more vigorous public debates about the future of their international adoption programs. Ultimately, at the end of that second day, Catherine was faced with the choice of which of the three young boys to adopt. She told me that she had "the most information on Tucker," who was also the youngest of the group: "And so that was how I decided. I knew he had been born full term. One little boy was a foundling, so they had no information on him. That was sort of it." Catherine made her decision based on the snippets of Tucker's health history that were available to her.

Catherine adopted Tucker right on the cusp of a sea change in international adoption policy and practice in the United States; over the last fifteen years, international adoption in the country has entered a new era. For several decades prior, international adoptions had been characterized by a ready supply of adoptable children, a lack of contact between adoptive parents and adopted children's biological kin, and relative bureaucratic ease. Throughout the first decade of the twenty-first century, however, international adoption became increasingly difficult for adoptive parents in the United States, as many systemic changes took place within both "sending nations"—the nations that send their children abroad in international adoptions—and the United States as a "receiving nation." Many sending nations closed their programs altogether, and regulations that restrict international adoption increased across the board. At the same time, intensely polarized disputes have arisen around international adoption as a commercial enterprise, the definition of children's "best interests," and the political and often nationalistic meanings that attach to the movement of "needy" children across national borders. Widespread evidence of fraud and corruption in international adoption programs around the world has also come to light, in part through adoptees and their adoptive parents sharing their stories, as well as through investigative journalism and critical social scientific research. This book investigates the experiences of a cohort of mothers who, like Catherine, adopted internationally amid this shift in practices, discourses, diplomatic relations, and reproductive politics. These mothers' stories provide a snapshot in time; because of when they entered into the process of international adoption, they were uniquely compelled to negotiate their desire to mother at a moment of growing societal awareness of international adoption as a flawed institution.

This book is about the ways that recent international adoptive mothers in the United States have navigated the unraveling of the marketplace and the shifting cultural logic of international adoption. These changes have compelled them to confront the complicated meanings attached to their reproductive and family lives. I start out by asking what happened to these mothers when they were swept up in a moment of change and what their experiences might illustrate about reproductive decision-making in a context of shrinking choice. I also ask how the ending of an era of relatively easy international adoption might inform the debates surrounding contemporary family life in our society more generally as well as the evolving, high-stakes reproductive politics that define so much of the contemporary United States. The context that frames these questions is rooted in multiple overlapping scholarly and public conversations. First of all, how and why was international adoption framed as good for children, good for families, and a civic good? How did this positive vision inform and shape the experiences of recent international adoptive mothers just as that vision was fracturing? Second, how does international adoption fit into the feminist debate around reproductive markets? The mothers I interviewed for this project were caught in the old double-bind of work and family life at the same time that they faced newly emerging controversies around international adoption—the way that they had elected, out of a universe of constrained choices, to bring children into their families. In this vein, it's worth asking how motherhood as an institution shapes the stories in this book. How might threads of compulsory motherhood run through these stories of navigating an unraveling reproductive market? The narratives at the heart of this book reflect our society's ongoing negotiation of the boundaries between love and money, between private caregiving and the public good, and between reproductive choice and reproductive justice.

International adoption began in post–World War II America as a response to war orphans in Europe and Korea. The historian Ellen Herman (2008) characterizes our view of international adoption as a "triumphal narrative" whereby U.S. parents, and the United States as a whole, function as benevolent actors that "save" children from desperate circumstances abroad while, at the same time, making the United States a more inclusive, multiracial, and multiethnic society. Spikes in the numbers of international adoptions in the United States have often followed cries for humanitarian aid in diplomacy and in the media—the end of the Vietnam war, the fall of the Soviet Union, reports of abandoned female infants due to China's one-child policy, political conflicts in Latin America, the AIDS epidemic in sub-Saharan Africa, and a handful of other political and natural disasters, including, more recently, the 2010 earthquake in Haiti. But despite these real crises, international adoptions in the United States have remained fundamentally demand-driven; war, poverty, and social dislocation alone do not cause U.S. parents to adopt children from overseas. Throughout the second half of the twentieth century, the number of international adoptions in the United States increased alongside some of the broadest and most basic changes in American family life: the entry of middle- and upper-middle-class women into elite professions, the delayed marriage and childbearing that followed, and the ramping-up of those delays—among women and men—that has accompanied the increasing instability of work life across the socioeconomic spectrum in a global, fluid, and precarious economy. As the century turned, demand for international adoption remained steady, while the supply of adoptable children became exceptionally volatile. Since the year 2000, one sending nation after another has shut down its international adoption program amid concerns over human rights abuses, corruption, and outright fraud; diplomatic disputes with the United States; or the political, social, and ethical implications of systematic migrations of children along traditional lines of global inequality. The debates that have emerged surrounding international adoption weave a complex web of internally contradictory concerns: preserving a child's cultural heritage by keeping him in his natal country, placing a child in a family rather than an institutional setting, protecting the rights of birth mothers in the face of unscrupulous adoption brokers, and balancing adoptive parents' desires for infants against more vigorous (and time-consuming) efforts toward family reunification. These debates, which I explore in detail in chapter 1, complicate a straightforward picture of international adoption as a humanitarian response to needy children and, more generally, as a public good.

INTERNATIONAL ADOPTION AS A REPRODUCTIVE MARKETPLACE

Feminist scholarship clearly places international adoption within the purview of reproductive markets, and much of the debate surrounding the politics and ethics of international adoption hinges on the ways in which it has operated as a commercial enterprise.[1] While our culture discourages thinking about having children as an economic activity, adoption has historically been rooted in the broader economic functions of the family. From the earliest days of colonial America, children would routinely be "placed out" and, practically speaking, adopted as apprentices or other types of household workers (Carp 2009; Herman 2008; Marsh and Ronner 1996; Zelizer 1985). But as our society's overall economic conditions shifted, children's economic and sentimental value changed as well. As their roles shifted from work to play and their economic contributions to their households decreased, our vision of childhood changed. Childhood came to be seen as a distinct stage of life best spent in protected exploration and education—and separate from economic production, commerce, and money. It is in this context that economic sociologist Viviana Zelizer argues that adoption as a social practice in the United States became emotionally rather than instrumentally driven.[2] Rather than adopting a child to benefit from his or her labor, Americans began adopting children out of a desire, as we might now say, "to parent a child."

But Zelizer also argues that during the late-nineteenth and early twentieth centuries, adoption in the United States became a uniquely commercial enterprise. The industrial economy and shifting views about the nature of childhood also led to a profound inequality in middle-class, working-class, and poor children's experiences of childhood (Mintz 2006). Governmental and nongovernmental social institutions cropped up in growing cities to care for the children orphaned and abandoned due to the social upheavals of urbanization and the industrial revolution. As the traditional social networks of preindustrial communities deteriorated and these institutions replaced them, money began to change hands in exchange for children. Ironically, perhaps, this exchange of money began to take place not only beside shifting ideologies about domesticity and the "pricelessness" of childhood but also alongside increasing bureaucratization and the involvement of professional social workers (Carp 2009; Herman 2010; Rothman 1989, 2005).

Viewed through a contemporary lens, adoption closely resembles other types of reproductive marketplaces, like those for egg and sperm "donation," gestational surrogacy, and fertility medicine more generally. Reproductive marketplaces—and adoption, in particular—occupy a complicated and internally contradictory social space. We are invested, culturally, in an idea of "family" and "the market" as separate spheres, but in the case of reproductive technology or adoption, family is created through the market. This can engender tremendous discomfort as adults of good conscience grapple with the practical, emotional, and ethical complexities of having their children through technology, commerce, and global inequality.[3] This contradiction is itself profoundly gendered; as Sharon Hays argues, motherhood specifically is "understood as more distant and more protected from market relationships than any other" aspect of family life (1996: 174). In this sense, reproductive markets rely on the gendered "altruism" and "care" woven into reproductive work. With respect to egg and sperm donation, several studies have argued that men see sperm donation as a job, while women see egg donation and surrogacy as altruistic endeavors in addition to potential sources of financial compensation (Almeling 2011; Becker 2000; Bertolli 2013; Nash 2014). In the context of gestational surrogacy, Heather Jacobson (2016) finds that surrogate mothers engage in tremendous amounts of work yet resist labeling it as such. Reproductive markets are also dependent upon the invisibility of reproductive work. With specific respect to adoption, Debora Spar and Anna Harrington voice what they understand to be a widely held view: "Most babies are clearly 'produced' outside the market—in the bedroom, for free, a product of love and not money. . . . Those who venture into the baby business, therefore, have good reason not to want to acknowledge the commercial side of their action" (2009: 43). In this light, surrogacy, egg donation, and, indeed, the role of birth mothers in international adoption can clearly be seen as a form of biolabor[4]—underpaid, donated, or simply invisible work that underpins a reproductive marketplace and that perpetuates the inequality inherent in that marketplace.

The international adoption marketplace also mimics markets for some of the most traditional forms of reproductive labor, such as domestic workers, nannies, and other types of childcare providers. The flows of genetic material (in the case of eggs and sperm), reproductive services (like surrogacy), and babies (in the case of adoption) from poorer women to richer women and from the Global South to the Global North follow the same routes as domestic and care workers like nannies and nurses from Asia, Latin America, and the Caribbean to the homes of affluent (and predominantly white) Americans (see, in particular, Glenn 1992, 2010; Hondagneu-Sotelo 2007; Parreñas 2001). This literature clearly frames reproductive labor and reproductive markets as sites of inequality and injustice, but the literature just as clearly reinforces the double-bind in which middle-class professional women, as employers of nannies and other domestic workers, often find themselves. Just as the outsourcing of cooking, cleaning, and childcare is a structural requirement of many women's professional lives, so, too, can these women enter into other kinds of reproductive markets due to delayed marriage and childbearing—a "labor-force induced infertility" (Briggs and Marre 2009: 17). Interestingly, though, the literature on transnational motherhood and stratified reproductive labor also shows us that mothering can be shared between mothers and nannies across national borders, where chains of caregivers enable multiple women's economic activity (Hondagneu-Sotelo 2007, among many others). In the case of many transnational mothers, the ironies of taking care of other women's children in order to support one's own do not corrupt motherhood so much as enable mothers' wage earning, thereby redefining traditionally gendered economic and family arrangements. Indeed, Zelizer's work beyond the specific history of adoption (2007, 2013) suggests that markets and money do not necessarily corrupt our social relationships but rather clarify their mechanics. This has inspired tremendous debate over the desirability—or even the ethical possibility—of consciously and openly applying a commercial structure to inherently stratified adoption transactions.

Our cultural tendency to separate commerce and care in the context of international adoption is even more challenged by the altruism built into the narrative of it as a public good. The parents I interviewed walked a fine line between a position of consumerism and an impulse toward altruism throughout their adoption processes. Interestingly, though, they also almost universally came to a broader, more nuanced, and more critical understanding of the tension between commerce and altruism in their own stories, as well as in international adoption as an institution. They spoke with a great deal of sensitivity about the confusion, contradictions, emotional turmoil, and ethical conundrums that cropped up in their adoption processes—largely, though surely not exclusively, because they entered into processes of international adoption just as programs were changing, norms were shifting, and the marketplace was, overall, shrinking and falling apart.

This meant that the parents I spoke with were forced, in one way or another, to confront, as Spar and Harrington put it, the "commercial side of their action" (2009: 43). Their forced awareness of this taboo—the overlap between money and love—disrupts a straightforward picture of an adoption marketplace in which adoptive parents remain shielded from messy truths by thick, intact layers of bureaucracy.

Motherhood, Markets, and "Choice"

With marketplaces come choices, and reproductive markets are no exception. In the context of motherhood, though, "choice" is a double-edged sword. In her study of single mothers "by choice," Rosanna Hertz (2006) uses the notion of compulsory motherhood[5] to explain the choices that single women make in order to become mothers. Hertz argues that in addition to broadening social norms surrounding single motherhood, new reproductive technologies and exponentially expanding choices in international adoption have rendered motherhood not more optional but, rather, all the more compulsory: "Compulsory motherhood has strengthened its hold as new reproductive technologies and the globalization of adoption have put children within every woman's reach" (2006: 5). The deepening of an ideology of compulsory motherhood is particularly apparent, Hertz argues, in the lives of single women who can now conceive children "naturally" without bearing the stigma of extramarital sexuality, thanks to a variety of reproductive technologies. Ultimately, Hertz suggests that the cultural sanctioning of single motherhood, lesbian mothers, and reproductive technologies themselves not only strengthens the cultural obligation for all women to be mothers but also reinforces the notion that motherhood remains a woman's most "natural" achievement. In this respect, Hertz echoes Angela Davis, who also argues that "motherhood lies just beyond the next technology. The consequence is an ideological compulsion toward a palpable goal: a child one creates either by one's own reproductive activity or via someone else's" (Davis 1993: 360). Here, Davis clearly articulates how contemporary reproductive technologies generate a range of reproductive "choices" and that a discourse of choice drives an ongoing ethos of compulsory motherhood for some women. In this sense, Davis also highlights the stratification upon which reproductive markets are built; medical technology and international adoption alike are certainly not within "every woman's reach."[6] Affluent women do not systematically sell their eggs to fertility clinics and poor women, in fact, lack access to assisted reproductive technologies (see, notably, Bell 2014; Wilson 2014). Wombs are not valued equally—the services of a gestational surrogate in India costs a fraction of what one might pay in the United States. And within the United States as well as globally, gestational surrogates are not the economic equals of the women who retain their services (Cahn 2009; Jacobson 2016; Markens 2007; Spar 2006; Twine 2011).

At the same time that a straightforward notion of compulsory motherhood glosses over the stratified nature of reproduction, it also negates women's experiences of pleasure and desire surrounding motherhood and mothering. Arlene Stein (1997) famously describes how, despite the goals of second-wave feminism, many women—including many lesbian women—never shook their "desire" to become mothers, which she primarily attributes to what she calls an "ethic of care." Other critiques of compulsory motherhood hinge on similar arguments about women's deeply felt desires for caring, interdependent relationships (see, notably, Chodorow 1978; Ruddick 1995). The literature on infertility in both historical and contemporary contexts suggests that women enter into reproductive marketplaces because of a combination of social compulsion and desire to mother for its own sake (Bell 2014; Cahn 2013; Marsh and Ronner 1996; May 1997; Wilson 2014). Yet again, in the context of new reproductive technologies, it often appears that a deep compulsion underlies that desire. Karey Harwood (2007) describes infertility treatment as a "treadmill," which keeps women coming back for one cycle of treatment after another, even when cycle after cycle has failed. This "fertility work" is deeply gendered; it is women, far more than their male partners, who take what are often extraordinary actions in pursuit of a pregnancy (Bertolli 2013). And even beyond the immediate pursuit of a pregnancy, Lauren Jade Martin (2010) describes women's pursuit of egg freezing as an exercise in "anticipatory infertility" and the mitigation of future risk. In this vein, Sarah Franklin (1995) argues that "choice" becomes a trap, while Michele Goodwin (2005) argues that any appearance of choice is "illusory." Indeed, the argument that an ethic of care can mitigate rather than strengthen the compulsory nature of motherhood relies on a presumption of choice.

The sociological literature on childbirth preferences, breastfeeding, and other types of embodied maternal decision-making further illustrate how this dialectic operates. These examples also illuminate how, as a result of fundamentally "forced" choices, motherhood can serve as a site of our societal emphasis on personal responsibility and personal "choice" in a neoliberal context.[7] Thus while all these technologies, from breast pumps to IVF, clearly create new *forms* of choices, they simultaneously create new forms of control over women's reproduction. And where compulsion goes, inequality follows; in her 2002 book *Beggars and Choosers: How the Politics of Choice Shapes Adoption, Abortion, and Welfare in the United States*, Rickie Solinger argues that our societal emphasis on reproductive "choices" not only subjects women to new forms of control but also turns women's reproductive lives into a consumer enterprise. While our choices are highly constrained, they exist in a stratified marketplace of options and alternatives. Ultimately, Solinger writes that "the contemporary language of choice promises dignity and reproductive autonomy to women with resources." But, she continues, "for women without, the language of choice is a taunt and a threat" (2002: 290; see also Hertz 2004). Motherhood, thanks to the discourse of "choice" surrounding it, can simultaneously be freely chosen and tightly controlled, "forcing" women into a stratified reproductive marketplace—for eggs, for sperm, for international adoption, or even just for an after-school nanny.

It is at this nexus of compulsion and choice—and of pleasure, desire, obligation, and responsibility—that the international adoptive mothers I interviewed for this project enter the picture. Their experiences illustrate how seemingly clashing understandings of motherhood—either as compulsory or as freely chosen—are in fact fused together, along with the inequality inherent in reproduction and reproductive markets. The women interviewed for this project also remind us that the reality of reproductive decision-making is for many mothers grounded in the more mundane (yet still deeply gendered) circumstances of everyday life, as they describe highly complex decision-making processes surrounding international adoption specifically and motherhood more generally. What drove these women to pursue and complete international adoption processes—to pursue motherhood—in the face of tremendous logistical, financial, emotional, and relational challenges is one of the more practical questions animating this research. How these mothers see themselves within the long arc bending toward reproductive justice is one of the more ideational ones. Broadly, these mothers' narratives illustrate the twenty-first-century decline and unraveling of international adoption as a reproductive marketplace, as well as the reproductive politics surrounding inequality, race, ethnicity, health, and disability wrapped up in the story of this decline. And the tangle of reproductive politics surrounding this "end" of international adoption is, like all reproductive politics, tethered to the puzzles and contradictions of our whole society's political moment.

A Note on Methods

The narratives that I present in this book are drawn from forty-three semistructured oral history interviews with mothers (and a few fathers) who adopted children internationally between 2004 and 2014. I conducted the vast majority of these interviews in the corridor between Boston and New York City. The women I interviewed were highly educated and, generally speaking, professionally active and successful. They were generally affluent, with a median annual income of over $100,000 for single parents and over $150,000 for married couples. A little more than half of the participants were married and a little fewer than half single. They were all white, though three of them had partners of color (none of whom participated in the interview process). In total, I spoke with six fathers—four together with their wives, one married heterosexual father without his wife present, and one gay-identified single father. One of the married women I interviewed was married to another woman, but she and the single father were the only LGBT-identified participants in the study. Overall, the parents I interviewed were more secular than religious and largely identified as politically liberal. They were, on the whole, affluent, well-educated, urban Northeasterners. More details about the characteristics of my sample and the interview process can be found in the methodological appendix.

The choice to write about adoptive parents in itself also deserves a qualification. Adoptive parents are one leg in a three-legged stool; social workers and adoption experts refer to the adoption "triad" made up of first families, adoptees, and adoptive families. Adoptees and, much more so, adoptive parents are already well represented in the sociological literature on international adoption, while birth mothers are essentially absent. When we do hear from birth mothers, it tends to be second- or thirdhand.[8] But I have chosen to turn to adoptive mothers again because of the ways that this cohort of mothers complicate reductive arguments about the ethics of international adoption and because of how their experiences may contribute to ongoing debates about the ethics and the future of reproductive marketplaces, what constitutes reproductive justice, and how reproductive politics shape our most intimate family relationships.

The Structure of This Book

In the next chapter, I present the evolving media coverage of international adoption both as a means of providing historical context for the adoption processes that my interviewees experienced and also as a framework for understanding their thinking on the politics and the ethics of international adoption. Much of this media attention has focused on the religious motivations of some adoptive parents, but the adoptive parents I interviewed were, with two notable exceptions, not religiously motivated. Rather, the parents I interviewed adopted children internationally out of a desire to parent, choosing international adoption from among the reproductive options available to them.

In chapter 2, I situate international adoption within the literature on reproductive markets and explore how adoptive parents understand themselves as participants in marketplace transactions. I argue that the parents I interviewed approached the adoption process as consumers and that because of their experiences in a shrinking and unraveling market, they developed an increasing awareness of the commercial nature of adoption. I question the existing literature on reproductive markets, insofar as it emphasizes the ways in which consumers of reproductive services and products do not see the commercial and highly stratified nature of the "baby business" (see, in particular, Ginsburg and Rapp 1995; Scheper-Hughes and Wacquant 2002; Spar 2006). In chapter 3, I explore in detail adoptive parents' decision-making processes with specific respect to the age, race, health, and disability status of their (future) children. I explore how parents' decision-making involves a delicate balance of preferences and concessions and reflects their aspirations and fears for their children's future lives. I relate this to the literature on racial formation, parental anxiety, and intensive mothering, and I argue that ongoing racial formation in the United States leads to fine-grained racial hierarchies in which children's perceived health and "fitness" contributes, at times in unexpected ways, to their racialization in their parents' minds.

In chapter 4, I present the stories of mothers who encountered—and often vigilantly sought to uncover—evidence of fraud and corruption in their children's adoptions. I also discuss the range of responses to fraud and corruption in my sample; while some parents sought to rationalize it, others experienced it as a deep betrayal of their children and of themselves. I argue that in the context of contemporary ideologies surrounding motherhood, adoptive mothers' encounters with fraud, corruption, and broader antiadoption sentiments create new and deeply gendered forms of emotion work and ideological work. In addition to managing the bulk of the day-to-day family work associated with adopting and caring for their children, the adoptive mothers in my sample faced the distinctly gendered work of reconciling their actions to prevailing ideologies about family, motherhood, and a triumphal narrative of international adoption.

In its heyday, international adoption represented a cheerful, optimistic modernism—a multiracial society that transcended colonial boundaries and hierarchies and embraced "brave new families." But ultimately, this project asks whether—or to what extent—the shrinking of international adoption in a postmodern, neoliberal context signals some kind of cultural reversal on those values. Our thinking about international adoption encompasses an internally contradictory tangle of interests and a jumble of polarized debates—about the nature of kinship, about women's agency and choice, about children's individual interests versus the agendas of the adults around them, and about the role of the United States in the world, at least when it comes to "saving" versus "stealing" children. The cohort of mothers whose stories I tell in the coming chapters captures a moment of change in the institutional structure of international adoption and may therefore shed light on the workings of some of these cultural contradictions.

CHAPTER 1

International Adoption in the Twenty-First Century

In 2004, the year that the number of international adoptions in the United States peaked, the *Cincinnati Enquirer* reported on two families, the Ingles and the Wallises, great friends who were about to move into custom-built homes on the same suburban street. The stay-at-home mothers had run a marathon together, and the fathers volunteered together at their church. Between them, they had twenty-two children, seven born to their parents and the other fifteen adopted through a combination of Ohio's foster care system, private domestic adoption, and international adoptions from South Africa and Ethiopia. There were financial and logistical struggles, moments of chaos and exhaustion, but Heather Ingle, one of the mothers, told the reporter with confidence, "I feel like I'm doing exactly what I'm supposed to be doing" (Johnston 2004). Almost ten years later, a story about international adoption on Fox News flashed across gyms, waiting rooms, and living rooms everywhere, about a Missouri family that adopted a sibling group of five older children from Peru. Children played happily in a large manicured yard while a reporter interviewed their parents. The mother described being "called" to adoption because it was "in her heart" to help orphans in need. The father discussed the pride and purpose that he felt in both providing for and having fought for his children. As the adoptive mother explained, "We got told 'no' a lot of times, and by then we were already crazy about these kids, so it was a rough part of the story. . . . And you had to keep trusting that we were fighting for something that you knew was yours to fight for . . . doing what God asks even when it seems crazy is worth it" (Tenney 2013).

Media coverage of Hollywood celebrities adopting kids from overseas has complemented this overwhelmingly positive spin. In 2005, ABC News claimed that American interest in adopting children from Ethiopia doubled in response to Angelina Jolie's adoption of her daughter Zahara (Good Morning America 2005). The *Huffington Post* called Jolie's and Brad Pitt's adoption of additional children a "race to keep their family more ethnically diverse than Madonna's"

(Matthews 2009). The phenomenon of celebrity adoptions is not new: in the late 1950s, jazz phenomenon Josephine Baker set out to adopt her own "Rainbow Tribe" and disrupt the ethnoracial order of the day. While *New York Magazine* claims that Baker started the trend of international celebrity adoption (Gaines 2009), neither Baker, nor Madonna, nor any other celebrity alone could have sparked the growth of international adoption in the late 1990s and early 2000s. Nonetheless, these celebrities have presided over the perceived triumph of international adoption as both a personal and a public good. Gail, a mother whom I interviewed for this project, recalled the triumphal mood in the first decade of the 2000s, when she began the process of adopting her daughter from Ethiopia, telling me, "Everybody was really celebrating international adoption at that point."

Equally celebratory but more complicated stories have also emerged. Writing in *Newsweek* in February 2013, National Public Radio host Steve Inskeep, himself an adoptee, shares the story of adopting his second daughter from China. Like many of the parents I interviewed for this project, Inskeep and his wife were thanked both for "saving" their daughter and for doing "a noble thing" (Inskeep 2013). And like several of the parents I interviewed for this project, Inskeep and his wife were also asked directly (by the taxi driver bringing them from their daughter's orphanage to their hotel) how much they paid for their new baby. Inskeep describes explaining to the taxi driver that, "according to Chinese documents," their daughter had been abandoned in a hospital hallway, needing surgery for a "common and correctable" heart murmur. At the same time that Inskeep rejects the notion that he purchased his child, he also rejects the notion that his actions were "noble," writing, "My younger daughter is one of my people. She is adopted like me. She is American like me, having arrived in this nation of immigrants. . . . We did not bring [her] home to save her or to change the world. We did it to add to our family, just as my parents did years ago. Our lives are richer for it."

In the same year that Inskeep wrote about his daughter's adoption, a CNN special investigation profiled a young woman named Tarikuwa Lemma. "When I was thirteen, I was sold," she said. The news piece explains that she and two sisters were adopted by a U.S. couple who were told that the girls' birth parents had died of AIDS. As Lemma explains, "The truth was that our mother had died as a result of complications during childbirth, and our father was alive and well" (Voigt 2013). CBS News also reported in 2010 on a separate set of three sisters, who alleged that their father had been paid by a U.S.-based adoption agency to place them for adoption in the United States (Keteyian 2010). In November 2017, CNN released an exclusive feature titled *Kids for Sale*, which was featured on their website, and was aired in prime time when Randi Kaye, the lead investigator, sat down to discuss widespread cases of financial corruption, fraud, and trafficking in international adoption programs across Africa with CNN anchor

Anderson Cooper (for the landing page displaying all the features of the investigation, see Kaye and Drash 2017).

The last thirty years of international adoption have been characterized by rapid program expansions, followed by temporary freezes and, often, indefinite shutdowns in one sending nation after another. This cycle began early in the history of international adoption, shortly after the Korean War, but the pattern solidified after the Cold War era, starting with Romania after the fall of the former Soviet Union. While the 1990s and early 2000s were a time of multiple disruptions to established international adoption programs, the number of international adoption in the United States grew overall. However, since the number of international adoptions to the United States peaked at 22,991 in 2004, the last fifteen years have been characterized by a series of indefinite closures to international adoption programs in both major and more minor sending nations, despite some smaller temporary "booms" in Ethiopia, Uganda, Liberia, and Haiti. The 2017 fiscal year saw the lowest number of international adoptions in the United States since 1973: 4,714 children were adopted internationally in 2017, a 79 percent decline from the 2004 peak (Bureau of Consular Affairs 2018). Moreover, in countries where international adoption remains open, the profile of adoptable children has shifted substantially, bureaucratic processes are far longer and more involved than they were fifteen years ago, there is far more emphasis placed on adopting children with special needs, and children are generally older. The average age of children at adoption has increased dramatically, and fewer than one in twenty international adoptees are currently adopted before the age of two, compared to 40 percent in 2004 (Bureau of Consular Affairs 2016). Today there is no international adoption program in existence that offers parents the opportunity to adopt infants.

In this chapter, I review the historical changes that shaped international adoption in the first part of the twenty-first century as well as the media coverage surrounding those changes in order to lay out the context of the bureaucratic circumstances, political shifts, and ethical debates that have defined our evolving cultural conversation about international adoption. The story in this chapter is about how many in the news media, with the help of critical scholarship in sociology, anthropology, and social work (see, notably, Briggs 2012; Briggs and Marre 2009; Dorow 2006; Dubinsky 2010; Leinaweaver 2008), worked diligently to uncover cross-national patterns of fraud, financial corruption, and the high costs and negative optics of both orphanages and large-scale out-migrations of children. The reporting on international adoption that I outline in this chapter changed our cultural conversation about international adoption and consequently set the stage for the stories that I tell in the coming chapters. It also provides the best data we have about patterned irregularities and structural changes across a variety of international adoption programs. I suggest that the contours of these patterns and the polarized ways that the media portrays them reflect broader cultural contradictions surrounding family life, child welfare, and reproductive politics.

Early History

International adoption in the United States originated in the context of post–World War II America, but its foundations are rooted in a longer history of adoption as a social practice and the evolution of that social practice in the modern United States. Informal but widespread adoption practices dating back to colonial America allowed for both the care of unparented children and the accommodation of childless couples. Children were often raised by adults other than their biological parents, usually by family members but sometimes by strangers. Both the "putting out" and the "taking in" of children was possible because "the household, and not so much the conjugal unit, constituted the colonial family." These arrangements depended on fluid, permeable boundaries, both between "family" and "community" as well as between "consanguine and non-consanguine families" (Carp 2009; Marsh and Ronner 1996). As the norms and practices of colonial America gave way in the nineteenth century, the same social, economic, and political forces that led to more nuclear family arrangements consequently hardened the boundaries between kin and nonkin. Simultaneously, as the conception of childhood itself began to shift with urbanization and the growing industrial economy, adoption became more organized. Viviana Zelizer (1985) famously characterizes the changing nature of adoption as a shift from the "instrumental" placement of children in foster families and apprenticeships to the "emotional" adoption of children as one's "own." Indeed, the term *adoption* itself was not used to describe the forging of family ties until the second decade of the nineteenth century.

At the turn of the twentieth century, adoption also became far more bureaucratized alongside new forms of social policy and governmental oversight, as well as the emergence of the social work profession during the Progressive era (Carp 2009; Marsh and Ronner 1996; May 1997). The first formal adoption code in the United States was a Massachusetts law passed in 1851, far more concerned with inheritance than the emotional aspects of kinship per se. Indeed, the formalization of adoptions remained uneven until well into the twentieth century; despite the passage of adoption laws across the country, it was uncommon for Americans to use them until the structure of the newly minted Social Security system, beginning in the 1930s, created material incentives to do so (Herman 2008; also see Marsh and Ronner 1996). The Massachusetts law, which would become the model for adoption laws across the United States, nonetheless "reflected Americans' new conceptions of childhood and parenthood by emphasizing the welfare of the child" (Carp 2009: 6). The demand for infant adoptions in the first decades of the twentieth century far outpaced the availability of adoptable children; Zelizer cites a 1937 headline in the *New York Times* that declares, "The Baby Market Is Booming" (1985: 192). The article, however, elaborates that the adopted child "needs protection as never before . . . [because] too many hands are snatching it." Indeed, the history of adoption has long been intertwined with fears of baby snatching, baby selling, "bad" mothers, and "good" mothers being wronged. As Zelizer (1985) illustrates, stories about adoption have long been a staple of the press, which magnifies and distorts our cultural anxiety surrounding kinship and motherhood more generally. At the same time, money has been a part of adoption since the very beginning. In the modern (and postmodern) contexts, market dynamics and marketplace analogies are interwoven with the concern for child welfare that has characterized the formalization and bureaucratization of American adoptions throughout the twentieth century.

INTERNATIONAL ADOPTION AS A NATIONAL PROJECT

As the United States emerged from the Second World War, Americans grew to see their role in the world, from rebuilding Europe to "fighting communism," as generous and benevolent. The emergence of this worldview coincided with the ongoing assimilation of the children and grandchildren of European immigrants, thanks in no small measure to the postwar economic boom. It was in this economic, cultural, and diplomatic context that both the United States as a nation and Americans as individuals came to see the breaking down of (white) ethnic barriers and a role for themselves in the international adoption of children. It was the children fathered by American servicemen in Europe, Japan, and Korea who initially generated the most interest and pity; reports of the mistreatment of mixed-race children—particularly the children of African American service members—filled the pages of the American popular press (Herman 2008: 216). At the time, military families stationed in Europe were able to adopt local children through a military screening process, avoiding both U.S. and European national authorities, but the trend quickly spread to nonmilitary families. Initiated by an emergency directive by President Truman in 1945, international adoptions of "eligible children from war-torn countries" proceeded with relatively little regulation and oversight until 1962. In the context of postwar America, "citizens' desires"[1] for children in the context of the nuclear family and the era's particular cult of domesticity coincided with contemporary views on America's particular role in the modern, modernizing world (see also May 2008).

International adoption and transracial domestic adoption took on important symbolic value within the ideologies surrounding American kinship in the late 1950s and early 1960s as the first wave of Korean children joined American parents and as the first organized efforts to promote transracial domestic adoption materialized in the mid-to-late 1960s. The humanitarian motivations behind the first postwar international adoptions reanimated a "rhetoric of rescue and religious fervor" (Herman 2008: 217) that had characterized the placement of orphans throughout the nineteenth and early twentieth centuries. This supported the "triumphal narrative" that has characterized international adoption as a statement of altruism, of America's political-economic and moral superiority, and of cultural openness, inclusivity, and diversity both within individual families and within U.S. foreign policy. International and domestic transracial adoption has, in this sense, come to reflect "a longed-for symbol of national progress" toward a pluralistic, inclusive, and multicultural society (Herman 2008: 288). A triumphal narrative not only naturalizes international adoption as a way of forming kinship ties but also allows international adoption to proceed as a widespread and relatively uncontested practice precisely because it reinforces broader ideologies of American citizenship.

This triumphal ideology was clearly at work in one of the most notable child-relocation operations of the twentieth century: Operation Peter Pan, in which more than ten thousand child refugees from Cuba—called "political orphans" in the media at the time—were placed in foster care in the United States throughout the early 1960s. The Cuban Revolution, having ushered in a new phase of Cold War rhetoric, set the stage for the media reports that described "saving" these children from "Castro's brainwashing" (Dubinsky 2010: 32). Publications by the U.S. Department of State, the Catholic Church, and other organizations described both the importance and the ease of these children's adjustment to American cultural and political values.[2] While Operation Peter Pan was framed as a fostering program and not, strictly speaking, as an international adoption program, it provides an instructive example of the triumphal narrative that underlies U.S. involvement in international adoption. Further, the rhetoric surrounding this program and the cycle of international adoption programs' openings and closures illustrates the relationship between U.S. diplomacy and international adoption.

This is not only true from the perspective of the United States. International political and diplomatic bodies have long sought to regulate international adoption. The 1993 Hague Convention on Protection of Children and Co-operation in Respect of Intercountry Adoption called for the application of international standards to prevent fraud, corruption, and abuse within international adoption. The Hague convention emphasizes children's rights to live in families, rather than institutions, seeking "to ensure that intercountry adoptions are made in the best interests of the child and with respect for his or her fundamental rights, and to prevent the abduction, the sale of, or traffic in children." In its primary objectives, the Hague convention calls for the establishment of a centralized authority to handle international adoptions in both sending and receiving nations and for nations' central authorities to cooperate fully and transparently with one another. The

United States, an initial signatory, did not officially ratify the Hague convention until 2007.

In December 2012, Russian president Vladimir Putin signed a bill permanently banning Americans from adopting Russian children, claiming retaliation against a U.S. law that sanctioned Russian officials for accused human rights violations (Flintoff 2012; Lipman 2012; Voigt and Brown 2013). Masha Lipman, writing in the *New Yorker*, quotes one of the Russian lawmakers instrumental in the ban's initiation, who was asked by a Russian reporter if she thought Russian orphans would be better off in Russian orphanages than in U.S. families. The lawmaker responded, "This is not the point. You're asking a wrong question. . . . Normally economically developed countries don't give up their children, not a single one of them. I am a Russian patriot" (Lipman 2012). But at that time, Russia was still "giving up" their children to Sweden, France, and Germany; the bill solely halted adoptions to the United States. When Putin held a press conference upon signing the adoption ban, a reporter asked him to comment on the notion that the ban was "excessive." Putin, in a direct reference to the United States' "humiliation" of Russia, responded, "Do you enjoy being humiliated? Are you a sadomasochist?" (Lipman 2012). The U.S. Department of State, as reported in the *New York Times*, "strongly criticized" the ban; as one State Department spokesman said, "We have repeatedly made clear, both in private and in public, our deep concerns about the bill passed by the Russian Parliament" (Herszenhorn and Eckholm 2012). Nobody in the U.S. State Department questioned the legitimacy of the abandonment of Russian children, nor were reports of a "gray market" at all operative in Russia's decision to end adoptions with the United States. The Russian adoption ban provides a clear case of baldly diplomatic and nationalistic motivations, including the blatant suggestion that the best interests of children are far *less* important than nationalistic concerns.

Russia had also temporarily suspended international adoptions in 2007 when—along with multiple other countries, including China and the United States—they began to shift their practices toward compliance with the Hague convention. After 2007, the numbers of international adoptions from Russia and China—the two leading sending nations to the United States at that time—declined as adoptive families began to face longer processes and additional paperwork. These slowdowns, which ultimately became the norm for the international adoption program in China, were wholly bureaucratic in nature and driven by the organized implementation of new policies rather than by the kinds of scandals that rocked Guatemala, Vietnam, Cambodia, and other nations. At the time of these slowdowns, journalist and adoption advocate Adam Pertman was quoted in the *New York Times*, explaining, "What is happening in Russia is part of a fundamental restructuring of international adoption across several countries" (Clemetson 2007a).

In May 2007, China instituted new and far more stringent regulations governing the eligibility of foreign adoptive parents. The new rules initially prohibited single people and those over the age of fifty from adopting. In 2011, China revised the restrictions, allowing single women to adopt children with special needs if the women sign an affidavit stating that they are not homosexual. The 2007 regulations also bar adoptive parents with a body mass index of more than forty (about 230 lbs. for a 5′4″ woman or 275 lbs. for a 5′10″ man) and those who have taken antidepressants or other psychiatric drugs. There are additional regulations related to the length of a couple's marriage, the marital history of the partners, and adoptive parents' income and assets (Katz 2006; Voigt and Brown 2013). As reported by CNN, a Chinese government spokeswoman explained that "the new rules were necessary to protect 'the best interests of children' as foreign demand for children outstripped the supply of orphans. . . . The rules ensure adopters 'are able to offer the Chinese children adopted the best possible environment to grow in'" (Voigt and Brown 2013). While there have been reports of baby-buying scandals in China that surfaced in the mainstream U.S. media (notably by Charlie Custer [2013], writing in the *Atlantic*), these reports have neither gained the same traction nor had the same impact as they have in other cases of sending nations.

Some of the clearest insight into international adoption from the Chinese perspective has come from the academic literature (for a full history, see Choy 2013). Dorow's investigation of the marketplace dynamics in U.S.-China adoptions reveals how Chinese adoption policies facilitate international adoption through a discourse of "clienthood," which serves the interests, both practical and emotional, of U.S. adoptive parents as consumers. Dorow argues that this also serves the broader interest of U.S.-China economic relations because "clienthood as a discourse is perpetually reproductive of modernity for China, [and] of the political economy of adoption" (2006: 124). Kay Ann Johnson (2016) offers a vivid and detailed account of the ways that the Chinese authorities and Chinese society more generally have responded to the "out-of-plan" children—the second and third children born to parents under China's one-child policy. Johnson argues that popular efforts to hide or traffic these children became central to the Chinese government's response to the country's international adoption program. Chinese adoption programs have outwardly espoused a "best interests of children" discourse, unlike the turn to nationalistic political discourse in Russia. Chinese adoption regulations can be seen as driven by a similar, if softer, nationalism, though, by carefully curating China's image while simultaneously placing restrictions on potential U.S. adoptive parents that directly judge their "fitness" as parents and as citizens.

Similarly, in her ethnography on child circulation—both local and international—in Andean Peru, Jessaca Leinaweaver describes the ways that nationalistic ideas can meld with child welfare discourse and take unexpected shapes in the context of international adoption. She frames international adoption in Peru within the context of centuries-old indigenous systems of child circulation and their contemporary expressions in a context of rural-to-urban migration, high unemployment, and the precariousness engendered by neoliberal economic policies. Casting Peru's participation in international adoption as only one part of a larger system of child circulation, she explains that in the 1990s, in the wake of decades of violence, "poverty intensified as neoliberal policies took hold, and revisions in family and adoption law—based proudly in international treaties, legislating Peru as a modern and internationally aware nation—reshaped poor and indigenous Peruvian families" (2008: 158). Referring to the procedural requirements of these treaties, Leinaweaver continues, "It's worth asking why the neoliberal state would want to take on the burden of additional children to care for. Why do the courts go to such lengths to . . . [produce] more wards of the state? The answer, I suggest, lies partly in a co-optation of the 'best interest of the child' standpoint so widely accepted in the international sphere" (2008: 158–159). Leinaweaver argues that this is how Peru "perform[s] itself" as a modern nation on the global stage (2008: 159). If Peru performs as a modern nation with modern Euro-American, "enlightened" social work practices, then the United States no longer plays the role of an exclusively enlightened savior-nation. The near-universal acceptance of the "best interest of the child" standpoint along with contemporary standards of practice in social work both illustrate the dynamism of the diplomatic relationships that underscore international adoption programs and disrupt the triumphal narrative in which the United States is so invested.

Following the collapse of the Soviet Union, Americans were outraged by media coverage of the deplorable living conditions in Romanian orphanages, first exposed on ABC's *20/20* special "Shame of a Nation." As Tara Bahrampour (2014) wrote in the *Washington Post* almost twenty-five years later, "News organizations across the world presented Romania's orphanages as a symbol of a decayed empire"—and, consequently, as a symbol of American triumphalism at the close of the Cold War. As the Soviet Union fell and the United States adjusted its self-image to meet a new global political reality, international adoption from Romania functioned as a site of that reinvention. In the news coverage of Romanian orphanages, Americans perceived a real crisis and a real affront to their values. Birth control had been banned in Romania as women were exhorted to produce new workers for the nation. When abandoned children, many disabled, ended up in orphanages, Americans' Cold War fervor was reinvigorated, and many flocked to "save" Romanian orphans. Adam Pertman, *Boston Globe* journalist and adoption advocate, called the rush to adopt from Romania "a wildfire."

In the chaos of Romania's regime change, many children found themselves unparented at a time when there was almost no regulation or oversight of international adoptions. Writing in *Foreign Affairs* in 2003, Ethan Kapstein explains,

"Changes in economic and social policies determined the sources of supply. With the end of the Cold War, market-driven economics were ushered into Central and Eastern Europe, causing the collapse of communist-era welfare systems and a surge in the number of abandoned children. Romania, for example, had allowed only 30 intercountry adoptions in 1989; in the year after the fall of Nicolae Ceausescu, it let more than 10,000 children leave the country." Indeed, more than 2,500 Romanian children came to the United States in 1991, a far higher number than in any year since (see Hamilton 2014 and Sullivan 2012 for additional journalistic coverage of Romanian adoptions). But in 2001, Romania shut down international adoptions for good, claiming to be responding to reports of irregularities at all stages of Romanian adoption processes. Elizabeth Bartholet, a Harvard law professor and strong proponent of international adoption, characterized the Romanian shutdown as wholly disconnected from concerns over child welfare or the conditions in orphanages, suggesting that it was initially triggered by what she calls a very limited baby-buying scandal. She alleges that "opponents of international adoption took advantage of this scandal to call for a moratorium on international adoption [in Romania] pending 'reform' of the adoption system. While efforts to enforce rules against baby buying are appropriate, these so-called reform moves in Romania resulted in denying adoptive homes on an on-going basis to thousands of children abandoned in institutions" (2005: 111). But the Romanians, like the Russians speaking to the news media and like the Peruvian officials in Leineweaver's ethnography, were also acting out of the embarrassment that flowed from both allegations of corruption and the widespread out-migration of children. Writing about the frenzy on the American side to adopt children from Romanian orphanages and about the shutdown that followed, Ana Ortiz and Laura Briggs suggest that the debates surrounding international adoption, broadly speaking, constitute an encounter with "powerful contradictions that lay bare cultural logics [and] identify the diverse stakeholders in social conflicts" (2003: 39). In this sense, debates about international adoption become a powerful way for children and child welfare discourse to signal the desires, aspirations, and interests of the state.

Making a Sending Nation

In 1996, following the end of a decades-long armed internal conflict, Guatemala surfaced as a willing and convenient sending nation for international adoptions, particularly to the United States. Throughout the late 1990s and early 2000s, adoptions in Guatemala were largely unregulated and relied on independent networks of foster mothers, doctors, and lawyers who enjoyed an almost total lack of governmental oversight. Guatemala ratified the Hague convention in 2002, temporarily freezing adoptions until the Constitutional Court of Guatemala reversed the country's course on the convention's implementation. While there was some ongoing tension between Guatemalan authorities and the U.S. Department of State over the Hague convention between 2003 and 2007 (see Clemetson 2007b), Guatemalan adoptions to the United States continued at a brisk pace during those years, ultimately peaking at more than 4,500 adoptions in 2007. Between 1997 and 2004, 79 percent of all adoptions in Guatemala were to the United States. After 2004, Europe and Canada pulled out of international adoptions with Guatemala, and the proportion of U.S. adoptive parents rose to 93 percent in 2004 and reached at least 99 percent by 2007 (for an overview of this history, see Dubinsky 2010; Selman 2009a). The sheer scale of Guatemala's international adoption program was massive; a 2006 Associated Press article claimed that "today every 100th baby born in Guatemala grows up as an adopted American" (Llorca 2006). And this was big business: by the early 2000s, U.S. parents were paying up to forty thousand dollars for a transaction that, according to calculations by a coalition of NGOs, actually cost about four thousand dollars (Dubinsky 2010: 108). At these margins, plus thousands of annual adoptive parents' tourist dollars spent on hotel rooms, restaurant meals, taxis, and souvenir handicrafts, international adoption was playing a serious role in the Guatemalan economy. In a case study of international adoption in Guatemala, Karen Dubinsky interviews a North American expatriate hotel owner in Guatemala who tells her, "If they shut down the adoption system, it will be like closing an auto plant" (2010: 108).

As adoptions from Guatemala were booming in the early 2000s, some of the first journalistic investigations of Guatemalan adoptions began to emerge. Writing in *Foreign Affairs* in 2003, Kapstein cites a 2000 U.N. report that links Guatemalan adoptions to "a variety of criminal offences, including the buying and selling of children, the falsifying of documents, the kidnapping of children, and the [improper] housing of babies awaiting private adoption." Peter Selman, writing in *Foreign Policy* in 2007, calls international adoption in general "a growing for-profit trade" and singles Guatemala out as a particularly egregious example of "baby buying." E. J. Graff, head of the Schuster Institute for Investigative Journalism at Brandeis University and a specialist in international adoption, describes Guatemala as having "the world's most notorious record of corruption in foreign adoption" (2008: 63). In February 2007, more mainstream media began to sound alarm bells, with the *New York Times* reporting that the U.S. Department of State "cautioned" parents interested in adopting from Guatemala that the situation was "volatile and unpredictable" (Lacey 2007a). But the *Times* article issues a distinct warning to U.S. adoptive parents to be careful rather than an indictment of the structural issues in Guatemala (and around the world)— war, poverty, corruption, legal impunity—that led to volatility in the adoption system.

At the same time, stories about U.S. adoptive families facing this uncertainty and grappling with its implications began to emerge. Writing in the *New York*

Times Magazine in October 2007, Maggie Jones, a contributing writer and mother of a daughter adopted from Guatemala, explains that she initially sought an open adoption because she was sensitive to the kinds of questions and emotions that could emerge around identity for adopted children. She writes that "before we went to Guatemala to adopt our daughter Lucia, we told our agency we hoped to meet her Guatemalan mother. But it was never clear that she was given the option of meeting us." Jones goes on to describe hers and several other adoptive mothers' stories of searching for their children's birth mothers in Guatemala, though her predominant concern is for the identity formation and peace of mind of the adopted children she profiles. In a similar vein, journalist Elizabeth Larsen shares her story of searching for her daughter's Guatemalan birth mother in the December 2007 issue of *Mother Jones* magazine, but unlike Jones in the *Times Magazine* article, Larsen dives directly into the ethical issues surrounding the systemic movement of children from poor women to relatively wealthy ones. Jones, at the end of her piece, settles into the uncertainty that accompanied not being able to locate her daughter's birth mother, while Larsen frames her article with the ethical uncertainty that she encountered in the project of international adoption as a whole. Larsen furthermore calls for greater journalistic attention to the issues of corruption, fraud, and abuse within international adoption.

In response to tremendous international pressure from the European Union, the United Nations, and a number of NGOs, as well as in response to its own wounded national pride, Guatemala passed a comprehensive adoption reform law in December 2007. This law reaffirmed Guatemala's commitment to the Hague convention, created a centralized national adoption authority, and effectively halted international adoptions. The law went into full effect on July 13, 2010, and negotiations between Guatemala and the United States about both pending and future adoptions have been ongoing since then. Years later, many cases remain unresolved, and new cases of fraud have emerged. In 2009, the Associated Press reported that the Guatemalan government officially acknowledged that children whose parents were murdered during the decades-long armed internal conflict that ended in 1996 had been adopted, many by U.S. families (Llorca 2009a). Additionally, in the several years that followed the passage of Guatemala's adoption reform law, several cases of outright kidnapping were documented and resolved. In 2008, a Guatemalan woman, Ana Escobar, was kidnapped at gunpoint along with her infant daughter. Thanks to DNA testing, which was always required but received additional scrutiny after December 2007, the two were reunited (Grainger 2009; Llorca 2009b). The Associated Press reported that a California couple, suspecting that their daughter's adoption was fraudulent, spent months in Guatemala, ultimately prompting a criminal investigation into the adoption brokers responsible for their adopted daughter's paperwork. Their daughter was reunited with her birth parents, from whom she had been stolen (Llorca 2008). In August 2011, a Guatemalan judge ordered the return of a six-year-old girl, adopted by a family in the United States, to her birth mother in Guatemala, who had argued for years that her daughter was stolen. Nine Guatemalans, including a judge, were indicted in the girl's kidnapping, but the order to return the girl to her birth mother was unenforceable in the United States, and the girl's U.S. adoptive parents have remained silent on the matter (Kirpalani and Ng 2011; Romo 2011).

Mary Anastasia O'Grady, writing in 2014 for the *Wall Street Journal*, has profiled the children "left behind" in orphanages and foster care placements since the shutdown of international adoption, and the end of Guatemalan adoptions has provoked the question of what has "happened" to the four thousand children a year who have not been adopted from the country since. About eighteen months after the final shutdown of international adoptions there, I was able to spend some time with a group of Mayan midwives and one of their North American colleagues. Just before I left, a baby was born in their birth center, about a month premature, with a club foot and several missing fingers. The mother was very young and unmarried; she had been abandoned by her own father because of her pregnancy, and her mother had died unexpectedly a few months earlier. The baby's mother had always known that she didn't have the resources to take care of her child. When the baby was born with complications, the mother asked the midwives if she could place her child in an orphanage so that he might be adopted by a family in the United States. Because of what might be considered a minor, correctable, or even largely preventable birth abnormality, a community's informal adoption network could not absorb this baby, whose needs would create financial hardship for the family that might have taken him in. This mother's story fits the way that feminist sociologist and adoption scholar Laura Briggs has called Guatemala "*the* essential precursor to any kind of massive intercountry adoption program," depending on "war or economic upheaval that so tears the social fabric that those who wish to raise their children cannot, and those who do not wish to raise their children cannot find help or friends or family who can take them in" (2012: 10). The growth of Guatemala's international adoption program depended directly on the profound social dislocation of Guatemala's poorest citizens, coupled with an absence of civil society—"a culture of impunity about crime from the mundane to the catastrophic, and a breakdown of community and trust" (Dubinsky 2010: 110) at all strata of society, including among the doctors, lawyers, judges, and other administrative professionals who brokered adoptions.

While Guatemala presents a clear-cut example and scholars have described it as a quintessential case, the conditions that create sending nations cut across specific national contexts. Investigative journalist E. J. Graff, writing in 2014, identifies Cambodia as the case that initially caught the attention of the U.S. Department of State, setting them on the course that led to investigations in Vietnam, Nepal, Ethiopia, Haiti, the Democratic Republic of the Congo, and a handful of other nations. Graff argues that a distinct pattern emerged in these countries, in which babies were "'produced' by unscrupulous middlemen who would persuade desperately poor, uneducated, often illiterate villagers whose culture had no concept of permanently severing biological ties to send their children away—saying that wealthy Westerners would educate their children and send them home at age 18, or would send a monthly stipend, or some other culturally comprehensible fostering plan." Likewise, when the U.S. Department of State froze adoptions in Nepal in 2010, they based their decision on similar reports. Graff goes on to suggest that there are important lessons to be gleaned from the "anatomy" of the Vietnamese case: "The State Department was confident it had discovered systemic nationwide corruption in Vietnam—a network of adoption agency representatives, village officials, orphanage directors, nurses, hospital administrators, police officers, and government officials who were profiting by paying for, defrauding, coercing, or even simply stealing Vietnamese children from their families to sell them to unsuspecting Americans" (2010b).

The history of U.S. adoptions in Vietnam has its roots in the end of the Vietnam War,[3] but the number of international adoptions from Vietnam climbed along with the overall increase in international adoptions throughout the 1990s and early 2000s. In 2007, Brad Pitt and Angelina Jolie famously adopted their son, Pax, from Vietnam. In 2008, the United States began investigating international adoptions in Vietnam due to widespread reports of corruption, fraud, and outright trafficking in babies. In what some journalists describe as a diplomatic "tit for tat," Vietnam ultimately shut down international adoptions within a year of these allegations surfacing (Boudreau 2014). As the *New York Times* reported at the time of the shutdown, "An investigation by the American embassy found many cases in which mostly poor birth parents had been paid or deceived into placing their child in an orphanage. In many cases, an embassy report said, 'orphanage officials told them that the child will visit home frequently, will return home . . . or will send remittance payments from the United States'" (Navarro 2008). In her piece "Anatomy of an Adoption Crisis," E. J. Graff describes how Vietnamese authorities were particularly unhappy that Americans were conducting criminal investigations on their soil, interpreting U.S. actions as an insult to their national autonomy as well as to their ability to adequately care for their nation's children. Graff also acknowledges that many U.S. adoptive parents were catapulted into emotional turmoil over fraud investigations of adoptions that they had considered finalized and that, in many cases, were even considered final under Vietnamese law. Based on her review of State Department documents, Graff maintains that the State Department and the United States Citizenship and Immigration Service (USCIS)—the governmental body responsible for issuing entry visas to the United States since the 2001 passage of the Patriot Act—seemed to have the best interests of Vietnamese children at heart. At that point, the United States was not quick to shut down adoptions; as Graff

(2010b) reports, adoptions did not stop until Vietnam shut them down. Indeed, the United States had shut down adoptions in Cambodia due to similar reports in 2001, and U.S. adoptive families had been reported as "stuck" in Cambodia at that time (Corbett 2002; Mydans 2001; Rotabi 2012).

As adoptions halted in Vietnam, Cambodia, and Guatemala, many observers predicted that Ethiopia would be the next place that U.S. parents would turn to, and by 2010, Ethiopia was the second-largest sending nation for international adoption, outpaced only by China. In 2010, the Associated Press reported that while the numbers of international adoptions were on the decline around the world, Ethiopia was "bucking [the] global trend" (Crary 2010a). A 2010 *Washington Post* headline declared that "Ethiopia provide[d] hope" for U.S. adoptive parents who had been shut out by other sending nations' tightening regulations (Crary 2010b). In early 2012, the *Wall Street Journal* reported that "Ethiopia has become one of the busiest adoption destinations in the world, thanks in part to loose controls that make it one of the fastest places to adopt a child." The same article quoted Karen Rotabi, an adoption scholar and professor of social work, as saying that Ethiopia is "a classic example of the next boom country where there are warning signs [of corruption and fraud]" (Jordan 2012). Writer, researcher, and birth mother advocate Mirah Riben, writing for the *Huffington Post* in January 2015, called Ethiopia "the new go-to adoption hot spot nation" for American parents during its boom period, and she went on to argue that Ethiopia fit the clear pattern of a sending nation in which disorganization facilitates the same confluence of fraud, corruption, rights abuses, and scandal that rocked Vietnam, Cambodia, and particularly Guatemala. Even before the surge in Ethiopian adoptions truly took hold between 2008 and 2010, an Ethiopian adoption official was quoted in the *New York Times*, saying, "I don't think we'll be able to handle it. We don't have the capacity to handle all these new agencies, and we have to monitor the quality, not just the quantity" (Gross and Connors 2007).

Critical, investigative journalism quickly emerged in response to the growth of Ethiopian adoptions. E. J. Graff, in a boldly titled piece in the *American Prospect*—"Don't Adopt from Ethiopia"—opened with the allegation that the 2012 *Wall Street Journal* investigation told "a deceptively simple story" that failed to acknowledge the ethical dilemmas and the "grey market" inherent in international adoption. The *Wall Street Journal* piece to which Graff was responding describes a girl who was enjoying a life of relative affluence in the United States, whose living father in Ethiopia had simply failed to understand the permanent and legalistic nature of U.S. adoptions. Graff's conclusion was more severe: "It's far more rewarding to love an individual child than to give to anonymous foreigners. I know; I'm parenting an adopted child. But no one wants to be complicit, even unknowingly, in defrauding a father out of his daughter" (2012b). Writing in 2014 for the *Pacific Standard*, Graff linked this kind of micro-level fraud to broader and more lucrative patterns of financial corruption, echoing the worries that Ethiopian governmental officials had expressed years earlier. Graff explained, "Many poor nations' international adoption programs started, as in the Ethiopia that [*Time* magazine, in a 2002 piece on AIDS orphans] portrayed, with a few genuinely humanitarian adoptions, saving children from desperate circumstances. But once word spread among hopeful Western parents that healthy little ones were coming quickly out of a particular country, far more people would sign up than a small, poor country could effectively manage. National governments would become unable to continue carefully supervising every adoption. Demand would begin to outstrip supply, leading to that obvious two-part capitalist solution: increased prices and increased production." Katherine Joyce, writing in the *Atlantic* in 2011, alleged that Ethiopia's total lack of regulation and accountability at the local level led to multiple cases of silencing and frightening shakedowns of adoptive parents, journalists, and other activists who sought to uncover patterns of mismanagement, fraudulent documentation, and financial corruption. At the same time, Ethiopian adoptees' own stories began to emerge in the media. Unlike previous cases in Southeast Asia and in Guatemala, in which most adoptees were infants or young toddlers, many more of the children that came to the United States from Ethiopia were older, with greater native language development and more established memories at the time of their adoptions. Indeed, it would seem, the voices of older adopted children have presented an unanticipated contribution to the conversation.

A New Front in the Culture Wars

In 2013, Katherine Joyce published a piece in *Mother Jones* entitled "Orphan Fever: The Evangelical Movement's Adoption Obsession." In it, she describes "an 'orphan theology' movement that has taken hold among mainstream evangelical churches, whose flocks are urged to adopt as an extension of pro-life beliefs, as a way to address global poverty, and as a means of spreading the Gospel in their homes." She reports on fly-by-night operators, corrupt middlemen, and Christian ministries with little international legal experience who facilitated waves of adoptions fueled by professional networks of pastors, word of mouth, social media, and online Christian women's magazines. Joyce describes these magazines as innocent-seeming women's journals peddling natural remedies, organic "modest clothing," and neoconservative "family values" alongside Liberian children. Many of the families that adopted these children, Joyce reports, had large families to begin with. Often adopting four or more additional Liberian "orphans," they frequently homeschooled and, more disturbingly, practiced severe forms of corporal punishment promoted by the same fundamentalist Christian networks that encouraged adoption. While Evangelical Christian involvement in international adoption had never been a secret—many well-established adoption agencies have always had an explicitly Evangelical mission—Joyce's piece was one of the first to directly link the Christian adoption movement to broader trends reported within the Evangelical community: neoconservative politics, homeschooling, missionary work, and the organized practice of extreme corporal punishment.

In 2013, after adoptions in Ethiopia had begun to decline, CNN reported a "boom" of adoptions in Uganda (Schwartzchild 2013). In an interview published in *Salon* in 2013, Joyce identifies Uganda as the next "go-to" spot for Evangelical Christians interested in quick and easy adoptions (Barcella 2013; see also Joyce 2013c). Many Evangelical Christian groups had already set up missionary operations in Uganda, and they easily crossed over to orphanages and adoption. Early news coverage of the adoption booms in Uganda and in the Democratic Republic of the Congo raised "red flags," comparing them to cases in previous sending nations that had been widely covered in the same publications. Nonetheless, when the Congo shut down adoptions in 2013, Fox News ran a piece detailing the disappointment, shock, and simultaneous determination of U.S. adoptive parents—some motivated by Evangelical Christianity and some not—who were "stuck" in the Congo, awaiting the "release" of their children (Chiaramonte 2014). The *New York Daily News* also ran a sympathetic piece, complete with photos of the adoptive parents wearing empty African-print baby slings (Kuruvilla 2014). As of November 2015, a few children "stuck" in the 2013 controversy were granted the necessary exit permits by the Congolese government and were able to join their adoptive families in the United States, but approximately one thousand cases remained unresolved (see Graff 2015; Ligtvoet 2014; Pham 2015; USCIS 2015).

Soon after Joyce's exposé on family life within the Christian adoption movement, Reuters published a report that detailed the practice of "rehoming"—of finding new homes for children in failed or disrupted adoptions. The Reuters report frames the rehoming phenomenon as a result of the unchecked growth of international adoptions. It opens with the story of a girl named Quita, who an American couple had "rescued . . . from an orphanage in Liberia, brought to America and then signed . . . over to a couple [that the original adoptive parents] barely knew. Days later, they had no idea what had become of her" (Twohey 2013). The report quotes multiple parents who rehomed their internationally adopted children, often transferring custody with nothing more than a simple power of attorney, claiming that they "couldn't handle," their adopted children, felt "in over [their] heads," and were rehoming the adopted children to "protect" or "save" other children in the home. Some child welfare advocates have argued that the disregard of local, national, and international laws and protocols by Evangelical Christian missionaries and organizations is a clear sign of a parallel disregard for not only social work and social welfare protocols but also the "integrity of poor families" (Shani King [2012], writing in *Harvard Human Rights Review*). One of the clearest grounds for this argument took place in the aftermath of the 2010 earthquake in Haiti, when a group of Christian missionaries who entered Haiti under the pretense of offering humanitarian aid were accused and ultimately convicted of smuggling Haitian children over the border into the Dominican Republic with the intention of transporting them to the United States (Delva 2010; King 2012; Thompson 2010; Voigt 2013). Advocates called for strengthening social work and human rights protocols—in law as well as in the cultural conversation—in order to prevent similar crimes from taking place in the future (Rotabi 2010a; see also Rotabi 2015).

The Christian adoption movement also has implications for reproductive justice and reproductive politics that lie beyond specific debates about international adoption. Writing for the *Huffington Post*, Joyce suggests,

> Domestically, there has been a squeeze as well. While in the days before abortion was legalized or single parenthood accepted, many women with unexpected pregnancies relinquished for adoption, today that number has dropped to around 1 percent in some demographics. But the demand for adoptable infants didn't fall with it, and conservative religious groups like the Family Research Council and crisis pregnancy centers have sought to turn those numbers around by encouraging more women to relinquish. One suggestion the FRC came up with after commissioning a study sounds familiar: changing the language around adoption to present adoption as heroic, selfless, loving and mature—and conversely, portraying young or unmarried mothers who choose to parent their children as immature and selfish. It's hard to look at this, or the message of one Christian crisis pregnancy ministry—that all children born to unwed mothers should be considered de facto "orphans" available for adoption (they say they're following the biblical definition of an orphan as a *fatherless* child)—without thinking that something is wrong here. (2013b)

After the 2013 publication of her book *The Child Catchers: Rescue, Trafficking, and the New Gospel of Adoption*, Joyce published a flurry of articles and was interviewed on NPR's *Fresh Air*, widely discussing what she saw as cluelessness as well as outright manipulation and abuse within the Christian adoption movement. But more important for a framing of the reproductive politics around international adoption, Joyce also links the Christian adoption movement to other aspects of family law and policy, both in the *Huffington Post* piece quoted above and in a later article on a cluster of private domestic adoptions in Northwest Arkansas of babies born to immigrants from the U.S. Marshall Islands. Writing in the *New Republic* in April 2015, she describes the exploitation of this community of immigrants, whose cultural conception of adoption is based in their islander practice of informal networks of shared childrearing and a cultural system in which children have multiple parents. Joyce alleges that Arkansas state law, which has some of the weakest protections for birth mothers in the United

States, allows unscrupulous adoption agencies to exploit these marginalized women. Joyce ultimately argues that so-called proadoption laws in Arkansas are an important part of an organized Christian conservative agenda that seeks to diminish civil rights more broadly for adult adoptees seeking information about their birth families, for women in terms of reproductive choice, and for gay and lesbian citizens.

The evolution of the media coverage of international adoption is as much a part of this story as the legal and diplomatic shifts that have directly affected the accessibility of international adoption to American families. The media appears to have played an important role in shaping the terms of our broader cultural debate, which has been as animated as it has been polarizing. While Evangelical Christians (primarily, many would argue) continue to fuel demand for a practice that the U.S. Department of State has joined more liberal activists in trying to regulate, those liberal activists continue to speak out against the abuses within international adoption. Mirah Riben, a vocal advocate on behalf of birth mothers and for greater regulation, argues that "the adoption industry has fewer ethical guidelines than guide real estate transactions and no incentive to police itself. Adoption is thus a free-for-all marketplace full of unscrupulous baby brokers. Those who pay top dollar for children are often victims of scams and rip-offs. Some sue. Some have won wrongful adoption suits. No such recourse however is available to the victimized mothers whose children are commodified" (2015). Riben's argument is in line with those who would protect the rights of birth mothers first and foremost and is highly attuned not only to the global inequality that underlies international adoption but also to the mismanagement, corruption, and outright fraud that recent investigative journalism has uncovered. The journalism reviewed here is a necessary ingredient in any so-called antiadoption activism.

Graff, the journalist who started the trend of critical investigations into international adoption, tackles those issues head-on, summing up, "Here's the rule of thumb: If you can get a healthy infant or toddler within a year, don't adopt from that country." Graff's implication is that if a sending nation (or international adoption agency) purports to have a "healthy" infant or toddler available for quick adoption, the ethical standards of that adoption are not up to par. Graff continues, exhorting U.S. parents, "Adopt, instead, from American foster care, or from countries that send abroad very few children, and when they do, the children who are available are older, or disabled, or come in sibling groups, or otherwise have had trouble finding new local homes. Or if you're adopting for humanitarian reasons, donate that money to an organization that helps children *stay* with their families, or brings clean water and mosquito nets and medicines to their villages" (Graff 2012b). It's no wonder that would be a hard pill for U.S. adoptive parents to swallow. For Christians determined to "save" orphans, it creates an ethical wrinkle in what they see as an otherwise straightforward scriptural obligation. For parents motivated by humanitarian considerations, it creates an inconvenient truth, and for mothers who delayed childbearing in order to advance other life goals, it puts them in an unfortunate double-bind—to be told, often not for the first time, that they can't have a baby, that they must have something that's second best, that they can't have it all.

In many cases, the mothers whom I interviewed for this project were trapped in that particular double-bind because of the delays to marriage and childbearing that have resulted from the profound economic and cultural changes in American society over the past half century. However, it seems that they also came into international adoption with an older set of assumptions based in the historical and cultural context of the twentieth century. They expected their international adoption processes to proceed with relative bureaucratic ease, and they had no expectation of the kinds of ethical questions that the latest wave of investigative journalism and diplomatic volatility would present to them. They were unexpectedly met with a practice that was in flux—pragmatically and politically. When I first sat down at a quiet suburban Starbucks on a Sunday morning with Ivy, a married mother of an older son by birth and a younger daughter adopted from Nepal, her first words were, "I can't talk to you until I know what your politics are." Taken aback and at a loss, I joked that I was a "lifelong Democrat." While I was relieved to have broken the ice, Ivy expressed her profound relief that I wasn't there "to talk about saving babies." She told me very clearly that she did not want to talk to a "cheerleader" or an apologist for what she perceived to be a corrupt and very damaged international adoption system. In that moment and throughout our interview, Ivy also expressed sadness; she had pursued international adoption primarily out of a desire to mother a child and secondarily out of a desire to "do good in the world." The best interests of her (future) child were forefront in her mind. Ivy, like so many of the mothers I interviewed for this project, learned that the political debates around international adoption center on the deepest contradictions within our contemporary ideas about family, childhood, and motherhood and that the unraveling of international adoption therefore demands a reevaluation of our reproductive politics. In the coming chapters, I tell Ivy's story—not only of adopting at a time of shifting policies, practices, and norms but also of learning that international adoption represents something more than a straightforward pursuit of children's "best interests."

Both the emergence of international adoption in the mid-twentieth century and the decline of international adoption in the early twenty-first century establish the parameters within which the mothers I interviewed are operating. This is clearly true in a pragmatic sense, as many lives were caught in limbo as a direct result of the bureaucratic delays, political impasses, and policy changes that most of the families I interviewed experienced. In the chapters that follow, I tell the stories of families caught up in the very circumstances I've described here: the slowing down of adoptions from China; the adoption shutdowns in Guatemala,

Nepal, and the Congo; the instability of the adoption program in Russia; and the frantic boom period of adoptions from Ethiopia, in which almost half of the families interviewed for this project were involved. On an immediate level, this review of the media coverage surrounding international adoption contextualizes their lived experiences, but this recent history also advances the theoretical aims of this project. It explains the assumptions that the mothers I interviewed brought to their processes of international adoption and illuminates the changes to practices and politics with which they were forced to contend. The chapters that follow explore how the contours and the broader implications of their experiences may contribute to our understanding of the reproductive politics and marketplaces that continue to define family life in the twenty-first century.

CHAPTER 2

"We're on the Market Again"

One hot June day, while in the early stages of this project, I loaded my two preschool-aged, bathing suit–clad children into their stroller and, in a cloud of sunscreen fumes, headed for the very best of the Cambridge, Massachusetts, spray parks. Usually a good chunk of the adult conversation overheard in that park is in a language other than English, spoken by graduate students taking their kids out, international professionals of all ages, and nannies and au pairs meeting up for playdates. But on that day, which I soon realized was in the middle of Harvard University's reunion week, English dominated. Most of the parents at the park were sporting straw hats and reunion lanyards. On the bench next to me, a well-dressed, wiry woman, who appeared to be in her midforties, looked up from her phone to greet an old classmate. They exchanged pleasantries and discussed the reunion events, their accommodations, and plans to visit Boston. Then their conversation turned to their children. The woman seated next to me had been vaguely supervising two equally wiry, fair-haired preteens. The classmate and her husband had, upon entering the park, released a very eager four- or five-year-old girl into the sprinkler. I stopped listening to their remarks on soccer, piano, ballet, and the quality of their local public schools until a snippet of their conversation caught my attention: "We're on the market again." Excited for gossip about real estate prices in a fancy suburb somewhere, I was all ears. But the couple with the four-year-old were not talking about the housing market; they were talking about international adoption. And then this international adoptive mother proceeded to tell her old classmate a story that I would hear again and again once I began to conduct the interviews informing this project: about the unexpected roadblocks that cropped up in adopting their daughter from China and the uncertainty and long wait time they faced in adopting a second child. They said they were looking for alternatives, because it didn't seem like adopting a "healthy baby" from China was a realistic possibility.

This chapter tells the story of how the international adoptive parents I interviewed for this project came to see themselves, like the parents I overheard that day in the park, as consumers within a reproductive marketplace. As the adoptive mothers I interviewed entered into a shrinking adoption marketplace, they sought to maintain their altruistic, triumphal view of international adoption as well as their full consumer-controlled reproductive choice. But as the adoption market tightened, they struggled to hold on to both. The cohort of parents in this study moved through their processes of international adoption while both the bureaucracy and the triumphal ideology surrounding international adoption began to splinter. The narratives that I present in this chapter are organized progressively. First, I share the stories of international adoptive parents' negotiation of the logistics and bureaucracies of the adoption programs that are available to them. Then I present stories of international adoptive parents who turned away from domestic adoption because they struggled with the power dynamics of those programs, which they perceived to favor birth parents. These parents' narratives illustrate the ways that they embraced a position of power—and a presumption of choice that consumers bring to an open market. I follow these stories with the narratives of several mothers who approached international adoption with strong altruistic motivations. While a distinct minority of the mothers I interviewed described their desire to adopt as primarily altruistic, most shared altruism as a secondary motivation (see Fisher 2003; Smock and Greenland 2010). As the stories at the end of this chapter illustrate, changes in the international adoption market drove many of these mothers to a confrontation between altruism, adoption commerce, and "choice," and it was through that confrontation that the commercial nature of international adoption revealed itself to many of the mothers with whom I spoke.

The mothers I interviewed generally spoke like consumers who had done "a *ton* of research," as Danielle, a married mother of an older daughter by birth and a younger daughter adopted from China, put it. As in other types of consumer decision-making, women overwhelmingly spearheaded the research, drove the process forward, kept tabs on progress, and sat down to talk to me about it (see Bertolli 2013; Harwood 2007). The women I interviewed were busy with logistically complicated lives, and their initial approach to selecting an international adoption program reflected that. More often than not, their choices were highly constrained by the myriad regulations that sending nations have put in place to govern adoptive parents' eligibility regarding age, marital status, prior criminal record, personal finances, and health history, mental and physical. At the same time, the constriction of international adoption programs that has taken place across the globe since the early 2000s began before the families I interviewed initiated their adoption processes, and so whether they were aware of this constriction or not,[1] it also limited their options. The mothers with whom I spoke were left to navigate a limited array of choices. Yet most of the mothers I interviewed remained determined to find an "appropriate" program despite each family's individual constraints.

This is consistent with the scholarly literature in sociology and social work on adoptive mothers' views of altruism, domestic adoption, and the process of international adoption.[2] But I share their stories in this chapter because of the particular ways in which they confronted a declining marketplace and the breakdown of both bureaucratic and ideological norms at the ending of an era of international adoption. Growing awareness of the complexities of international adoption disrupted a triumphal narrative about international adoption as both a public good and a private good in the "best interests" of children. On that growing awareness, Andrea, who adopted her daughter from China, mused, "So much of the decision to adopt is a balancing game between what you think is in the best interest of the child and what's in the best interest of you as the adopting parents. It's a mixture of well-thought-out, rational things and completely gut-level reactions, which may or may not be in accord with what's in your head." The complexity of competing needs and interests—as well as the cultural contradictions between family, care, altruism, and the market—raises a unique set of questions. Neither pure altruism nor pure commercialism can adequately characterize international adoption. In some ways, though, their coexistence renders the commercial nature of international adoption clearer when an exchange of money jolts parents who had previously seen altruism and commerce as mutually exclusive.

ON A DECLINING MARKET

Alyssa, a younger married mother of a daughter adopted from the Democratic Republic of the Congo, described her first steps in selecting a country from which to adopt, illustrating the ways that her personal limitations were inconsistent with the programmatic limitations of many sending countries. She explained, "We did a lot of research looking at South American countries, but in those countries, you have to go and live there for a couple months. And with my husband's job, he couldn't take two months off. And I could not live by myself for two months in a foreign country. I took six years of Spanish, but [*laughing*] that only takes you so far." While some might consider living in Latin America for two months to be an adventure (or six years of Spanish instruction to be a solid foundation), Alyssa clearly did not. She continued, "In a lot of those countries they want both parents there to bond with [the] child, to make sure that it's a good match. But it just wasn't something we were really wanting to consider." Alyssa brings up a fundamental tension in the requirements that sending nations impose. On the one hand, a sending nation obviously should act responsibly in terms of child welfare, and U.S. parents should not feel entitled to adopt children without sufficient oversight. But at the same time, Alyssa illustrates how U.S. parents are structurally set up as consumers in international adoption arrangements. Through a combination of factors beyond her control (her husband's job) and only partly outside of her control (her own willingness to spend time outside of the United States), Alyssa assumes the role of a consumer and actively solidifies that position through her attitudes, choices, and actions. The choice of sending nation was hers, and she clearly chose against programs that required adoptive parents to remain together "in-country" for long periods of time.

Arden, another mother who adopted from the Democratic Republic of the Congo, was in her midthirties when she married an older man with two teenage sons from a previous marriage. Arden and her husband had a young daughter by birth when they began a process of international adoption in 2010, after most countries' programs had already reorganized or closed. Arden's case clearly illustrates how an adoptive parent can sound like a consumer when faced with a number of market-based constraints. Explaining her and her husband's choice to adopt from the Congo, Arden laid out the facts: "They didn't have age restrictions, and my husband was about to turn fifty. Adoptions were moving quickly at that time, and they had babies available. We had a year-and-a-half-old daughter, and we did not want to jump birth order." Indeed, Arden had come into her adoption process with a number of "deal-breakers"—some, like her husband's age, which were out of her control, and some, like her adoptive child's age, which were only partially out of her control. While, in general, social workers will only place children who will be the youngest in their families, Arden also expressed a clear and distinct preference for an infant. Regarding the other choices of sending nations available to her, she related, "We would have loved to adopt from Haiti, but I think you have to be married ten years to adopt from Haiti. That's one of their many restrictions, and that doesn't fit us." But while Arden could not change the length of time that she had been married, she could also have waited. Thus while Arden describes a constrained choice, she describes a choice nonetheless.

Erin, another married heterosexual mother, tells a similar story. She and her husband are both public school teachers in their early thirties, living in an expansive suburban town. Erin suffered from a childhood illness that compromised her fertility, and so she and her husband began looking into adoption soon after they married, ultimately adopting a son from Ethiopia. Regarding their initial research and decision-making surrounding sending nations, Erin explained, "[We] both teach, so some countries were ruled out because they require you to be in-country for such a long length of time, or they require multiple trips, and that just wasn't something that we thought would be feasible." Indeed, the inflexibility of Erin's workplace proved to be a major factor in her decision-making. So was her age. "At the time," she explained, "I was not thirty, so that ruled out several other countries who require you to be thirty to adopt, to even just submit your application, even though their wait list is three or four years." One of the youngest mothers in my sample, Erin expressed sadness that adoption appeared, at least to her, to be designed for older parents, who came to adoption through their own choices to delay childbearing. Erin felt that she, on the other hand, did not have a choice. But despite the sense of personal tragedy that she felt at the loss of her fertility, Erin nonetheless describes making a series of choices. This is particularly apparent with respect to her child's age. Continuing, Erin explains, "We knew we wanted an infant so we sort of narrowed it down to Ethiopia. Our social worker initially had talked about Guatemala. That was right around the time that there were questions of it shutting down, and ultimately we went [with] Ethiopia instead." Erin and her husband's choice of an infant was clear.

Amid all these mothers' preferences, limitations, and appetites for risk, they proceeded into international adoption as consumers who made distinct sets of choices regarding their future children as well as the processes in which they were willing to participate. But the mothers I interviewed also had distinct feelings of altruism and ethical responsibility with which to contend, and these feelings often interacted with their impulses and their structural position as consumers in interesting ways. Andrea's story of adopting from China after several years of failed fertility treatments illustrates the range and complexity of consumer-like decisions when emotions and ethics enter the picture. Andrea approached her decision-making surrounding adoption, at least in retrospect, with notable self-awareness. She reflected that "the whole decision-making process was a combination of good reasons and not-so-good reasons. At the time, China had a very predictable timeframe, which was very appealing after trying for so long to get pregnant." She described the circumstances surrounding her decision to adopt as a difficult time in her life, punctuated by a major career transition in addition to the mourning associated with giving up on carrying a pregnancy to term.

In the midst of her feelings of sadness and loss, Andrea sought out an international adoption program that met her and her husband's needs—pragmatic and emotional but also ethical. Speaking about her thoughts and feelings at the time, Andrea explained, "China had a reputation at the time for being a relatively 'clean' program. There was a central authority, there weren't all kinds of corrupt lawyers or brokers. There was an obvious and clear reason that so many kids were available for adoption—the one-child policy. We weren't worried about trafficking or money under the table; that was the reputation." Andrea and her husband shopped for a program that they felt would not exploit mothers and children in the sending nation and, at the same time, would protect her—an emotionally vulnerable adoptive mother. Andrea explained,

> I am *completely* in support of policies and laws that, you know, increase the rights of birth mothers and give them the time they need to make the decisions they need and allow them to change their minds. I think that's hugely

important. But I also knew for myself, having gone through years of uncertainty and the huge roller coaster of infertility treatment . . . that we could be matched with a woman who would like us to parent her child when she was maybe four months pregnant, and then go through this process with her for five months, and then have her change her mind. Which I completely support her right to do, but it was really scary. That would be completely emotionally devastating for us.

Andrea was clear, however, that she was particularly emotionally vulnerable at the time that she made the decision to adopt, quipping, "I don't think I was the most rational I've ever been." She further explained that as she learned more about China, international adoption as a system, and adoption more generally, she felt "a little embarrassed that we didn't look more seriously at the foster care system. I had a lot of the same prejudices that other people have—you know, too concerned about the impact of trauma. But now I know that international adoptees have the exact same trauma." Andrea is a primary example of a mother whose views on adoption evolved—the norm in my sample. Nonetheless, despite the fact that they changed, her ethics and sense of altruism—as they stood at the time—played a major role, alongside her own emotional needs, in her overall decision-making. Andrea's story highlights how many of the international adoptive mothers I interviewed wrestled with conflicting desires. The conflict between the mothers' sense of altruism and their desires for control over their reproductive choices is even more apparent in the narratives of those who, prior to adopting internationally, actively turned away from the possibility of a private domestic adoption.

Turning Away from Domestic Adoption

Private domestic adoption was the first arena in which many of the mothers I interviewed encountered a blurring of one of our strongest cultural boundaries—the line that we draw between private familial love and the marketplace. They entered into a commercial adoption process in which they were the paying consumers, yet one of the primary features of the matching process between adoptive parents and birth families in private domestic adoption is that the choice of an adoptive placement rests with the birth mother, who selects potential adoptive families for her child based on detailed profiles, letters, and photographs that the prospective adoptive parents provide. In this way, private domestic adoption strives to balance the interests of adoptive families and biological kin. But many of the international adoptive mothers I spoke with experienced this power dynamic as profoundly unsettling and cited it more often than any other factor as a reason that they turned away from private domestic adoption and toward international adoption.

Angela is a divorced heterosexual mother who adopted her daughter, Olivia, from Colombia while still married to Olivia's dad, Troy. She said, "I had a real problem with the idea of advertising yourself to potential birth mothers . . . it really felt like marketing." Angela insisted that she supported the rights of birth mothers but that it didn't feel right to "market" herself. Anna, a married heterosexual mother of a son adopted from Nepal, described the letter she was asked to write to potential birth mothers as a "begging letter" and insisted that she should not have to "beg" in order to become a mother. Leah is a married heterosexual mother of two children, a girl adopted from Ethiopia and a boy adopted from South Korea. She was one of the few stay-at-home mothers I interviewed, and her husband, Eli, works very long hours as a financial manager. Leah called the letter a "bragging letter" and balked at her social worker's fixation on her (very comfortable) material circumstances. Donna, who adopted her son from Ethiopia as a single mother but subsequently married her partner and became a stepmother to his biracial daughter, was one of the few women I interviewed not firmly ensconced in the upper middle class. An administrative assistant, she and her husband, a chef, lived comfortably in a family-oriented suburb with their multiracial, blended family. While Donna told me that she adopted from Ethiopia primarily was because it was less expensive than private domestic adoption, she also described submitting a "Dear Birth Mother" letter to an adoption agency as "just like an online dating profile" and the prospect of "selling" herself to a birth mother as distasteful and unfair. Leslie, a married lesbian mother who ultimately adopted a daughter from Nepal, summed it up: "I just couldn't face advertising. I just couldn't." Further, uncertainty over getting selected at all was a factor for some women. Deirdre, a married heterosexual mother of two boys adopted from Ethiopia, described completing her "Dear Birth Mother" letter and then waiting two years without being selected by any birth mothers. She explained, matter-of-factly, "I was getting very close to the age of forty. And in my head, I had the idea, 'I don't want to be well past forty, getting children.' And because with domestic adoption, you have no control, you're really at the when-and-if of the birth mother, I decided that's when it was time to look at international adoption."

Another major factor that deterred families from domestic adoption was openness—both official and potential, given the legal structures surrounding adoption in the United States. Danielle and Mark—a married couple who adopted a daughter, Elianna, from China after experiencing secondary infertility following the birth of an older daughter, Rachel—simply did not want an open adoption. In this respect, they exemplified many families' discomfort with open adoptions, which many felt had become the norm and expectation in private domestic adoption. At first, Danielle and Mark gave the simple explanation that in adopting Elianna, they "wanted [the adoption] to be cut-and-dry, starting new." Mark, one of the few fathers present for our interview, however, went further. He expressed concern around "uncertainty about the laws and transparency" regarding domestic adoption in general. He emphatically did not want his child to have connections to her biological kin because, in his view, this compromised his legal protection as his child's father. Marjorie, a married heterosexual mother of three children adopted from China, similarly explained that her biggest fear in domestic adoption was the idea that biological kin would try to take away her children. She exclaimed, in this case with reference to public adoption through the foster care system, "Some Great Aunt Matilda out in the middle of nowhere decides, 'I want this kid. I'm like sixty-five and I have no job, but I want this kid.' They can take them at any time. I don't want any relatives popping out of the woodwork." But Marjorie's uneasiness extended to official, predetermined openness in domestic adoption as well. She told me that she feels that open adoption "really messes with the kids," who are forced to meet with relatives for whom they have their own ambivalence. Ivy, a married heterosexual mother who adopted a daughter from Nepal after experiencing secondary infertility, couched her discomfort with open adoption in the context of a birth mother's potential lack of dependability. She explained, "We did a lot of research about domestic—domestic open, foster care—and to be really honest, we did not want an open adoption. The ones who forget to call on the birthday, that's like twice as painful as the one who just disappeared."

Kate, a married mother in her early forties, was one of several mothers who struggled with political and ethical ideals that complicated her adoption choices from the outset. Kate told me very clearly that she found domestic adoption to be cold, economic, and transactional compared to her experience of international adoption, which she found to be more about children's best interests, despite the ethical ambiguity that she recognized. A highly educated professional, Kate lives in a single-family home in an affluent and, in her words, "overwhelmingly white" suburb with her husband, Greg, and their two children, both adopted from Africa. In our interview, Kate described her affinity for Africa, African cultures, and the needs of African children living in poverty. Yet Kate describes how she and her husband had initially pursued domestic adoption, recounting, "We put together these, like, family albums. And it didn't feel natural, it just felt too vulnerable to have to put ourselves out there and be picked." Kate was also extremely uncomfortable with her social worker's emphasis on the more material aspects of her and her husband's lives, in particular when they did not align with her values. Kate explained, "They wanted us to say all these weird things like 'MBA dad' and 'oh, you're a lawyer but you'd stay home.' And it didn't feel like us. Like parts of us, certainly, but not the core of us, not who we really were." Indeed, for Kate, her discomfort with "marketing" was part of a broader feeling about private domestic adoption:

> I never felt like anybody was representing us or advocating for us in a domestic adoption; it was always about what was in the best interest of the birth mother.

I totally understand that they need a lot of support and a lot of advocacy and what they're doing is a gigantic decision. . . . We lasted about a month and then we pulled out. I just couldn't do it; I just felt like nobody had my back. It was very transactional . . . I think that's the right word for how I felt when we were doing the domestic [adoption]. With [our new international adoption social worker], it felt much more collaborative; it felt like they were representing us. I know that that's not really how it is. I am smart enough to know that it's really about the child and about the birth parents, but I felt like we had a voice for the first time.

For Kate, "transactional" meant cold, clinical, and without attention to the nuances and the humanity of the people involved—and to her needs in particular. Her experience of international adoption felt "more collaborative" and less "transactional" than domestic adoption. Kate felt free to acknowledge her feelings and desires as a part of the process, as well as free of what she perceived to be her social worker's fetishization of her husband's MBA. Throughout our interview, Kate was highly attuned to issues of inequality, discussing her pro bono legal work, her involvement in international aid organizations, and, quite unlike the majority of those interviewed for this project, the importance she placed on adopting children of color in a domestic context. Kate nonetheless felt objectified by her relative privilege and wealth, and she wanted her voice heard as a participant in more than a simple economic exchange; she was, after all, growing her family. Kate's story in particular illustrates how a turn away from private domestic adoption can force adoptive mothers to acknowledge their position as consumers in a market because of how their turn toward international adoption signals a desire for greater control and agency in the adoption process.

Jane, a married mother of a daughter adopted from China, expressed similar worries about both private and public domestic adoption, but she framed them in broader terms. "It just seemed like it would take a long, long time," she confessed. And echoing the same concerns expressed by practically all the parents I interviewed, she continued, "You have to be *chosen* by the birth mother. . . . We were really in a hurry at that point." Jane also brought up concerns over legal status, similar to Danielle and Mark's, mentioning the "Baby Veronica" case, which made news headlines over the summer of 2013. In this case, a child, "Veronica," had been adopted by a Caucasian couple and had been in their custody for two years when her biological father, himself part Cherokee Indian, decided that he wanted to regain custody of his daughter. He went to court with the claim that his parental rights had never been legally terminated. The U.S. Supreme Court ruled in favor of the father, citing the Indian Child Welfare Act of 1978, which was instituted to redress systematic removal of native children from their families and communities. Jane was bothered by the outcome of this case, explaining, "The father was a very, very small part Cherokee, never lived as a Cherokee, never accepted that part of himself. I see why the law is there, certainly, for some kids, but maybe it goes too far in the other extreme." The reaction that Jane and her husband, Tom, had to this case ultimately played a substantial role in their decision to forego domestic adoption; as Jane explained, "We were a little concerned about the possibility of it just going wrong and then having some kind of possibility that the child would be taken away." Mary, a single mother in her midfifties with a son adopted from China, likewise explained, "I thought about domestic, but you hear so many stories about the birth mother coming back or a grandparent coming back, and I think our civil rights are too strong here and it scared me . . . Why would I go through the heartache here over and over again?"

Indeed, in the narratives of many of the mothers I interviewed, fears of disrupted adoption placements blended together with overall discomfort with open adoption. But for some mothers, the fear of losing a child was particularly acute. Robin is a married heterosexual mother with two adopted children—an older boy from Guatemala and a younger daughter who she and her husband, Bill, adopted through a private domestic adoption after international adoptions were frozen in Guatemala. Although she did ultimately adopt domestically, she explained that at the time she adopted her son, she was terribly afraid of "going to the hospital, holding the baby, and then the birth mother—who has every right—changing her mind. Or another birth [relative] coming forward." More than one mother described the possibility of a disrupted placement as "scary": Arden, who adopted a daughter from the Democratic Republic of the Congo, recounted, "Very close family friends had a bunch of [domestic] adoptions fall through. That seemed really scary to me." Deirdre, a married heterosexual mother who adopted two boys from Ethiopia, described the pain of her own "failed placement" through private domestic adoption before "moving on" to international adoption.

Similarly, Marjorie, a married heterosexual mother of three children adopted from China, explained her immediate turn toward international adoption with a story in which friends of hers had tried without success to adopt through their state's foster care system for six years. When, after six years of waiting, they were finally matched with an infant, they raised her for four years with, reportedly, no contact from the biological mother. But when the girl was four years old, Marjorie recounted, the social worker reportedly said to her friend, "We're going to give Mom one more try." Marjorie's implication, in telling this story, was that domestic adoptions, in general, privilege the rights of birth mothers over adoptive mothers, even under the most nonsensical and painful of circumstances. In the same vein, Erin, a married mother of a son adopted from Ethiopia, explained her thinking to me:

> Domestic adoption is very scary. You're sort of putting yourself out there. You have to put together your profile, and you put yourself out there, but there's

always that risk of one parent who either doesn't know or doesn't sign . . . and
we just felt like the risks domestically were so great that we weren't willing. We
actually started [an adoption through the state foster care system], and we had
a child that we were asked to take. At the last minute, Mom decided she wanted
to parent. So we were ready for this child, and they said, "No, she's not coming.
Mom wants to parent." At that point, we had done the [required training] and
everything, and we said, "OK, we put everything on hold to open our homes
to this baby, and it just sort of shattered in front of us." At that point, we said,
"OK we're going forward with international."

Similarly, Anna, a married mother of a son adopted from Nepal, explained,

We looked into domestic adoption, but once we heard about the corruption
issues they had, and also the number of people in line, and the letter that you
have to write in order to get approval from the legal parents . . . The birth
parents [in domestic adoptions] are essentially demanding more and more
money before they give birth and then, essentially, changing their minds after
thirty days. There's no way of vetting what's going on, who's a serious parent in
terms of willing to give up their child and who's out there trying to make money
off of it . . . We had friends who had had way too many failed placements, and
we just didn't want to have that kind of heartbreak. We knew there were risks
with international adoption, but at the time we were looking, in 2010, we didn't
know anybody who had had any failed placements with international adoption. It just seemed the quote-unquote safer way to go.

Anger and suspicion toward U.S. birth mothers were often barely veiled among
some of the mothers I interviewed, including in Anna's case. And like many of
the mothers I interviewed, Anna is also clear that she desires an adoption process that skews control in her favor. In turning away from domestic adoption,
the main thing these adoptive mothers have in common is their desire to maintain agency in their adoption processes. The desire to maintain full consumer-
controlled reproductive choice is ultimately what drove them to international
adoption.

Many of the mothers I interviewed also saw international adoption as a more
attractive opportunity than domestic adoption precisely because, at the outset of
their processes, the commercial nature of international adoption remained hidden to them while they maintained a sense of control. That sense of control felt
natural; as Kate said about domestic adoption, it didn't feel *natural* to "have to be
picked." The loss of agency and control that many adoptive mothers experienced
(or simply feared) allowed them to glimpse the transactional and commercial
nature of adoption. In Kate's case, this was explicit—she herself felt objectified and commodified by the touting of her and her husband's academic and
professional achievements. The more generalized feeling that private domestic

adoptions involved adoptive parents "marketing" or "advertising" themselves also contributed to the adoptive parents' view of adoption as a commercial transaction—though perhaps ironically, since they often saw birth mothers as the financial beneficiary. Through their discomfort, they came face-to-face with what Debora Spar and Anna Harrington call "the commercial side of their action" (2009: 43) and retreated to a position—international adoption—where they hoped they could protect their interests. They felt more comfortable in a "buyers' market."

WHEN ALTRUISM MEETS THE MARKET

For many mothers, their desire for agency and control remained interwoven with their sense of altruism. Linda—a married mother in her midfifties with five children, the youngest two adopted from Russia—summed it up: "I want a child that's really an orphan. That nobody's coming back for." Linda echoes the same fundamental discomfort that many parents expressed with the legal and social work paradigms that leave U.S. birth mothers with more rights and greater agency than birth mothers abroad. Yet the majority of the parents I interviewed began their processes of international adoption with an abiding belief in the triumphal narrative that Ellen Herman (2008) describes. Several mothers called international adoption "a chance to do something good." Indeed, many of the parents whom I interviewed expressed altruistic motivations not only as a factor in their decision to adopt internationally but also as impacting their choice of sending nation. All the parents I interviewed who adopted from China—including those who ultimately adopted boys—expressed horror at reports of female infanticide related to China's one-child policy and explained that the policy had impacted their decision to adopt from China. Several families expressed interest in adopting from Haiti in the wake of the earthquake in 2010, although only one family in my sample ultimately did. Several mothers described wanting a child who "needed" them, and others described turning away from domestic adoption because the children available for adoption internationally were "needier." One devoutly Catholic mother bemoaned what she perceived as a shift away from the social justice orientation of the Catholic Church she remembered from her childhood and was clear that she had elected to adopt two school-age children from Russia in part as a way to "give back." Clearly, there is a natural overlap between altruistic and religious motivations for adoption, and indeed, the few very religious Christians in my sample (both Evangelical Protestant and Catholic) expressed some of the strongest altruistic motivations. But altruism remained a secondary motivation for all of them, save one exception.

While several of the mothers I interviewed called international adoption a "win-win" for adoptive parents and adopted children, Lisa, one of the few Evangelical Christian mothers I interviewed and the only mother I spoke with who chose to adopt for primarily altruistic motivations, called international adoption a "win-win-win." She explained that as adoptive parents, she and her husband, Vin, "won" by growing their family, while their adopted children "won" by being spared from life in an institution, and the world would "win" through one "small act of healing" at a time. A white married mother of three older biological children as well as two school-aged children adopted from Ethiopia, Lisa spoke to me from the plush couches of her immaculate, high-ceilinged living room in an affluent outer-suburban community. A devout Christian, she explained that she had become interested in international adoption after attending a presentation at her church and seeing video footage of impoverished children in Ethiopia. Describing the beginnings of her desire to adopt, she said, "I didn't feel like I needed more children, or even wanted more . . . but hearing [about] these children in need, that's what really did it." She told me that she was worried that she was being "overly emotional" about the decision, like "any woman who gets emotional and wants a puppy." She explained, however, that when her husband decided that he, too, wanted to adopt and himself took the first steps to contact adoption agencies, she knew that it was truly the right thing for her family. If her husband took the initiative, she reasoned, then adopting would not be an irrational, emotional decision. Of course, Lisa's deference to her husband's initiative is consistent with the Christian doctrine that she espoused throughout our interview. Nonetheless, in her gendered language, Lisa clearly distinguishes between what she sees as an "emotional" motivation for adopting versus a "genuinely" altruistic one.

Lisa was unique in my sample in her insistence that she was not trying to fulfill a "mothering desire" but rather wanted to "help out a family in need." She elaborated, "I don't see it as, those are our kids. They are, but they are also someone else's. I see it more as merging a blended family. We care for them, we love them fully, we treat them as our very own, but they know they have two sets of parents, one in America and one in Ethiopia." Lisa explained that she felt she had a lot in common with her Ethiopian children's biological family and that she and her husband were united in their Christian faith with the children's biological father, who "was praying for a family to take his children in, [while] we were praying to help some other family." Lisa was comforted—and felt that her adopted children were comforted—by the fact that their biological father "reads the Bible every day, and my husband reads the Bible every day." Lisa's shared faith with her children's biological kin not only made her feel confident in her altruism and her actions but also made her feel like part of a global community. As Lisa herself said, "It takes a village." Lisa even went so far as to say that if anything happened to her and her husband, she hoped another family "somewhere in the world" would do for her children what she had done for someone else's. Seen from one perspective, Lisa's altruism and sense of a global village betray a blindness, whether unconscious or willful, to the kinds of systemic inequality that underlie international adoption. Her moral certainty, guided by Evangelical Christianity, runs up against the ambivalence, nuance, and critical perspective that so many of the mothers I interviewed expressed. Yet while Lisa is exceptional in my sample by being motivated, as she claims, solely by altruism, she is far from unique in her view of international adoption as a fundamentally altruistic enterprise—at least at the outset of the processes that the participants in this study experienced.

Joan and David, a white married couple with a large blended family, expressed a sense of altruism similar to Lisa's, but from a profoundly irreligious point of view. After marrying and bringing their biological children from previous marriages together, they decided to adopt from Ethiopia because of what Joan described to me as the "tremendous need." For Joan, adopting was a marriage of her desire to mother and her progressive politics. Over coffee at a busy café in her diverse urban neighborhood, I asked her if she and David had considered adopting from any countries besides Ethiopia. She replied that they had initially been drawn to Liberia but turned toward Ethiopia because of irregularities that they perceived in the Liberia program. Ethiopia, Joan explained, was a more established program, and to her mind, the agencies involved were more reputable. About her and David's overall motivations, however, she was clear: "Something about Africa—there was just something so viscerally appealing to us. And there were so many kids. There still are so many kids." Unlike Lisa, Joan expressed mixed feelings about adoption as an institution, as well as a profound understanding of the loss that accompanies adoption. She was clear in her opinion that "the best thing for all adopted kids would be if they were able to be raised in their first families. We are a very, very distant second. But," she continued, "every child needs a family." Ultimately, Joan said that she thought adopting was the right thing to do; had one of her daughters remained in Ethiopia, Joan suspected that she may not have survived. "When we brought her home," Joan explained, "we found out that she was positive for TB. That makes us feel like we did a good thing." Similarly, Leslie, the sole lesbian mother in my sample and one of the most vocal about her feminist politics, expressed profound sadness at the outcomes faced by abandoned girls in many parts of the world and explained that a major factor in her decision to adopt internationally, rather than to pursue a pregnancy, was to protect a girl from sex trafficking. On this point, Leslie was blunt: "Girls who grow up in orphanages do not have good options." But despite the discomfort that Leslie described with the language of "saving" children, she nonetheless believed—and not without grounds—that in adopting, she was genuinely saving her daughter from a life of domestic and sexual servitude.

Feelings of altruism, however, can be tricky, and the exchange of money can make them even trickier to negotiate. Many of the parents I interviewed were, like Leslie, partially motivated to adopt out of a sense of altruism, but they also expressed the same discomfort as she did with language that framed adoption as a way to "save" children. More significantly, most of the parents I spoke with expressed a stark disconnect between any potential altruism and the market dynamics that underlay their international adoption processes. If their actions were even partially altruistic, they reasoned, then their actions could not be simultaneously commercial. Commerce precluded altruism and care because family stood so firmly outside of the market in their cultural imaginations. And so it was precisely when parents began to see through their presumptions and claims about international adoption as an inherently altruistic endeavor that they began to more clearly see the ways in which their international adoption processes were part of a commercial enterprise. The mothers I interviewed came to see themselves as consumers precisely because they had initially seen themselves (even if only in part) as altruists. Their triumphal narratives fell apart when altruism met the market. Ivy's story exemplifies how this happened for several mothers with whom I spoke.

A married mother of a biological son and a daughter adopted from Nepal, Ivy vividly described her growing awareness of international adoption as a reproductive market through the lens of her initial approach to adopting. A tenured university professor, she spoke about her initial desire to adopt a child from India, which was based on her personal and academic ties to India as well as a desire to "do good." She explained that at the time that she and her husband, Paul, were considering adoption, they were very committed to adopting a child who "needed" them, because then, Ivy reasoned, the adoption would be mutually beneficial. About the "millions of children without families" in India, Ivy was certain that "there [was] no question they need[ed] help." Elaborating on the context of her and Paul's initial decision-making, Ivy explained, "It was in the wake of 9/11, I just felt . . . it was like our personal lives and politics just came to a head. The world was going to hell, I had tenure but was dissatisfied in my job, I can't conceive . . . let's do something for one person. The books I write, who cares—maybe three people in the world read them—I mean, it was that pie in the sky: I can't fix the whole world, [but] maybe I can help just one person." In retrospect, Ivy questioned her initial assumption about the benevolence of her desire to adopt. Mocking what she perceived as her own naivete, she self-deprecatingly quipped, "What, I was going to be Gandhi, Mother Theresa all wrapped into one?" Ivy's rosy outlook was stripped down early and often by the very process of going through an adoption—ultimately, of a daughter from Nepal—that was brokered for money.

Ivy described the first moment she realized that she was participating in an essentially commercial endeavor as both eye-opening and fundamentally unsettling. She spoke softly, with a sense of betrayal: "We were told to show up at [our adoption agency's U.S. office] with five thousand dollars cash. In new one-hundred-dollar bills. So I went to the bank, made a withdrawal, popped over there, and to this day, I don't know what that money was for, where it went—was it for [the agency's Nepali representative's] plane ticket? I have no idea." She went on to explain that her agency had, in her opinion, failed to provide proper services and support in terms of transportation, food, accommodations, shopping for baby supplies, medical care, and even the bureaucratic process of finalizing her daughter's adoption. She felt that she and her husband had been forced to figure things out themselves, and they hired a private driver, recommended to them by other American adoptive parents. Dismayed, Ivy said, "[The private driver we hired in Nepal] did everything."

Throughout our conversation, Ivy toggled between anger that she had been forced to fend for herself despite a substantial outlay of cash and sadness that she now saw her adoption as a commercial transaction despite her initial altruistic motivations. Ivy's story suggests a shift in her critical perspective, and indeed, Ivy explained how her "politics" shifted as a result of her experiences in Nepal and afterward. Ivy was clear that while she did not see her story as a straight-forward narrative of "baby saving," she didn't see it as a straightforward case of "baby buying" either. Ivy described taking her newly adopted daughter on outings in Kathmandu while waiting for the adoption to be finalized and how "everybody took one look at us and said, 'Nepali baby? How much did you pay?' That was the immediate question, every single time." Ivy told me that this insinu-ation made her profoundly sad and that her sadness emanated from "both the truth and [the] lie" within it. Describing the profound depression that she fell into upon returning to the United States with her daughter, Ivy attributed it, in part, to living with that "truth"—that she had indeed exchanged money for a child—and the "lie" that she had straightforwardly bought another human being. Ivy *had* been motivated by the desire to mother, and she certainly had strong evidence that her actions—bringing her daughter out of an orphanage, into a family—benefitted her daughter on an individual level. Ivy, ever-critical, came home to inhabit a profound ethical and emotional dissonance among altruism, care, and the market.

Ivy seriously wrestles with the material reality that would have circumscribed her daughter's life had she not been adopted: "If she had stayed there. . . . She didn't have a bright future. They still have indentured servitude, so families sell their daughters to go work for a period of time on someone's farm. She wasn't going to be going to school, she would not have had a good life. I do take seri-ously the criticisms of these naive Americans—they think everything is going to be a Hallmark greeting card, they're going to go out and fix the world—but. . . . But." But, Ivy implies, there is no straightforward solution to the question of international adoption. While many scholars point out that we have a cultural difficulty with the idea that money is determinative in the intimate arena of reproduction because we separate the "market" from the "personal," Ivy's nar-rative suggests a further difficulty. We also separate the market from the altru-istic or the charitable. And while Ivy was clear that she was motivated to adopt because she wanted another child, she was equally clear regarding her altruistic motivations as well as her abiding belief that adoption provided her child with a "better" life.

Confronting Choice Head-On

For some of those I interviewed, consciousness of the commercial side of international adoption came about through a direct experience of consumer choice. Pat and Rich are a primary example, as a married couple in their midfifties with two daughters, Laura and Jessica, whom they adopted from Guatemala. One of the very few traditionally middle-class families with whom I spoke, they live in a cozy single-family home in a small ethnically diverse, working-class city. Rich is a retired blue-collar worker and Pat, a decade younger than Rich, is self-employed. Having married "later in life," their journey toward international adoption is quite typical of my sample: they initially pursued having a biological child but shifted their focus to adoption relatively quickly, bypassing all but the slightest medical interventions into their fertility. Their process of adopting their two daughters was dramatic and fraught and yet also not atypical of the stories I heard from many parents. Pat and Rich described themselves as "politically progressive" and as having a cultural affinity for Latin America. Earlier in her life, Pat had lived in Mexico, working with indigenous Guatemalan refugee women fleeing their country's decades-long armed conflict. As a result, she had traveled throughout Guatemala on multiple occasions and felt a particularly strong emotional connection to the region, in addition to having a high level of cultural competency and Spanish-language fluency. Nonetheless, Pat was clear that her motivations for adopting were distinctly related to parenting.

Pat described how, when she and Rich began to search for an adoption agency, one thing quickly led to another: "We hadn't been parents before; we wanted to try for a younger child, rather than an older child who might have had more challenges than we could handle. So we were looking at Mexico, and I was corresponding with all these adoption agencies working in Mexico, and then this agency working in Guatemala just emailed me and said, 'Hey, we have this child, are you interested?' I think we had filled out an initial interest form, but not the home study, not any of that yet. That should have been our first red flag." Pat and Rich nonetheless proceeded with that initial referral, for a baby named Elsa. They completed their paperwork and began receiving periodic updates. They had poor communication with their agency, however, and became particularly suspicious when the pictures they were receiving of Elsa appeared, all of a sudden, to be of a different child. So Pat and Rich bought themselves a couple of plane tickets. As Pat explained to me, "We just decided, 'You know what? We should just go see what's going on in Guatemala.' I speak fluent Spanish, and I just thought, 'You know what, this is weird.' We had been getting pictures, and then we were getting other pictures that didn't look like the same child. And the [adoption agency representative] was like, 'Oh, kids change as they get older,' and we were like, 'Oh, this is really weird.' So we went to Guatemala." By this point, Elsa's birth mother had given birth to another baby girl, Laura, and Pat and Rich completed the paperwork to adopt her as well.

Upon arrival in Guatemala, Pat and Rich were met with utterly unexpected circumstances and quickly realized that, essentially, they had been victims of fraud. As Pat recounted, "So we went, and my parents went with us. And we found out—Elsa, we found out, just by looking at her, she had cerebral palsy. Her legs were crossed and rigid, she cried all the time, she couldn't stand. While we were there, we called the lawyer, because [Elsa] wasn't the child [we'd been receiving pictures of]. It was a different child." In the meantime, Pat, Rich, and Pat's parents brought Elsa and her sister Laura back to their hotel and spent the next few days caring for them, although, as Pat recalled, they barely interacted with Laura because Elsa required their constant care and attention. At fifteen months, Elsa was unable to sit, crawl, walk, or make any prespeech vocalizations. "Her legs were so tightly locked together," Pat explained, "that you could barely change her." Continuing her story, Pat recounted,

My parents were very good. Rich and I, we were just so stunned by this. . . . So every day, we were just trying to deal with the reality of what this would mean for us. Laura was just a baby, just a three-month-old baby. My father suggested, "Why don't you call a doctor who you know will come to the hotel?" And [the doctor] told us, "Why don't you have an MRI and all that stuff?" So we did all of it. The lawyer was pretty upset that we were doing it. . . . She thought this would jeopardize the adoption. And it did. At the very end of our stay, Rich and I made the decision, and we talked to the lawyer; this is not—and this is a very sad thing to talk about, but we made the decision not to adopt Elsa, because we just felt that we couldn't handle it.

I thank goodness that my parents were there. They were a stabilizing force for us. My mother said, "This is not your biological child. This is a child you are choosing to adopt. And yes, you are choosing to care for [her]. You have the opportunity to make the decision now, and you need to make the decision that's right for you." She said, "If it was your biological child, obviously you would take the steps and do what you would need to do, but you have a deci- sion here." And it was very, very hard, but we don't have any regrets.

Pat and Rich proceeded with their plans to adopt Laura, but they chose to leave Elsa behind. They would later pursue a separate adoption process for their daughter Jessica.

Pat and Rich's story brings the reality—that adoption is ultimately a choice—into sharp focus. As Pat's mother advised, "You have a decision here."

Despite what she perceived as a deep familiarity with "how business is done," Pat had truly not dreamed that she could have been placed in such a position. The fact that she and Rich were faced with this decision clearly resulted from the fraudulent activities of their adoption agency. Yet faced with the prospect of adopting a severely disabled child, Pat and Rich were ultimately able, due to their position as consumers, to make the decision of whether to adopt Elsa or not. Indeed, Pat and Rich had never shirked their privilege as consumers. Describing her initial turn toward Guatemalan adoption, away from Mexico, Pat said,

> Mexico seemed like a really good prospect at the time; you could go to the border town and get to know the woman who was giving birth to the child and actually apparently be there for the birth, but you would have to live in Mexico for four or five months, and we were both working at the time. I mean, we would have done it, but Guatemala just seemed so much simpler and less challenging. All the adoptions from Guatemala, they were babies. They were happening much, much faster. It was expensive, but all the reports at the time, they were really good.

Pat entered into this process with knowledge and experience but also with the sensibility of a North American consumer making a consumer choice: adopting from Guatemala was more expensive but seemed much more convenient than adopting from Mexico—and seemingly without any additional risk. Pat and Rich went on to face a situation that, while more painful than some, proved to be common among the parents who participated in this project. Fraud was a common experience among those I interviewed for this project, a theme that I pursue in detail in chapter 4. But Pat and Rich's story is particularly instructive in the context of how international adoptive parents came to see themselves as consumers in a—albeit, deeply flawed—reproductive marketplace precisely because "the commercial side of their action" was revealed through fraud. Pat and Rich came to understand their positions as consumers more clearly because of the gut-wrenching, ethically fraught decision that they were forced into by the circumstances of a poorly regulated international adoption marketplace.

Pat and Rich's experience is not a straightforward story of profit-driven corruption. Clearly, given better regulation and oversight, the type of fraud that Pat and Rich encountered should be avoidable. But beyond the pain caused by those fraudulent activities, the agency's corruption, as well as its overall mismanagement, clash with North American consumer expectations and, in that clash, reveal the commercial mechanisms of international adoption to U.S. adoptive parents. Like the other parents I describe above, Pat and Rich operate as consumers—specifically, as North American consumers with a set of assumptions and expectations surrounding the privilege of regulation and transparency in the marketplace. But when their unconscious expectations are not met, when their assumptions prove ill-founded, the commercial mechanisms of the process are revealed. For Pat and Rich, this happened on a macro level as well as on a personal micro level. As Pat explained, "Right after [the situation with Elsa] happens, Guatemala shuts down for three months. Our lawyer, who we had hired, said it's because of international pressure. But his take was, right now, lawyers get all the money for international adoption in Guatemala, and it's a lot of money. And the Guatemalan government wants a hand in it . . . they want a cut of the money." Pat's experiences led her to abandon her adoption agency, strike out on her own, and hire an independent attorney. In the process, she was forced to rethink the entire nature of adoption, and she came to the ultimate conclusion that adoption leaves her, the adoptive parent and paying customer, with the power to make her own decisions.

However, Pat's experiences also exposed her to the very real issues of corruption and adoption fraud being reported in Guatemala. At the same time that Pat confronted a marketplace, she found it was a corrupt and fraudulent one, which further disrupted her initial assumptions about the institution in which she had elected to participate. Pat explained,

> And then all the stories come up, of mothers supposedly selling their babies, and we're like, "Oh my God." But at this point, and even now, I really feel that we know [because] the birth mother signed three times, [and] we had two— no, three—DNA tests done on the birth mother, because we're like, we're going to make sure right and square that everything's right at this point. We're not going to have any problem in the future, that someone would say, "That's not a legal adoption." Because that was part of wanting an international adoption in the first place; we wanted to make sure that this kid is going to be our child and not have something come up later on that—yikes. And even then, the stories weren't coming out as fierce as they did later on.

Just like many others, Pat and Rich had turned to international adoption for a sense of certainty, but the shifting landscape around them—the changing market dynamics and the changing bureaucracies—ruptured their sense of ethical certainty.

Later on, Guatemala would indeed shut down international adoption in the face of tremendous international pressure, citing multiple cases of outright kidnapping as well as gross mismanagement and greed on the part of multiple adoption professionals (for a concise overview, see Graff 2012a; Voigt 2013). Parker, another mother who adopted from Guatemala, was clear about her take on the situation; the first thing she did after signing the consent form and beginning our interview was to offer a flat-out indictment of international adoption as a byproduct of dislocation and trauma, on both a macro and a micro level. She declared, "I'd just like to point out the absolute irony that it was the U.S.'s systematic destruction of Guatemala that caused my son to need a home," connecting her individual circumstances and global inequality in the broadest sense. For Pat and Rich, this corruption and dysfunction allowed them to see the system as a commercial enterprise, and their circumstances led them to understand themselves as consumers with choices. They caught a glimpse behind the veil, and the ideology of a clean, triumphal, and child-centered adoption system came tumbling down.

The narratives in this chapter illustrate several things. First, they show us how international adoptive parents function as consumers and, indeed, can embrace the position of power and privilege that comes with being a buyer in a marketplace defined by inequality. But the mothers whom I interviewed, unlike mothers in other studies of reproductive markets, also came to see themselves as consumers. Perhaps these mothers depart from previous studies in this respect because of the ways that my sample is a snapshot in time: the vast majority of the parents I interviewed began their process of international adoption at the precise moment that those processes became more difficult and unpredictable from the adoptive parents' perspective. The narratives that I present here suggest that these changes may have cracked the ideological facade of international adoption as a purely benevolent enterprise. This would have allowed (or forced) adoptive parents to more easily see the multiple dimensions of their own ethically ambiguous positions in a shifting and complex reproductive marketplace. Pat and Rich provide one painfully clear example of parents who confronted fraud and corruption in the adoption agency they worked with and who came to see the entire project of international adoption in a different light because of it. The stories throughout this chapter point to more generalized experiences: globalization, information technologies, the booming of social media, and increasing investigative journalism (in addition to critical scholarship) on international adoption have rendered the commercial character of international adoption increasingly visible. But while camps of activists coalesce around a binary "pro" and "against" vision of international adoption in politics and the media, parents live out the ambivalence and uncertainty that an expanded awareness has engendered.

Second, these stories show how altruism played a substantial, if secondary, role in how the mothers I interviewed perceived their actions. It was the mothers' sense of altruism that systemic changes to international adoption shook the most, and it was through the fracture of that feeling—their individual version of a "triumphal narrative"—that they were able to first glimpse adoption commerce. Pat and Rich provide a dramatic example of the limits of adoptive parents' altruism and, consequently, a clear illustration of the adoptive parents' fundamental position as consumers. But the ethical questions raised by Pat and Rich's individual decision to leave Elsa behind are less germane to this point than the fact that, like any buyer, they were free to walk away. Indeed, the real ethical questions—as well as the theoretical problems—with treating adoption as a reproductive market center on the fact that the "commodities" in this market-place are not commodities. While international adoption certainly functions as a reproductive marketplace, it is distinct from markets for genetic materials and reproductive labor in important ways. Exchanges of genetic material for money clearly entail complex ethical problems, as does contracting the labor of a surrogate. But adoption is a transactional exchange of a human being. One solution, voiced most strongly in the sociological literature by Viviana Zelizer, is simply to foster greater transparency and an open acknowledgment of the already commercial nature of adoption. But the critical response to Zelizer's position cannot be erased: What would it look like for an adoption—inevitably born of inequality, violence, and displacement—to be, in Zelizer's words, a "life-enhancing" economic arrangement? Given the enormity of the gulf between parties, it can seem like an impossible proposition. Politicians don't like impossible propositions, and so despite calls from some academics and activists to streamline and regulate the adoption marketplace, the more common response to allegations of fraud and corruption—sometimes on the part of the U.S. Department of State, sometimes on the part of the sending nation—has been to simply shut programs down.

Third, this chapter introduces important themes that speak to the broader context of this book—the continual renegotiation of family life and caregiving in the twenty-first century. In this chapter, we see the tension that these mothers experience among altruism, maternal obligation, and "choice." These mothers work hard to balance their own desires, aspirations, fears, and limits against their perceptions of care, ethical behavior, and obligation to others. However, simultaneously, their every action is directed in large measure by marketplace externalities of which they often, at least at the outset, are ignorant. At the same time, these mothers express complex emotions and navigate difficult decisions surrounding adopting and raising children with special needs. This is a theme that rests at the center of many of their narratives but, as we have already seen, is in tension with other aspects of their decision-making. Ultimately, the ways that these mothers interacted with the shrinking international adoption marketplace in which they found themselves shows how these mothers were forced to renegotiate their visions and experiences of family, the meanings of motherhood, and the lopsided nature of reproductive "choice." In the next chapter, I turn to the ways that adoptive parents negotiate their decision-making surrounding their children's race, age, health, and disability status in more detail. In a market context, stigmatized children, whether by race or any other factor, are less "adoptable," something that Pat and Rich bring into painful relief. But my findings suggest that parents' calculus is nuanced and the hierarchies of desirability that they establish are both unexpected and internally contradictory. Indeed, I argue that parents' decision-making is a reflection of their deepest anxieties and aspirations for their children in the context of more permeable racial boundaries and a precarious new economy.

Parental Anxiety and Interwoven Decision-Making Surrounding Race, Health, and "Fitness"

Danielle is a married white mother in her late forties with a teenage daughter by birth and an elementary school–age daughter adopted from China. Sitting down in her expansive, newly renovated suburban home, Danielle told me that while she and her husband, Mark, were very open to forming a multiracial family, her own parents were more traditional. She explained, "When we first told my parents we were adopting from China, they said, 'Why? Don't you want to have a baby that looks like you?' And I was like, um, no. I said, 'We are not concerned about that; we want a healthy child.' We could adopt from Russia or Ukraine, but those are not healthy children, generally. We would rather go with a more known quantity, and just have a child we can love, who will just be healthy." Many might applaud the fact that race is—at least in a limited sense—no longer a deal-breaker in parents' images of their future children. In Danielle's case, she seems to see her own colorblindness as a generational achievement—she could handle a multiracial family, even if her parents couldn't. Danielle's "abstract liberalism" (as Eduardo Bonilla-Silva might put it) is consistent with shifting ideas about race and, particularly, about "honorarily white" Asian Americans in U.S. society more broadly. But beyond a degree of colorblindness, Danielle reveals that the primary driver of her decision-making is her desire for "a healthy baby," a near-prerequisite for a child she can "just . . . love."

Alyssa and Keith are a white married couple in their early thirties with a three-year-old daughter, Isabella, whom they adopted as an infant from the Democratic Republic of the Congo. They live in a neighborhood full of young families in a midsized rural New England town. I sat down to talk with Alyssa on a snowy February morning at her local Starbucks, right after she dropped Isabella off at her half-day preschool. Wondering if Alyssa had arrived first, I pulled into the parking lot next to a shiny black SUV sporting a red, yellow, and green "Africa Love" bumper sticker. I found Alyssa inside—friendly, bubbly, and eager to participate in the project, as well as very happy to engage in what she called "some mommy talk" about preschools, toys, behavioral challenges, and funny parenting moments. We left the interview agreeing that if we lived closer to one another, we might have arranged a playdate for our kids. But during the interview, Alyssa also expressed frustration with some of her fellow young parents, whom she felt did not understand or appreciate the differences between their own experiences and hers as a transracial adoptive mother. Alyssa used the example of a "typical three-year-old tantrum" to illustrate her point, explaining, "I had a lady call the cops on me at Target because they thought I was kidnapping [my daughter]." Alyssa felt that her white friends could never understand the discrimination that her daughter faces because their experiences are limited both by their children's whiteness and by their own unquestioned biological ties to their children. Wanting to be "just like" her young-parent friends but also needing the recognition that her circumstances were unique, Alyssa echoes a long-understood paradox in adoption; as Judith Modell (1994) first described, adoptive parents want to replicate the arrangements and relationships of nonadoptive families, yet simultaneously be recognized for their distinctiveness.

This paradox that Alyssa identifies—of being (and wanting to be seen as) "just like" others but also distinctive—takes on additional meanings within transracial adoptive families and highlights the tension between race-awareness and "colorblindness" that permeates all kinds of debates about race in our society. Ellen Herman puts this in historical perspective, explaining that unlike in the past, when "the paradoxical point was to design kinship so seamlessly that adoptive families did not appear to be designed at all" (2008: 121), adoption no longer strives to "appear natural" above all else. As Herman explains, other concerns have risen above race-based matching; although not without controversy, domestic and international transracial adoptions are more visible than ever. But set against the history of racial formation in the United States, white mothers of black children signal—and literally embody—centuries of conflict and contradiction; as if speaking directly to Alyssa in the aisle at Target, Barbara Katz Rothman writes, "We've crossed a racial boundary in our motherhood. . . . We have a baby that 'can't be' ours" (2005: 193). In this chapter, I explore what adoptive parents have to say about race but also about health, age, and ability/disability as an interwoven set of factors that they consider early on in their adoption processes. While some white adoptive parents clearly prioritize adopting a white child, the vast majority of the adoptive parents with whom I spoke emphasized, above all else, their desire for a healthy child. The narratives that I explore in this chapter reveal the complicated meanings that parents attach to their children's health. Locating race within this constellation of parental considerations certainly tells us something about both race and racism among white adoptive parents, but may also illuminate something about the ongoing racialization of circulating ideologies about health and fitness, as well as the racialized nature of contemporary parenting in today's anxious, risk-obsessed times.

Alyssa's narrative exemplifies the overlapping concerns about the age, health status, and race of adopted children that ran through all the interviews I conducted. One of the youngest mothers in my sample, Alyssa told me that after a year of trying to get pregnant, she was diagnosed with polycystic ovarian syndrome, a hormonal imbalance that is the leading cause of female infertility. She tried some pharmacological interventions but stopped short of pursuing IVF because of both the expense and the uncertainty. Turning to international adoption, she wanted to find a program that would be as quick and as "certain" as possible. She also wanted a baby. Alyssa explained, "For our first child, we really wanted a child as young as possible. We knew we would be better suited to an infant rather than a child of four or five. I was a special ed teacher before my daughter came home, and just seeing those behaviors that come with older adopted children . . . I didn't want to bring my work home. I don't know if that sounds bad, but it's just one of those things; you have to know your limits. We just knew what we wanted, at least [for] our first child: an infant as young as possible." Immediately, Alyssa links age to disability. But Alyssa's emphasis is on behavior—and, by implication, on typical social, emotional, and neurological development. Indeed, Alyssa explains that she wants to adopt "an infant as young as possible" as a hedge against the kinds of atypical neurological development that she saw in the older adopted children she had worked with professionally.

Continuing, Alyssa described her and Keith's first steps in pursuing international adoption. Given their relatively young age and their desire for a quick process, few international adoption programs struck Alyssa as viable options when they began the process of adopting in 2010. Filtered through these constraints, Alyssa's priorities become more visible. Discussing her and Keith's choices of sending nations from which to pursue an adoption, Alyssa quickly made it clear that health trumped national origin and, as a corollary, race. She recounted, "We had to research countries and agencies. We did them simultaneously. Some countries weren't even an option for us; we weren't even going to consider [them]. Well, Russia and Eastern European countries. I had worked with so many children who were adopted from orphanages in those countries and had significant [reactive attachment disorder] and other behavioral issues that are so common coming from those hard orphanages. It wasn't even something I would consider, even infants. So really, we're left with Africa, because there aren't really adoption programs in England, or whatever." Alyssa's narrative certainly demonstrates the interwoven nature of concerns over age, health, and ability/disability in adoptive parents' thinking and decision-making about their future children. But perhaps the most striking thing in Alyssa's narrative is the colorblindness with which she discusses her child's race. In this text, Alyssa is quite clear that her primary concern is her child's neurological and social-emotional health and development. At the same time, staking out a position of colorblindness whitewashes the fact that, as in the stories of several other parents presented in this chapter, black children were adopted as last resort—and often only as "unspoiled" infants. Furthermore, Alyssa's startling inattention to power and privilege—the false equivalence she draws between "Africa" and "England"—illustrates precisely how colorblindness, as Bonilla-Silva famously argues, can function as an "elastic wall that barricades whites from the United States' racial reality" (2006: 47). Bonilla-Silva argues that colorblind racism is most clearly manifest in whites' (like Alyssa's) downplaying of structural inequalities related to race, but he also suggests that it can be seen in the kind of "abstract liberalism" that the majority of parents with whom I spoke expressed in their openness to adopting children of color.

The changing nature of international adoption (the changing "supply" of children, in particular) has forced parents to consider a range of possibilities that previous cohorts of international adoptive parents were not structurally forced to consider: older children, children with documented medical needs, and black African and Afro-Caribbean children who, by and large, were not available for adoption in the United States. It was only in the early 2000s that U.S. adoption agencies opened new programs in Ethiopia, Liberia, Uganda, Haiti, and the Congo to meet ongoing demand after programs in Russia, China, and Guatemala were interrupted. Indeed, Alyssa acknowledged that she would have liked to adopt from Guatemala or from China. She was disappointed that Guatemala had shut down and that the wait time for a "healthy baby girl" from China was "like seven years or something." Ultimately, Alyssa and Keith's decision-making process hinged on multiple factors and revealed some of Allyssa's pragmatic and emotional limitations.

In this chapter, I argue that the ways in which parents weave these factors together in their decision-making reveal their most profound desires—and anxieties—surrounding their children's futures. Further, I argue that structural changes to international adoption, coupled with the new, emerging shape of parental anxiety in the twenty-first century, complicates adoptive parents' calculus. Thinking about children's futures implies a particular kind of preoccupation with their "fitness" to meet the demands of a precariously shifting economy and society. In an era where work and even citizenship depend on cognitive "fitness" and flexibility (see Pitts-Taylor 2010), the task falls to mothers—and their imperative to mother intensively—to prepare their children for success in a neuroscientific, hypercognitive age (Wall 2010). Our knowledge economy and hypercognitive society demand developmental, cognitive, and social-emotional "fitness" at the same time that dramatic advances in medical technology have made birth defects like cleft palate malformation or certain congenital heart defects entirely correctable through surgery. Indeed, the mothers that I interviewed universally tried to avoid adopting children with cognitive, behavioral, and social-emotional disabilities, while many were willing to adopt a child with what they considered to be a "correctable" medical need. These mothers illustrate how our ideas and ideals about health and fitness change in relation to both the demands of our economy and the capabilities of medical care and technology. But health itself has long been a racialized construct, from ideas about "cleanliness" in the British Empire to far-reaching debates about eugenics in the twentieth century (see, for example, McClintock 1995 on the colonial context and Carter 1997 on the contemporary U.S. context), and whiteness has routinely been defined in contrast to supposed deficiencies in the cleanliness, health, and fitness of indigenous, immigrant, or other nonwhite groups. Racialized notions of fitness are apparent today in the disproportionate labeling of black students, particularly boys, as "special needs" (see Blum 2015 for an overview). In this context, racialized notions of health and fitness—and therefore race itself—rest at the center of adoptive parents' decision-making, barely acknowledged, except, ironically, when white parents insist upon adopting white children. For the vast majority of the parents I spoke with who adopted children of color, the prevailing discourse of colorblindness—considered its own form of racism—is what allowed them to elevate health above race as a primary consideration.

Much has been written about the unacknowledged racism of many white adoptive parents, particularly with respect to black children that they either do or do not ultimately adopt (see, in particular and most recently, Gailey 2010; Seligman 2013). That black children remain particularly "difficult to place" through public and private adoption is both a clear fact and a profound tragedy. Here, however, I ask specifically how white adoptive parents' decision-making processes reveal the ways that race is intertwined with other ideas about adoptive children's desirability, with particular attention to health, ability/disability, and the gendered discourses and family arrangements that feed contemporary forms of parental anxiety. The ability to even ask this question rests on the inexplicit and complicated nature of colorblind racism, as well as the dynamism and fluidity of some racial categories, but perhaps not others, in the contemporary United States. The stories I present in this chapter speak directly to the intersection of two distinct literatures within sociology: the literature on racial formation—how the boundaries and perceived hierarchies between racial groups form and change—and the literature on parenting and parental anxiety in the face of preparing their children for an uncertain political and economic future.

INTERNATIONAL ADOPTION AS A SITE OF RACIAL FORMATION

The narratives of the mothers I interviewed emerge from an increasingly complex ethnoracial order in the United States. The 1970s and 1980s saw dramatic increases in the numbers of domestic transracial adoptions in addition to the increasing international adoptions of the 1980s, 1990s, and 2000s. Interracial adoption has a storied history in the United States, having been (sometimes simultaneously) forbidden, encouraged, discouraged, vilified, and extolled as a means of achieving racial justice.[1] Yet at the same time that arguments against transracial adoption promote family preservation and seek to advance reproductive justice for mothers of color, such arguments may also reinforce racial separation and, indirectly, the purported biogenetic basis of racial categories. This tension also runs through more fundamental questions about how racial categories form to begin with. If race and ethnicity are rooted in ancestry and kinship, then adoption must be a site of ongoing racial formation.

Recent studies of both contemporary immigration and the children of racially or ethnically mixed couples question the ongoing meanings of categories like "white," "minority," and "mainstream" (see Alba 2009; Alba and Nee 2005; Kasinitz et al. 2009; Lee and Bean 2012; Waters 1999; Yancey 2003). In particular, Jennifer Lee and Frank Bean (2012) argue that children of both white-Asian and white-Hispanic interethnic couples increasingly view themselves as white.[2] Lee and Bean suggest that these children's identity flows in large part from being monolingual English speakers who experience their Asian or Hispanic ethnicity as increasingly symbolic—relegated to foods and occasional holidays, just like their peers of Italian or Irish heritage. This kind of symbolic ethnicity for a monolingual English speaker, most scholars of international adoption have long argued, is exactly what international adoptees experience (Dorow 2006; Howell 2006; Jacobson 2008). Thus as Richard Alba and Victor Nee argue, contemporary patterns of racial formation must rely on "new ways of theorizing assimilation as a social process stemming from immigration" (2003: 9). Likewise, Philip Kasinitz and his coauthors write, "Today's immigrants and their children challenge us to examine the nature of our racial definitions, the ways in which race operates in American society, and how nonwhite immigrants and their descendants will be incorporated into the society as members of racial categories" (2009: 302).

For black adopted children, neither race nor symbolic ethnicity is simple. The parents I interviewed who adopted African children also went to great lengths to expose them to the food, language, religion, and other traditions of their natal countries. But I would argue that these parents did so in part because they were forced to wrestle with the question of whether their child is Ethiopian American, Congolese American, or just African American—that is, black. Linda Seligman, comparing the parents of Chinese adopted children to the parents of African American domestic adoptees, notes that "although adoptive parents use 'heritage' with respect to transnational transracial adoptions, they tend to use 'race' in the context of domestic transracial adoptions" (2013: 11). I take up this observation with respect to the white parents of black African adoptees whom I interviewed. Their narratives suggest a particularly finely grained exercise of boundary-work. They emphasize their black children's national heritages while simultaneously (though not always) distancing themselves and their children from U.S.-born blacks. In the context of a shifting ethnoracial hierarchy in the twenty-first century United States, George Yancey (2003), among other scholars, suggests that the new racial divide in our society is between blacks and nonblacks rather than between whites and nonwhites. In line with Lee and Bean (2012) as well as others who look at model minority discourses, Yancey argues that assimilation is, in some ways, inevitable for nonblack racial minorities but that the African American experience is "unique" (2003: 153). The narratives of the white mothers of African children that I present in this chapter certainly highlight white adoptive mothers' (likely futile) efforts to exempt their black children from that "unique" experience.

Michael Omi and Howard Winant frame their argument in *Racial Formation in the United States* with the general critique that much of the sociological literature on race has a "tendency to *reduce* race to a mere manifestation of other supposedly more fundamental social and political relationships" (1994: 2)—a disembodied construct. They alternatively define race itself as "a concept which signifies and symbolizes social conflicts and interests by referring to different types of human bodies" (1994: 55). This definition means that when a person's body is racialized, it carries with it a full history of ethnic, class, and national-level conflicts, among others, and that it reflects contemporary social hierarchies. It is precisely in this way that race can transcend other elements of the social structure, as well as other axes of transracial adoptees' identities. This is how adoption can make a child upper-middle-class but cannot make a black child white. And this is where "race-awareness" has emerged as an important part of the transracial adoptive experience and brought many adoptive families to embrace their children's cultural heritage, from Chinese New Year festivals to language classes to "heritage trips." But in the context of white families who adopt black children, the "social conflicts and interests" that black bodies carry for life are particularly weighty, as well as particularly immutable. As Rothman writes, "For a while, your black child will have a white family, the protective cloak of your whiteness cast over the child. But eventually, that child goes off, as children eventually do, and your whiteness won't do a thing for that kid" (2005: 233).

Stephen Cornell and Douglas Hartmann (1998) diverge slightly from Omi and Winant in their thinking. They argue that while the formation and maintenance of both racial categories and individual racial identities rely on an ascribed status based in racialized histories, race also depends on the ongoing efforts and actions of individuals. In the context of interracial adoption, domestic or international, this begs the question of whether being adopted by white parents can, indeed, "whiten" a child of color to some extent. As the history of racial categories over the twentieth century has shown, "white" is far from an immutable category; it greatly expanded in the post-World War II era to include formerly not-quite-white groups (see, for example, Brodkin 1998 on Eastern European Jews; Ignatieff 1995 and Roediger 2007 on Irish immigrants). But the Irish, Italian, and Jewish immigrants who "became white" largely did so by distinguishing themselves from U.S. blacks, upholding a persistent black-and-white binary in U.S. race relations. Indeed, Kasinitz and his coauthors remind us that the conceptual treatment of blackness remains central because, as in prior models of assimilation, we continue to "risk essentializing central-city black culture in the image of the underclass" (2009: 8). For many Afro-Caribbean immigrants to the United States, Mary Waters writes that "becoming American also entails becoming Black" (1999: 93). For children of mixed black-white parentage, Lee and Bean (2012) argue that the one-drop rule continues to operate in a way that has never applied to children of mixed white-Asian or white-Hispanic parentage.

With respect to Asian Americans, Lee and Bean hold up their "model minority" and "honorarily white" status as evidence of a dramatically shifting ethnoracial hierarchy in the United States, given the derisive and violent discourse surrounding Asian immigrants at the turn of the twentieth century. But Lee and Bean are clear about what has "whitened" Asians, writing that "what changed was not Asian immigrants' skin color or other physical characteristics but the way they are now perceived by native-born whites after having achieved both economic and social mobility" (2012: 139). Money and "respectability" are what "whiten." It is in this vein that the notion of a model minority is fundamentally attached to an anti-model—poor African Americans—and reinforces our cultural association of black Americans with cultural deficiency and inescapable poverty.[3] As Michèle Lamont has argued, these boundaries rely on our basic, ongoing work of refining and reasserting what distinguishes us from others. The mothers that I interviewed described this kind of boundary-work as a central part of their decision-making surrounding both the sending nation from which they chose to adopt and the perceived risk-profile of the children they adopted, particularly with respect to neuropsychological health and development. As Nadia Abu El-Haj (2007) and Dorothy Roberts (2009, 2012) have both argued, health, "fitness," and race are continually reinscribed upon one another as our cultural conversation about health increasingly centers on genetics, "responsible" decision-making, and risk management. The narratives of the mothers that I interviewed reflect this cultural sensibility; in their decision-making surrounding their children's adoption, health served as an agent of racialization, albeit in sometimes unexpected ways.

PARENTAL ANXIETY IN A RISK SOCIETY

When the mothers I interviewed spoke about health and fitness, they did so in the context of a particular set of discourses surrounding motherhood and our current cultural relationship with risk more generally. The late twentieth century and the outset of the twenty-first century have heralded an age of "intensive mothering" (see Hays 1996, most notably) in which women in particular are exhorted and expected to devote tremendous amounts of time, energy, and money to the project of raising their children. Sharon Hays argues that this is a distinctly gendered phenomenon and that intensive mothering results from the intractability of the gendered arrangements of work and family life. From Arlie Hochschild's 1989 description of a "stalled revolution" to Kathleen Gerson's 2010 description of an "unfinished" one, the middle- and upper-middle-class heterosexual mothers that populate such studies have remained both psychologically and economically saddled with the great majority of care work, despite substantial (though uneven) shifts in the gendered ideologies that women and men bring into marriage. The stubbornness of these gendered work and family arrangements is apparent in the Pew Research Center's finding that the share of "stay-at-home" mothers has increased across the socioeconomic spectrum since 2000 (Cohn et al. 2014). Moreover, that a norm of intensive mothering has completely saturated our culture is perhaps best illustrated by the finding that employed mothers at the outset of the twenty-first century spent more time actively engaged with their children than nonemployed mothers did in the 1960s and 1970s (Bianchi et al. 2007). Expectations for mothers' (and, arguably, all parents') involvement in their children's lives has never been higher because, as many argue, the stakes are so high due to economic precariousness, the shrinking of the middle class, and the overall splintering of full-time work, from subcontracted janitors to subcontracted lawyers.

Recent literature on parental anxiety tells us that parents—but of course, mothers, most particularly—feel that they must cultivate the kinds of attributes, advantages, and skills that they suspect will best prepare their children for an uncertain future. As our overall cultural shift in focus from treatment to prevention highlights a shift in our understanding of practical and moral culpability for health outcomes, new perceived risks and threats emerge in the forms of environmental pollution, chemical exposure, suboptimal (or excessive) nutrition, and even genetic risk. Mothers are specifically exhorted to mitigate these risks.[4] The generally affluent mothers in my sample certainly reported subscribing to the class-based stratagems of "concerted cultivation" that Annette Lareau (2003) describes. But they also spoke about their decision-making surrounding adoption in a way that resembled what Joan Wolf (2010) calls "total mothering." Writing in the context of ideologies surrounding breastfeeding, Wolf argues that contemporary mothering ideologies demand a total mitigation of all potential risk—an impossible proposition, of course, but one that drives mothers to extreme measures. These multiple and complicated anxieties run through the narratives of the mothers I interviewed. While these mothers' anxieties and intensive mothering practices are largely class based (see Hays 1996; Lareau 2003; Nelson 2010), they are also linked to the intellectual requirements of a knowledge economy as well as, increasingly, the social-emotional acumen required to remain employed in the "gig economy." For nervous middle- and upper-middle-class parents who perceive shrinking professional—or simply decent—job opportunities for their children, the demands of a truly "hypercognitive" society collide with the increasing medicalization of childhood, and this has led to heightened scrutiny of children's social-emotional, behavioral, and neurological development.[5]

The parents whom I interviewed for this project almost universally expressed a distinct hierarchy of health over whiteness. This is consistent with the existing literature on parental decision-making in international adoption, which establishes that adoptive parents privilege their future children's health status over other factors when selecting a country from which to adopt (see Jacobson 2013; Khanna and Killian 2015; Kim 2008; Quiroz 2008; Seligman 2013; Sweeny 2013; Zhang and Lee 2011). This literature is inherently intersectional because the country from which a child is adopted is, of course, largely determinative of that child's racial status in the United States. Heather Jacobson (2013), Nikki Khanna and Caitlin Killian (2015), and Yuanting Zhang and Gary R. Lee (2011) in particular find that white, upper-middle-class American adoptive parents like Danielle elect to adopt "honorarily white" Asian children over white Russian children, whom parents perceive to be at risk for a variety of health problems. These parents' racial imaginaries and racialized visions of health are particularly relevant because the international adoptive parents I interviewed envision a "healthy baby" as, first and foremost, psychologically and neurologically typical. Additionally, where other studies show that adoptive parents will adopt "fully" healthy children over potentially atypically developing ones, my findings suggest that in a constricting adoption marketplace, some parents elect to adopt children with documented physical health care needs—but whom they hoped would be "neurotypical"—over children whom they perceived to be at too great a risk of atypical neuropsychological development. And particularly in the context of African adoptions, the parents in this study's overarching emphasis on neurotypical kids highlights a unique intersection of race with evolving ideas about what constitutes health, fitness, and disability.

In this chapter, I share parents' narratives around three themes. First, I discuss the ways that the mothers I interviewed drew racialized boundaries around what constituted a "healthy" child and expressed their absolute preference for adopting "neurotypical" children. Second, I turn to the narratives of mothers who elected to adopt children with physical health care needs, which further illustrate the ways that neuropsychological health functions as the primary marker of fitness among the mothers in my sample. Finally, I present the narratives of mothers who adopted black children from Africa. For the mothers whom I interviewed, race—but blackness in particular—took on different meanings at different health statuses. These mothers were able to articulate these different intersectional racial imaginaries because of both racialized stereotypes of sending nations and also because of the prevailing colorblind discourse that characterizes much of the discussion of race in the United States.

A "HEALTHY BABY"

Many of the parents I interviewed were clear that they turned to international adoption out of trepidation toward domestic adoption. The previous chapter discusses some of the ways that they felt uncomfortable with the transactional dynamics of private domestic adoption. But the parents I interviewed also pursued international adoption in the belief that they might hedge against potentially unhealthy American children and risky American birth mothers. Building off of Ortiz and Briggs's 2003 analysis of international adoption in Romania,[6] Sara Dorow calls this "the transracial imaginary of white America, which includes the vilification of poor mothers of color, [and in which] nonwhite orphans abroad are deemed more rescuable and desirable than domestic nonwhite children" (2010: 71). Ortiz and Briggs take their argument a step further with specific respect to U.S. foster kids, arguing that Americans are motivated to adopt abroad because of "the racialization and biologization of poverty" (2003: 40) and the subsequent "creation of moral panics over the scarcity of white children for adoption or the medical fragility of crack babies" (2003: 41). In this chapter, I take up Ortiz and Briggs' argument that international adoption relies on the "racialization and biologization of poverty" in international adoption, asking precisely how adoptive parents' desires for a "healthy" baby affect their thinking and decision-making surrounding race.

Almost thirty years after panic over an "epidemic" of "crack babies" ensued—and the myth was ultimately debunked (see Okie 2009)—Ivy, a married white mother of a child adopted from Nepal, fell back on its old panicked language to explain why she opted against domestic adoption. As she explained, "We did a lot of research about domestic, domestic open, foster care, and to be really honest, the domestic scene was scary—you had to take five siblings and three of them were crack babies. Not the direction we wanted to go." As Ortiz and Briggs (among many others) establish, "crack babies" are black in our cultural imagination, and this white mother hit two of the most classic negative tropes about poor black mothers right on the head: drug use and uncontrolled fertility. Ivy's description leaves little doubt that the faces she imagined in her domestic adoption "horror story" were black. While Ivy was particularly explicit in her phrasing, other mothers used somewhat more coded language. Arden, a married white mother who adopted a daughter from the Democratic Republic of the Congo, explained,

> As part of my research, I looked into private and foster care adoption. Private didn't make sense for us because we didn't have fertility issues and the supply cannot meet the demand in domestic adoption. The need for those kids, it's not the same. So there was no reason to do private infant adoption for us; we could just have our own biological kid. As far as domestic foster care, it wasn't a good match for us because of the age of the kids. And the needs of those kids

are extremely severe. So because of the age and the special needs, we decided not to.

Here, Arden is particularly emphasizing what she herself called "the needs of those kids": "But of course," she said, it was "the needs of the children" that caused her and her husband to adopt from the Congo. Echoing Dorow, Arden explained that she felt a domestic infant did not "need" her. And by emphasizing her own fertility, Arden reinforced the fact that she was adopting a child who did. Arden also made clear that she went to the Congo because "they had babies available," and so, for Arden, a black baby in Africa was more rescuable and far more desirable than a "damaged" black child in the United States. Arden rested her decision-making on a discourse of colorblindness as well as a racialized discourse of health and fitness.

Presented with the choices inherent in international adoption, parents' colorblind language enabled them to explain their hierarchy of preferences in terms of age, health, and race: parents wanted babies as young as possible as a hedge against atypical social-emotional and neurological development. Perhaps more important, parents consistently expressed a distinct hierarchy of health over whiteness, with the exception of the parents of the five children (8 percent of the children in the sample) who were adopted from Russia. Jane, a fifty-year-old married mother of a daughter adopted from China, turned to adoption after "a year or so" of trying to conceive but without pursuing any kind of medical intervention. She was uninterested, she explained, mostly because, as she said, she was "getting a little older." When I asked her why she and her husband had chosen to adopt from China specifically, she explained,

> We just ruled out other places. China seemed to be very organized, they had the experience of doing this for a decade or more at that point, and it seemed very efficient, and we would be taken care of in-country as well . . . and then, just knowing that statistically, the children from China seem to do very well—they have less attachment issues and things like that, that I've heard, [compared to children] from other countries. Russia we kind of considered a little bit, but it didn't really feel right to us. I mean, I've heard a few things about Russia; it's not really fair, but it just seemed like . . . it was partly emotional and partly intellectual, but it just seemed like China was a better fit and would go more smoothly.

Jane articulated her trepidation about Russia as a positive decision to adopt from China, where the process was streamlined and the children "seem[ed] to do very well." Jane hardly masked her priorities: whiteness was unimportant in the face of the attachment issues "and things like that" for which Russian adoptees are infamous. Yet Jane's quick dismissal of whiteness was enabled by the model minority status enjoyed by many groups of Asian immigrants, including, ultimately, the adopted Chinese daughters of white middle-class professional parents who, as Jane put it, "seem to do very well."

In a similar vein, Beth, a mother with an older biological daughter and a younger daughter adopted from Russia, told me that she felt comfortable with international adoption in general because of the contrast between adoptees from Asia and U.S. foster kids in our collective imagination. She explained, "I never really thought about domestic adoption. I only really thought about international. I mean, I wonder to what extent it has to do with the wave of Chinese and Korean adoption and how successful those kids are in the outside world. And how foster care has a very different image to middle-class Americans—of being like forgotten kids, messed up kids, messed up families, baggage. And I wonder first to what extent that was in my psyche deep enough that I couldn't even consider it as a valid option." While Beth did ultimately adopt from Russia and not from China or South Korea, she highlights the dichotomy between model minority status and "deficiency" that seems to enable many of the parents I interviewed to adopt Asian children, as well as the particular ways that health—and a biologization of poverty—can cut across sometimes fluid, sometimes permeable racial categories. Indeed, she illustrates the idea that U.S. society can assign model minorities differing degrees of whiteness.

The discourse of a model minority—and its dialectic opposite—certainly illustrate the ideas that many white adoptive parents have about the health of black American children. But the model minority discourse does not address precisely why many white adoptive parents in the United States hesitate to adopt white children from Eastern Europe. Anna, a married white mother of a son adopted from Nepal, described her turn away from Eastern Europe as guided by her adoption agency as well as a discourse of colorblindness. Speaking specifically to what she means by "health," she explained,

> We started with Eastern Europe because it was what we knew . . . but then our adoption agency asked us to prioritize what was most important to us in terms of health, age, ethnic background, and we didn't care about age and ethnic background at all, but we did care about health, and that's when they said, "Well, then, Eastern Europe is not for you." So we went back to the drawing board a little bit, and that's when we realized that Nepal is a Hindu and Buddhist country, and that leads to very little abuse and neglect. That was the main way we saw it then . . . compared to Eastern Europe there's probably very little abuse and neglect and very little exposure to alcohol and drugs.

Anna was not concerned about bacterial infection or malnutrition—very real, deadly problems in Nepal. Rather, she uses "health" as code for a lack of fetal exposure to drugs and alcohol and a lowered risk for disordered attachment, social-emotional challenges, and atypical cognitive development, at least in her estimation.

Anna's barely coded language runs through the narratives of many other mothers with whom I spoke and dovetails with ideas about exoticism and "naturalness" among transracial adopted children. Catherine, a single white mother of a son adopted from Kazakhstan, also framed her choice of Kazakhstan over Russia in terms of Kazakhstan's ethnoreligious character: "Kazakhstan is an Islamic country," she explained, "so there's less incidence of fetal alcohol syndrome." Another single white mother, Betty, a PhD in Russian literature with a son adopted from Mongolia, told me that she originally wanted to pursue adoption from Russia because she speaks fluent Russian, has a deep cultural and historical understanding of the region, and had lived in Russia for extended periods of time. But her concerns over the "health" of the children living in Russian orphanages trumped her intellectual interest and cultural affinity. Betty also framed the health—defined as less prenatal drug and alcohol exposure—of Mongolian children in terms of Mongolia's Buddhist character, despite the fact that Mongolia's rate of alcohol abuse is actually three times the overall rate in Europe (see Lim 2009). Indeed, these mothers exoticize their children and their children's native countries, casting them as "healthy" because they're unspoiled by drugs and alcohol and are therefore closer to their "natural" state. Echoing a trope as old as Orientalism, one mother said, "We were very open to ethnic cultures." These mothers clearly illustrate how a hierarchy of "health" over whiteness operates, as well as how "health" itself is racialized along the new lines of fitness and desirability that we've drawn as best we can to meet the demands of the new economy.

At the same time, it is absolutely the case that for a few mothers in my sample, adopting a white child was very important. Yet it's simultaneously clear that this struck them as a risky preference. Those who adopted white Russian children also experienced tremendous anxiety surrounding their children's social-emotional, behavioral, and neurological development. These parents were exceptional in my sample in the sense that health did *not* trump race, but health was still a fundamental concern. Indeed, all five of these mothers explained that they had chosen to adopt from Russia *only* because of race and in spite of serious trepidations related to attachment issues and fetal alcohol and drug exposure. Linda, a married white mother, with two children by birth, had adopted a school-aged brother and sister from Russia when her two older children were teenagers. She told me that she simply did not feel she could navigate the complexities of an interracial family, explaining, "We went with Russia because the kids would blend into our family naturally. And there was nothing wrong with getting a child from Ethiopia or China, I think. It's just that then my older kids would have to talk adoption all the time. Because that child . . . you know how it is. They don't look like them, so everybody has to say, 'Oh, they're adopted.' So I figured we wouldn't have to, you know, have to talk about our kids being adopted to everybody all the time." Similarly, Abby, a self-described "older" single white mother, specifically sought out a Russian adoption because she wanted a child who would "look like" her. Abby was not particularly nervous about fetal alcohol syndrome because, unlike almost all other participants in this project, she set out to adopt an elementary-aged child from the start. As a result, she explained, the presence of severe fetal alcohol syndrome would have been apparent. She was apprehensive about attachment, however, and described this as the only factor that made her doubt her commitment to motherhood and adoption.

Karen, a single white mother of a daughter adopted from Russia as a young toddler, was also very explicit about her reluctance to form an interracial family, as she felt her daughter would already face disadvantages as the child of a single mother in a traditionally religious Jewish community. Karen also shared with pride—if not a little bemusement—that acquaintances often comment on how alike she and her daughter, Leora, look (Karen showed me several pictures on her phone to elicit my opinion on the matter, as well as to show off Leora's recent social studies project). But Karen made no secret of her fears of fetal alcohol syndrome and other developmental disorders. She told me explicitly, "I wanted someone who wasn't institutional looking." Further, on multiple occasions during our interview, she described the scrutiny she gave to Leora's philtrum (the vertical groove between the nose and upper lip). Karen and her parents poured over Leora's photographs when Karen received the match, trying to determine if it was "flat"—a possible sign of fetal alcohol exposure. Karen also described immediately focusing on Leora's philtrum when the two met at the orphanage. Ultimately, Karen bonded with Leora before fully formulating her thoughts on Leora's risk of facing developmental challenges, and she decided to proceed with the adoption. Karen also explained, though, that after making the decision to proceed but before finalizing the adoption, she felt "tremendous relief" to see that Leora "was all there." Taken in concert with Danielle's stated desire in the opening of this chapter for a "healthy" child whom she and her husband could "just . . . love," these comments highlight the ways that neurotypical development not only rests at the center of mothers' preferences but also largely defines children's overall health and disability status.

Making Trade-Offs

Parents' discomfort with—and even fear of—domestic adoption loomed large in their decisions to pursue adoption internationally. As one mother summed up her feelings on international adoption, "It just seemed like it would go more smoothly." But as almost all the parents I interviewed discovered, international adoption rarely proceeds smoothly or quickly, particularly in the context of the massive changes to international adoption programs that were taking place as they pursued adoption. As a result, many of them reported making trade-offs in terms of the age, race, and health of their adopted children, and this decision-making sheds light on the interplay of race and "fitness" that characterizes these parents' narratives. Marjorie, a married white mother of three children adopted from China, was very explicit in her rejection of "damaged" foster children, alcohol-exposed Russian children, and children with atypical neurological and social-emotional development in general, but her language surrounding the trade-offs and compromises that she did make is telling. Initially explaining how she and her husband had ruled out adopting through domestic foster care, Marjorie was succinct: "We went to one state [foster-to-adopt] training group and the kids were significantly damaged." Telling me about her preferences with respect to international adoption, though, Marjorie elaborated,

> We specified zero to three, because of language, emotional, and other developmental things. The kids in foster care, the average age was seven or eight. We looked at a lot of different countries, but Guatemala was closed, Kazakhstan was closed, Vietnam was closed. So we looked at China, and they have a special focus program, which is kids who have minor correctable medical needs. So on the advice of some of our physician friends, we went with cleft palate kids. The wait [for them] was twelve to eighteen months, whereas a healthy child from China would have taken four years or more.

Here, Marjorie is clear that her children's age at adoption was paramount among her concerns. She is also clear that she was willing to make certain concessions in terms of her children's health. But Marjorie goes on to specify in no uncertain terms what she means. As she explained, "Russia was completely out because of [fetal alcohol syndrome]. I had worked in a drug rehab; I knew some of those behaviors. Our kids just needed surgery, and then they were fine. We could not have handled it, like, medical versus emotional issues."

Most recent adoptive parents have faced the decision to adopt an "older child"—a child over the age of one or two—or a child with a documented disability or health concern because "healthy infants" have become increasingly unavailable for international adoption as regulation and oversight has increased, both in the United States and within sending nations. This is the case even for parents adopting from China, a country that did not "shut down" or experience any major diplomatic shakeup. But Marjorie's story pinpoints what the vast majority of the parents I interviewed remained closed to: the prospect of adopting a child whom they perceived to be at risk for neurological, psychiatric, behavioral, or social-emotional challenges. Alyssa and Keith, introduced in the opening of this chapter, were able to bring their daughter home from the Congo at eight months old, but that program—one of the last to make "healthy infants" available—shut down soon after. Overwhelmingly, parents who were unable to adopt "healthy infants" revealed that when they choose "special needs" or "special focus" adoptions, they wanted to adopt a child with a diagnosis that, as more than one mother put it, was "correctable" or at least "medically understood." These mothers clearly excluded children whom they deemed to be at risk for atypical social-emotional development. As Alyssa's calculus clearly illustrates at the outset of this chapter, the best hedge against atypical neurodevelopment that parents could identify was a child's age. This concern came to the forefront for many parents as adoption processes grew longer, particularly in once-predictable China. Jane, another mother who adopted a daughter from China, explained, "Nobody was getting referrals as quickly as they thought they would . . . it was very disheartening and very hard to wait. When we finally got the referral, she was older than we had said we wanted, but as soon as I saw the picture, I knew this was right. I had dreams about her eyes, that I was looking in her eyes—she has these huge eyes; it's so sweet." Jane illustrates that age is paramount. But beyond age, Jane is focused on an intangible cognitive quality—she looked into her daughter's eyes and knew it "was right," just like Karen, who looked into her daughter Leora's eyes and knew she was "all there." Of course, in the case of a white mother adopting from China, a daughter with "huge eyes" hits on a classic trope in the racialization of Asian women who seek out "whitening" double-eyelid surgeries (Kaw 1993). Jane's focus on her Chinese daughter's "huge eyes"—a feature of white women—is deeply interwoven not only with ideas about health and cognitive fitness but also with racial assimilation in U.S. society.

Mary, a single mother in her early fifties, provides a striking example of the trade-offs that parents make when a sending nation's regulations change and then slow down the process of adoption. Mary described having focused on her business career earlier in life and, despite always wanting children, having "never met the right guy." When she turned forty-five, she decided to adopt from China, acting on the advice of a colleague who had adopted two daughters from China after experiencing several failed domestic placements. Mary elaborated on her decision and explained what happened next: "It was a fairly quick process from China at that time, and most importantly, they took single women. I made my application in September 2006 and I was logged in April 13, 2007. So at that time—up until that time—it was thirteen to fourteen months; it was a fairly manageable wait. I went to China because they accepted single women. So there was a flood of applicants, and that, coupled with all the other changes in China, economic and whatever else . . . So the wait became a big wait, and so you wait." Four years passed. Mary made a career change, got a graduate degree, moved back to her hometown, and climbed Mount Kilimanjaro because, she said, "I thought, 'What should I do now that will be more difficult with a child later on?' and I had always wanted to do that."

Meanwhile, since Mary saw no end to her waiting, she began to search for a way to expedite her process. She explained,

> I was looking at the waiting children pictures [online] and I thought, "I'm just gonna ask about this one little girl," and I asked to see her file. I went over to [Children's Hospital] and I thought, "I'm way out of my league," you know, "I'm a single mother, this isn't going to be fair to either one of us"; it was far more complicated than I wanted to deal with. I said [no], but then the director of the waiting children program called me again and said, "Listen, we have this child, we didn't know if you would want it, it's special focus," which means that it's not a real extenuating circumstance but because the child had a heart murmur and because they had identified it, they had to put the child into a different category. So I said, "Sure, I'll look at the file." I didn't want to see the picture but it was the cutest little picture and I was looking at the file and thinking, "This is so insignificant." I was looking at the EKG and I sent it to my mother by email and I said, "Why would I say no?" And she said, "You wouldn't." So I said, "Sure, I'll accept."

Mary's trade-off may seem minor, but she highlights the process that many parents I spoke with experienced: roadblocks were met with alternatives, and parents adjusted their thinking to accommodate what they considered to be minor, correctable medical needs. Mary's privilege—and the privilege of these adoptive parents, in general—speaks volumes because they have the resources to address a variety of "correctable" medical needs but would not relinquish their intergenerational privilege by adopting irreversibly damaged children with disordered attachment or damaged brains.

Parker and John provide another example of parents who were willing to adopt a child with a medical need that they considered "manageable." They are a white heterosexual married couple in their early thirties with two sons, eight-year-old Gabriel, adopted from Guatemala, and six-year-old John Jr., adopted from China. At the time of our interview, they lived in a modest apartment in an affluent inner suburb. John was employed full time, and Parker combined adjunct college teaching with a postdoctoral research fellowship. Despite the family portraits on the walls, the futon on which we conducted our interview was much more "grad student" than "upper-middle-class professional." Parker and John decided to grow their family through adoption before getting married in their early twenties and initially considered adopting through the state-run foster care system. They decided against that route primarily because Parker's career could lead them to move out of the state at any time, which would have disqualified them from any adoption in process. While they were exceptional in their interest in adoption from the foster care system, they were less of an exception in other ways. Parker was very clear that for their first child, they wanted "a baby, as young as possible," and they chose to adopt Gabriel from Guatemala—when adoptions in Guatemala were still open—primarily for that reason. By the time they were ready to adopt a second child, however, adoptions in Guatemala had stopped. They were old enough to adopt from China by that time, though the wait time for a healthy infant had grown to several years. Parker and John considered the range of disabilities they were willing to take on knowingly, and they ruled out severe physical limitations as well as mild, moderate, and severe developmental delays, including autism. As Parker related, "I didn't think we could handle major behavioral problems, or problems like autism." Instead, Parker and John selected a number of relatively minor, surgically "correctable" issues—cleft palate, missing digit, minor congenital heart defect. In relatively short order, they were matched with John Jr., who, after corrective surgery, is "doing great" with "no restrictions on his activities."

While there are certainly families in the United States who consciously and specifically adopt severely disabled children, they represent a tiny minority of adoptive parents. One mother I interviewed told me about an acquaintance who adopted a daughter with both severe disabilities and a chronic life-threatening illness. This devoutly Christian couple was strictly motivated by the desire that the girl would "know a family and know Jesus" before she died. But the mother who told me this story did so out of curiosity and a desire to distinguish herself and her own motivations from those of her acquaintance. Again and again, the parents that I interviewed told me that they were primarily motivated by the desire to parent, not by the desire to "save," neither spiritually nor in any other sense. This was as true for the few very religious Christian parents with whom I spoke as it was for those with a more secular outlook. This was so true for Pat and Rich, whose adoption processes in Guatemala I discussed in the previous chapter, that they backed out of an adoption of a child with severe disabilities. But Pat and Rich's circumstances, while extreme, were not atypical, as the parents were concerned with both severe physical limitations and impaired cognitive development. Many parents, including Pat and Rich, said they "just couldn't handle" the prospect of parenting a child with such severe special needs; Parker and John referred to it as "advanced parenting," emphasizing that for their first child, they were still "beginners."

Adopting Black Children

The narratives above suggest that these parents' expressions of colorblindness function as one way that they reveal the true meaning of their preferences surrounding their future children's health and fitness. Yet most of these parents' colorblindness had an implicit limit, revealed through the omission of any mention of black children. Of the parents I interviewed, the only ones who mentioned the possibility of adopting black children were those parents who actually did. There was a singular exception—Wendy, whose story I tell at the close of this chapter. One possible explanation for this omission could be parents' lack of awareness of adoption programs in Africa; these programs were simply not very large until other major sending nations shut down or significantly slowed their programs. In fact, many U.S. adoption agencies only opened programs in Ethiopia (the African country with by far the largest number of adoptees living in the United States) after Guatemala shut down international adoption with the United States in 2008. Correspondingly, Ethiopia only saw adoptions to the United States exceed 100 per year in 2001. Adoptions from Ethiopia surpassed 500 in 2006 and peaked at more than 2,500 in 2010 (see Under Secretary for Public Diplomacy and Public Affairs 2012). It was during that period that the majority of the parents I spoke with who adopted from Ethiopia began their processes, motivated in part, like Kate and Joan in the previous chapter, by what they described as an "affinity" for Africa. Since 2010, the number of adoptions from Ethiopia has declined by more than half, and all Ethiopian adoptions today are of children over the age of two. Other African countries represent a trickle of adoptions in comparison. In this context, what can we make of the narratives of parents who *do* adopt black children? How do parents elect to adopt from Africa? And how do their decision-making narratives surrounding race and "fitness" parallel or differ from the narratives of parents who do not?

Discussing why she ultimately chose to adopt from Africa, Kate, a married white mother of two adopted African children, explained, "We knew we weren't comfortable with Eastern European countries because of some of the issues with connections and how the kids are doing emotionally—the kids' emotional connections with the caregivers. But with Africa, we know enough Africans to know that the kids would have been held. They would have been tiny and they would have had stomach issues, but they would have been held and they would have been looked at and they would have been spoken to. And we wanted that for attachment reasons." Kate goes so far as to describe herself as happy to take on real physical health issues like malnutrition in lieu of "damaged" Russian children. Additionally, Arden, whose objections to children from U.S. foster care hinged on a desire to avoid the special needs I discussed above, expressed substantial confidence in African orphanage care: "We knew that [our daughter] would get a lot of individualized attention and loving; that's just in the African culture. Kids are worn until they're two or three." In contrast, Deirdre, a married white mother of two siblings adopted from Ethiopia, described her suspicion of Russian caregivers: "The communist system of childrearing and the mentality of that era is so . . . *cold*." Like the mothers of children adopted from Kazakhstan, Mongolia, and Nepal, described above, these mothers of African adoptees sound classically racist tropes of exotic, baby-wearing, "natural" African women, thinly veiled by their expression of colorblindness and "abstract liberalism." The "typical" development that makes African children different than African American children, in these mothers' minds, represents a new kind of boundary-work in an ever more fine-grained American ethnoracial order.

In order to explore the question of these mothers' boundary-making, I consistently asked the parents of African children about how they balanced exposing their children to the culture of their birth with exposing their children to African American culture. Did they find one or the other more important? More complicated? What strategies did they use? One mother, Deirdre, described her ongoing efforts to teach her two boys about African American history—slavery, Reconstruction, the civil rights movement. Among my sample, she was entirely alone in that effort. While some parents expressed a desire for their children to be exposed to well-educated middle-class African Americans, even more described the distance that their children (or, perhaps, they themselves) felt from less advantaged African Americans. Lisa, a mother of three children by birth and two biological siblings adopted from Ethiopia, explained, "I find that [my] kids relate better to other immigrant kids than kids of color specifically, because they have similar experiences rather than just looking the same. I have some friends with Ethiopian kids who live in a more diverse neighborhood closer to [the nearest large city]. They just don't get along with those kids, because they don't have a lot in common." The eighteen mothers in my sample who adopted African children all described conscientious efforts to expose their children to a diverse group of children and adults as well as to black adult role models. Some parents were more aware than others of their children's needs to navigate the complexities of an "African American" or "black" identity more broadly. All the parents of African children in my sample described efforts to keep their children connected to Ethiopian or Congolese culture specifically, whether through churches, community groups, adoptive family groups, or individual family friends.

Many of the children adopted from Ethiopia whose parents I interviewed came to the United States as older children, with memories, identities, and native language fluency. Perhaps because of this, their parents expressed both a great deal of fluency with Ethiopian culture and with some of the psychological and social-emotional issues facing older adopted children. For many parents, the depth of their children's trauma, pain, and anger was unexpected. Despite the distance that these families maintained from African American communities, history, and culture, they described going to great lengths to eat in Ethiopian restaurants, participate in Ethiopian community groups, visit Ethiopia, and attend Ethiopian churches. Marty—a devoted atheist and a single mother of five children, all biological siblings adopted from Ethiopia—described her discomfort with her oldest son's deep involvement in a local Ethiopian church. She explained, however, that as an adolescent who came to live in the United States at age twelve, the church was crucial to her son's identity as he negotiated the complexities of black masculinity and how they intersected with Ethiopian immigrant culture. And so Marty encouraged her son's church involvement because she saw it not only as an opportunity for him to speak his native language and maintain community ties but also as a salve against the very real dangers—both physical and psychological—that face black men in America.

Lisa, the mother of five who sought to distinguish her Ethiopian children from African Americans, nonetheless revealed, like Marty, deeply perceptive instincts about other people's visions of black masculinity. When it came time to integrate her newly adopted, six-year-old Ethiopian son into his new neighborhood and school, she became immediately race-aware. She described the process:

> The biggest reservation I had about it was the color difference in our neighborhood. It's not that people are hateful; it's more that they're just fascinated. But the lack of diversity in our town is very poor. They're not colorblind; they know exactly the deal. I homeschooled [my youngest son] for a while because I knew, in our school system, he would get labeled. I knew he would have a hard time, and then act out, and then adjust, and they would label him as ADD or something. But that's not him; he was just adjusting. The school administration was offended; they were like, "You don't think we can do it?" And I was like, "Well, I'm not using my son as an experiment for that."

Lisa homeschooled her son for his first few months of first grade in order to manage his adjustment, in large part because she was intuitively aware of the kinds of labeling that disproportionately affect black boys. Lisa's insight rings true with Linda Blum's finding that "mothers raising vulnerable sons of color might also pose risks [in addition to protection], inviting . . . the harsh, unfair framing of any disruptive behaviors" (2015: 234–235). But like the majority of parents I spoke with who adopted African children, Lisa saw her child as different from African American children and therefore saw the issues he faced as inherently distinct from issues facing them. In keeping her son out of school until she felt he was ready, she wanted to ensure that his peers and teachers would not label him along racially biased lines.

The narratives of what happens when children adopted from Africa enter school in the United States offer additional insight into the ways that parents' decision-making and concern surrounding age, race, and fitness are woven together. Jen, a mother of two daughters adopted from Ethiopia, noted that her older daughter, Ruby, a struggling student, gravitates toward other international adoptees in school, even though her teachers often see her as African American. When teachers see that Jen is white, Jen said, they have then assumed that Ruby was adopted domestically or was in foster care. Jen suggested that while she sees (or initially saw) her Ethiopian adopted daughter as "brown," others quite clearly see her as black, particularly because of her academic difficulties. Jen's narrative shows how Ruby's teachers see learning challenges as specifically linked to U.S.-born blacks rather than international adoptees; Ruby's teachers, who see her socializing with other international adoptees, had no reason to assume that she was adopted domestically other than racialized stereotypes about children with learning disabilities.

Lisa's and Jen's stories illustrate the ways that African American adopted children are often presumed to have learning disabilities, as well as the interwoven discomfort that can arise for white adoptive parents when their African children are seen as African American. Consistent with Seligman's (2013) observation that international adoptive parents generally focus on their child's "ethnic heritage" rather than their race, the parents I interviewed who adopted children from Africa went to great lengths to identify their kids as African—Ethiopian, Congolese—rather than as African American or simply as black. But the parents of African adoptees whom I interviewed did not simply focus on language, religion, food, or heritage trips as a means of instilling their children with a sense of ethnic identity. They also focused on typical neurological development and school performance, as well as good mental and behavioral health, as a means of actively distinguishing their children from images and stereotypes of U.S.-born blacks.

Writing about domestic adoptions, Randall Kennedy notes that "nothing more succinctly evinces the broadly disfavored status of black children on the adoption market than the fact that they are conventionally described as juveniles with 'special needs,' or pegged as 'hard to place'—labels created for and routinely attached to children with physical or mental disabilities" (2003: 449). Indeed, the very language and structure of adoption programs draw an equivalence between blackness and disability. Kennedy points to the echoes of a "biologization" of poverty argument, the ways that U.S. black children are so often pathologized for seemingly little beyond their race. The parents I interviewed who adopted from Africa saw their children very differently—not as African American but as Ethiopian or Congolese. Like parents who adopted from China, they routinely set Eastern Europe up as a negative to the positive of an African culture of baby care. Not only did they focus on a lack of fetal alcohol and drug exposure; they insisted—and expressed tremendous relief—that their children had been held and nurtured, unlike children from Russia. Wholly unlike "cold" Russian orphanages, parents described African caregivers as "loving" and "warm," emphasizing that they "held," "looked at," and "spoke to" the children in their care. And so for the parents I interviewed, the liabilities of disordered white children were held up as the opposite of "healthy" African children, whom they believed were primed for normal attachment and typical social-emotional development.

"To Be 'Excited' Is Very White"

Wendy is a married white mother in her late forties. She lives with her husband, two sons, and their ten-year-old German shepherd in a large single-family home, tucked behind the central business district of an ethnically diverse middle-income urban neighborhood. As I arrived for our interview, Wendy was settling her older son, James, into a YouTube video on giant deep-sea creatures. Wendy homeschools James and explained that it was a treat for him to watch a video. Wendy's home is tastefully filled with objects that seem to have been collected over many years of world travel, and the semiopen floor plan betrayed several cooking projects in progress in the kitchen. As we settled into the living room and James followed us, his head buried in his iPad, Wendy apologized for a pile of astronomy equipment—her husband and the boys were tracking a comet. Nondescript on the exterior, the home is a quirky yet intentional jumble of activity and display of taste. Wendy, with a Southern twang moderated by many years of living in the Northeast, began her story. She and her husband Charles had agreed that they wanted to grow their family through adoption before getting married, she told me, and they began to pursue adoption through the state foster care system soon afterward. They put that process on hold when Wendy unexpectedly became pregnant with James. Then when James turned two, they tried to pick up their adoption plans where they left off.

The bureaucratic challenges that Wendy and her husband faced in their interactions with state agencies were ultimately what led them to international adoption, despite both a strong financial disincentive and their even stronger ideological commitment to public domestic adoption. Wendy explains that she only "went international" grudgingly and not because of any perceived advantages. Indeed, she and Charles struggled with international adoption emotionally more than financially; Wendy told me that they felt like they were "buying" a child. In order to avoid a long waiting period, they elected to adopt a child with disabilities. In line with other parents interviewed for this project, they ruled out intellectual disabilities. Ultimately, they brought their son Preston home after a relatively short waiting period due to his challenging (but not at all life-threatening) diagnosis of albinism. Yet Preston's homecoming was cold comfort after a devastating loss in the state-run adoption system. Wendy explained that she and Charles had been matched with a baby girl in foster care but that they were deemed an inappropriate placement at the last minute because of, of all things, their ten-year-old German shepherd. Wendy was indignant that this had not come up in their home study and became disillusioned with the foster-to-adopt program—both its bureaucracy and its rigidity. She had wanted to "do the right thing," and her dog, "the sweetest darn dog you're ever going to meet," forced her out of the only adoption program that she considered wholly ethical.

"To say I was upset," Wendy told me, "would be an understatement of *epic* proportion. To say my husband was upset . . . we were devastated."

Wendy, in many ways, presents an exception to the majority of those interviewed for this project. Her initial preference was to adopt a child through the
state-run foster care system. She felt that foster-to-adopt was the "right way" to
adopt, and she felt deeply betrayed by a system that was so rigid and unreason-
able that she felt "forced" to adopt internationally. For Wendy, being open to a
"harder-to-place" child was the answer to her discomfort with international
adoption and her deep ethical and political commitment to public, domestic adoption. She and her husband briefly considered private domestic adoption after
their public adoption process fell apart, but as she explained,

> I have a lot of issues with private domestic adoption, moral and ethical. I have
> a lot of issues with adoption, period, moral and ethical. We looked briefly [at
> private domestic adoption], and we're talking about women in a very compro-
> mised situation, where someone from an agency is swooping in and saying,
> "You can have all of this money." And that, the coercion . . . just struck me as
> horrid, just horrid. It was going to be the rare exception that there was some
> happy-go-lucky high schooler who really wanted to place her *unexpected* child
> in a happy home and go get her PhD and move on, whole, with her life. These
> were drug-addicted, compromised, needy women . . . there's a huge coercion
> in my opinion.

In her ethical objection to private domestic adoption, Wendy is somewhat exceptional in my sample; the majority of mothers who expressed objections to private
domestic adoption did so because, as I discussed in the previous chapter, it weak-
ened their position of power in the transaction.

Wendy is particularly exceptional because she and her husband, even before
having James, had planned to have a multiracial family. I asked Wendy if she was
"excited" by the process of forming a multiracial family, and Wendy explained,
"We anticipated it. [We were] excited about having a family member, excited
about embracing who he or she was. But," Wendy continued, "to be 'excited' is
very white." In this sense, Wendy clearly signaled to me that she did not exoticize
or idealize the prospect of mothering a black child. Indeed, she mocked mothers
who do, voicing their seemingly suspicious motivations, "Like, check me out,
my bad self with my black child. Like Angelina Jolie. Like a social accessory, like
Madonna." As for her own motivations, Wendy was clear: "[We were] excited
about the process, not about the color."

The opposite of Bonilla-Silva's designation of "colorblind," Wendy is clearly
quite "color-aware." Nonetheless, she criticized a woman from her state-run
foster-to-adopt training group whose own awareness was, perhaps, not up to
Wendy's standard. In what she called "a sad, racist, funny example," Wendy

recounted how the woman "said she would take someone who was Hispanic, but not black. OK . . . my whole head was like, *Did you just say that out loud?*" Wendy, responding directly to the assumption that there is a clear-cut line between "black" and "Hispanic," expressed her outrage at the antiblack racism she perceived among white adoptive parents. Among the parents I interviewed, Wendy was unique in her attention to race and ability to talk about blackness. When Wendy and her husband decided to pursue adoption through the foster care system, they went through a transformative process of self-scrutiny and emerged ready, willing, and—they believed—well-prepared to adopt an African American child. But Wendy's experience with the state-run foster care system involved trauma and betrayal. Initially an exception among adoptive parents, Wendy and her husband ultimately elected to do the same thing as many of the other parents in my sample. In making their own set of trade-offs, they adopted a child from China with a "manageable" genetic condition that "doesn't really affect his life."

Neuropsychological "Fitness" and Race in the New Economy

The child that the parents I interviewed wanted to parent, by and large, was a neurotypical one—remember Danielle, who said she wanted to "just have a child we can love, who will just be healthy." The parents I spoke with were clear that their top priority was to have a "healthy child," but I argue that their ideas about health are bound up with the particular character of contemporary parenting, parental anxiety, and their perceptions of the demands of the new economy. The vast majority of the parents I spoke with considered health to be more important than race per se in this respect. This position is enabled by model minority discourses around Asian Americans in particular, as well as some increasing flexibility in the American ethnoracial order more generally. But parents who adopted black children prioritized "health" over race as well, and their stories much more clearly illustrate how views of health and "fitness" can be racialized. Taken together, the stories in this chapter illuminate a number of ways that international adoption has played a role, however minor, in the ongoing processes of racial formation in the United States.

It is curious that in our highly racialized (and racist) society, white parents would choose "healthy" children of color over potentially "damaged" white children. As the narratives above illustrate, it is partly a liberal cultural commitment to colorblindness that enables these decisions. Further, in the context of a model minority discourse, Asian children may be particularly desirable; as one mother I interviewed described them, they are "successful" and "cute as buttons, bright and shiny . . . outstanding members of their community," quite unlike the "messed up kids" from U.S. foster care that this same mother described. While all the parents I interviewed described efforts to introduce their internationally adopted children to their "cultural heritage," the meanings attached to this vary greatly by the adopted child's race and ethnicity. For white (Russian), Asian, and Hispanic international adoptees living in white families, ethnicity can be purely symbolic (see Jacobson 2008 on "culture keeping"), as it is for the children of (part) Asian and Hispanic ethnicity that Lee and Bean (2012) describe. I argue that the narratives of the white parents of African adoptees whom I interviewed suggest a particularly finely grained exercise of boundary-work. They emphasize their black children's national "heritage" while simultaneously distancing themselves and their children from U.S. blacks, but race functions differently for U.S. blacks than for other people of color in contemporary America.

The lengths to which adoptive parents went to distinguish their African-born children from African Americans support the idea that our real problem—with international adoption, as well as with race more generally—concerns the full integration, inclusion, and acceptance of black Americans in American society. Yet the American society that continues to exclude black Americans, immigrants and nonimmigrants, is a moving target. In the context of post-1965 immigration, Alba argues that thinking about the "assimilation" of nonwhite immigrants into "white" society is "informative but ultimately inadequate" because there is no monolithic society for immigrants to be "assimilated" into (2009: 15). He maintains that "ethno-racial hierarchies, at least in democratic, economically dynamic societies, are less rigid than they are sometimes thought to be" (2009: 21). As racial categories shift in the United States at the same time that socioeconomic inequality, driven by educational and occupational success, becomes all the more intractable, the mothers in this study reveal a presumption—or a hope, perhaps—that neuropsychological health and fitness might be a better bet in terms of future success than whiteness, plain and simple. The white parents that I interviewed for this project are both actors in the ongoing drama of racial formation in this country and a part of white racism in our society. It is a prevailing discourse of colorblindness that allows them to frame their children as international adoptees rather than as black Americans as well as to justify the importance of "health" over race. Christine Ward Gailey (2010) argues rather bluntly that middle- and upper-middle-class professional adoptive parents desire, if not entirely expect, a "blue-ribbon baby" who will attend a prestigious university and achieve a high professional status. In many of the stories I heard, however, parents' anxieties far outweighed their aspirations, and parents' fears—primarily of atypical neurodevelopment—led them to make a series of intricately racialized decisions.

Changes in international adoption on a programmatic level have forced parents to consider a variety of children that they would have previously overlooked: children over the age of one or two, children with documented health care needs, and, crucially, black African children. These structural shifts to international adoption have readjusted the balancing acts parents perform with the characteristics that they elect (or do not) in their future children. Perhaps, in turn, the ways that adoptive parents conceive of risk, desirability, and fitness have also changed, not only in response to constricting international adoption marketplaces but also in response to our ever-evolving enthnoracial landscape and the tremendous economic anxiety that characterizes the new millennium. The colorblindness of our racial discourse and our racism also enables the adoptive parents' position. As one mother described her black son, "He's so magnetic that I think sometimes people don't see his color." Another mother described her black daughter by saying, "I guess this is assuming things, but she's *beautiful*. And she has a very strong, outgoing personality. And I think sometimes, people see her, and they don't necessarily see the color of her skin because of her personality." These white mothers' blindness points out just how profound and painful a liability blackness is in our social world. The extent to which parents avoided children with cognitive disabilities in the face of such racism raises important questions about how parents view children, childhood, and, indeed, parenting itself, as we settle into the twenty-first century's knowledge-based but wholly uncertain economy.

CHAPTER 4

Murky Truths and Double-Binds

"I began to read a little more about how complicated it is and that it's not such a cut-and-dry thing," Danielle told me. After bringing her daughter home from China, she and her husband, Mark, had become very active in online discussion groups about international adoption, including a group just for parents who adopted from the same region of China as they had. Through these groups, they began to read more about irregularities, controversies, and scandals in international adoption programs around the world, including in the same orphanage where their daughter had lived. When I asked Danielle what she made of the stories she encountered, she responded, "There is no such thing as a real orphan, and we don't really know much about these kids' circumstances. We don't have any guarantee that these children are legitimately and authentically available. It's hard."

Gail is a single mother of a daughter, Peyton, whom she adopted from Ethiopia as a young toddler, and, like Danielle, she began to follow the media coverage of international adoption much more closely after bringing Peyton to the United States. Gail explained to me that she had come to view international adoption, as an institution, much more critically than she had prior to adopting Peyton. Reflecting on that time, she said, "About the ethics of international adoption, I think I didn't want to know. I wanted to be a mom. I wanted this to happen. I'm not proud of this. I just said, 'OK, I accept this,' and I went ahead and did it. Everybody was really celebrating international adoption at that point. There wasn't a lot of encouragement to probe more deeply."

Unlike Gail and Danielle, who went into their processes of international adoption with relatively little knowledge of their children's birth countries—and relatively little international experience in general—Kate, who adopted her son Jonah from Ethiopia, had worked in Africa and in the United States as an immigration and human rights lawyer. Also unlike Gail and Danielle, Kate was one of the many mothers I interviewed who discovered that the circumstances of their own children's adoptions were fraudulent. "We were told both parents were deceased," she explained to me. "Mom bled out giving birth to him, dad died of malaria a few months before he was born. We have since learned, the summer we went back and met them, [that] none of it was true."

In this chapter, I tell the stories of families who encountered and often vigilantly sought to uncover evidence of impropriety, corruption, and fraud while adopting their children. These stories illustrate how programmatic and political shifts in international adoption, alongside the gendered family arrangements of adoptive families, created a particular emotional and ethical double-bind for the mothers I interviewed. The stories in this chapter are full of the struggle, confusion, and pain that many international adoptive mothers felt as they reckoned with the social inequality, market dynamics, political battles, and ethical complexity that defined their experiences with international adoption. I tell these stories here not to privilege the pain of adoptive mothers over that of adoptees or their birth families; rather, I share these adoptive mothers' narratives because of what they reveal about how we, as a society, understand contemporary American families. The upheavals that international adoption programs have undergone over the past fifteen years have lifted the veil on any supposed simplicity regarding what constitute children's best interests and have shattered the triumphal narrative whereby U.S. involvement in international adoption functioned as a benevolent project that both saved orphans abroad and created a more open multiethnic society in the United States. The narratives that I heard from the mothers I interviewed are, on the whole, hardly "triumphal." They are stories about struggle and loss as much as they are stories about triumph and success, but the mothers I spoke with nonetheless all fought unrelentingly to bring their children to the United States. They never gave up, even under circumstances that observers—or they, themselves—might have considered to be ethically questionable. I use this chapter to explore the ways in which these mothers' actions—and the stories they tell about them—were driven by a deep ideological commitment to the intensive, totalizing norms of contemporary American motherhood, which colluded with a triumphal narrative of international adoption and drove these mothers to often extraordinary actions.

As they entered into the process of adopting internationally, many of the mothers I interviewed were not fully aware of the commercial structure of international adoption, nor were they all equally sensitive to the political and ethical complexity of international adoption arrangements. But just as most of the mothers I spoke with became more aware of the ways in which their adoptions were brokered for money, most mothers' sense of a broader triumphal narrative was fractured by mounting evidence that their children were often not "orphans" in the classical sense, nor was the world necessarily a better place simply because of the U.S. families who adopted "orphans" from abroad. At the same time that their awareness grew, a triumphal narrative of international adoption came under direct assault in international politics and the media. This grow-ing awareness of both the structural inequality and the systemic corruption in international adoption forced adoptive parents to defend themselves against alle-gations of misconduct, even if only to themselves. Many of the mothers I inter-viewed decided to more deeply investigate the circumstances of their children's adoptions and discovered that their children, presumed to be "true orphans," in fact had one or two living, healthy biological parents, as well as relatively intact extended families of biological siblings, grandparents, aunts, uncles, and cous-ins. These discoveries forced the mothers I interviewed to confront head-on the ways in which their mothering was predicated upon not only corruption within international adoption programs but also global inequality more generally.

The discoveries and upheavals faced by the mothers interviewed for this project drew out a distinctly gendered maternal response: an intensive, total-izing commitment to mothering, in which adoptive mothers did anything and everything they could to resolve uncertainties in their adoption processes and, as many adoptive parents say, "bring their children home." In the wake of the finan-cial corruption, political power plays, deception, and fraud that underscored so many disruptions to international adoption programs, the mothers calibrated their own behavior to our contemporary ideologies and expectations of inten-sive motherhood, stopping at nothing in pursuit of what they determined to be their children's interests. Back in the United States, these are mothers who would go on to hire private tutors, educational consultants, psychotherapists, and sports coaches for their newly adopted children. But before coming home to the United States with their children, these mothers described hiring pri-vate drivers, attorneys, investigators, doctors, and even foster mothers to help them finalize their threatened adoption processes. They pursued all paths and exhausted all options in pursuit of their (future) children, and the extraordinary circumstances in which they found themselves drew out their fiercest exercise of maternal obligation. Ultimately their intensive actions reinforced old ideas about the "triumph" of international adoption by, literally, triumphing over bureau-cratic holdups and political disputes. But these mothers' intensive actions also reproduced gendered family arrangements in which their husbands were largely absent from both the day-to-day family work of resolving these adoptions and the emotion work inherent in living within the ethical and emotional double-bind that these adoption processes created.

Gender, Family Work, and International Adoption

When problems emerged in the international adoption processes, it was the mothers I interviewed who assumed the bulk of the work to resolve them, illus-trating the utter persistence of gendered inequality in who performs the bulk of family work. This is by no means unique to adoption; gendered inequality

defines the ways that heterosexual couples proceed through other kinds of reproductive markets as well. Writing in the context of heterosexual couples experiencing infertility, Andrea Bertolli (2013) demonstrates the gendered inequality
of "fertility work," whereby women assume the primary responsibility for managing medical appointments, procedures, medications, and schedules related to
becoming pregnant. Writing in the context of markets for eggs and sperm, Rene
Almeling argues that men and women "calibrate their actions in ways that align
with cultural norms of maternal femininity and paternal masculinity" (2011:
178).[1] The adoptive mothers whom I interviewed also calibrated their actions,
desires, and priorities to reflect the distinctly gendered expectations and arrangements of intensive mothering in the twenty-first century. The actions undertaken
by the mothers and fathers in my study affirm the long-held understanding not only
that women remain disproportionately responsible for all kinds of reproductive work but, more important, that when families are stressed, the gendered
inequality in family arrangements grows (see Casper and Bianchi 2002; Cooper 2014; Hochschild 1989; Jacobs and Gerson 2004; Ochs and Kremer-Sadlik
2013; Stone 2007). This is particularly true of high-status professionals who work
in highly demanding fields and in jobs with expectations of long hours[2]—the
norm among parents involved in this project. Scott Coltrane, writing specifically
about high-status professionals, argues that mothers and fathers in high-status
professions "are likely to share breadwinning, but the accommodation of [their]
careers to family concerns is limited by nostalgic family ideals and gender stereotypes" (2004: 214–215).[3] Mothers, equally or nearly equally responsible for paid
work, remain primarily responsible for unpaid family work[4] despite the increasing involvement of many fathers.[5] Indeed, the most progressive and egalitarian
men are still simply called "involved" while mothers so often remain seen and
treated as the "primary parent" (Wall and Arnold 2007). Kaufman (2013) finds
that fathers, today, fall into three broad categories—"old" dads, "new" dads,
and "superdads," but characterizes the majority of fathers as the "new" kind
who ultimately make only minimal changes in their work schedules, mainly
to accommodate "fun" things like soccer practices and dance recitals.[6] Despite
exceptions on both ends of a spectrum, the norm of "involved"—but hardly
egalitarian—fatherhood provides a crucial lens for understanding the narratives
of the mothers whom I interviewed.

Of the twenty-five heterosexual couples that participated in this project, I
spoke with only five fathers—four together with their wives, and one stay-at-
home dad without his wife present. I also interviewed one single father. The
remaining interviews I conducted were all with women—seventeen single mothers, nineteen married heterosexual women without their spouses present, and
one married lesbian mother (also without her spouse present). Many mothers
squeezed interviews into their weekday schedules—no small feat, given that fifteen of the seventeen single mothers and twenty-two of the twenty-six married

women with whom I spoke were working at least part time. Beyond participating in this project and taking the lead on the initial logistics of their adoption processes, it was the mothers in my sample who assumed the monumental task of organizing and resolving the problems that came up in their children's adoptions. As the stories in this chapter illustrate, that was no simple task and was often accomplished thanks to a tremendous and intensive amount of organizational, emotional, and ideological work on mothers' parts. When Hochschild (1989) uses the term *emotion work* to describe the ways that mothers accept an unequal division of family work—as well as their husbands' fundamentally differing gender ideologies—she argues that mothers engage in this work in order, in part, to preserve their marriages. When Sharon Hays argues that mothers engage in "ideological work" to resolve their deeply held ambivalence surrounding contradictions between mothering and professional achievement, she writes that they do so as "a means of maintaining their sanity" (2011: 43). I argue that the mothers I interviewed engaged in profound kinds of emotional and ideological work in order to maintain their families' legitimacy. In the face of changing public discourse surrounding international adoption, these mothers had to make use of prevailing ideologies—both intensive motherhood and a triumphal narrative of international adoption—that validated their day-to-day lives. Perhaps their willingness to sit down with me went beyond an affirmation of traditional forms of gender inequality in family work and signaled their investment—as the "primary" parent—in an emotional and ideological resolution to their families' ordeals.

"SHE HAS A *FABULOUS* LIFE"

For some mothers in my sample, the possibility of fraud and corruption remained abstract, and these mothers used the scaffolding of a triumphal narrative of international adoption to justify systemic ethical difficulties after the fact. They acknowledged that there may have been improprieties in their children's adoptions but happily moved on, sweeping human rights abuses and extreme global inequality under the rug by relying on the presumption that their children were better off in families in the United States. This was particularly true for the nine families with whom I spoke who adopted from China. From these nine families, I spoke with three single mothers, four married heterosexual mothers without their spouses present, and two married heterosexual couples. Without exception, these parents reflected on the confidence they had in China's adoption program before they began their own adoption processes. These families all believed that China's system was efficient, relatively transparent, and corruption-free. Danielle, cited at the opening of this chapter, said that initially she saw adopting from China as the best way to avoid fraud, corruption, and even bureaucratic holdups. She related, "China seemed to be very organized, they had the experience of doing this for a decade or more at that point, and it seemed very efficient." Robin—a married heterosexual mother of two children, one adopted from China and another adopted from Vietnam—expressed comfort that most orphanages in China were (in her belief) state-run. "At least," she reasoned, "the communist system is efficient and organized." But as China's adoption program slowed down, some mothers began to question its reputation. Mary, a single mother of a boy adopted from China, explained that when her process had come to a practical standstill, she began to research Chinese adoption in greater depth, scouring the internet for any clues to explain the slowdown. Conveying her findings to me, she reported, "One of the stories was that they found a child in one of the southern provinces that they realized had not been abandoned but, indeed, had been taken off the street. So supposedly the [central adoption authority in China] took everything and made all the orphanages double-check each child, which brought everything to a halt." Other parents, like Lynne and Mike, began to read about the various scandals that rocked international adoption in a variety of sending nations, including China, after they had already brought their children home.

Lynne and Mike are a married couple with an older biological daughter and a younger daughter adopted from China. Discussing their feelings about media coverage that emerged after their daughter had been living with them for several years, they both expressed profound sadness that something they had considered benevolent and ethically straightforward had turned out to be so complicated and ethically fraught. Mike explained that he had been drawn to adopting from China because it seemed to have a "well-run" program relative to other, more "disorganized" sending nations, naming Guatemala in particular. Active in an email group of parents who adopted children from the same orphanage, Lynne and Mike were, at the time of our interview, regularly exchanging articles and information about various international adoption scandals, including a high-profile trafficking ring that was discovered in the region of their daughter's birth and implicated their daughter's orphanage. Lynne and Mike recognized elements of their daughter's story in the articles they were reading about other children and came to the realization that they may have adopted a baby who had been trafficked. Tearfully, Lynne related, "I think the government's trying to crack down. When we went into this, we weren't aware of that. The first media coverage on this came out within a year of bringing [our daughter] home. It's heartbreaking. There's a high likelihood that [our daughter] was one of these trafficked babies . . . Would I adopt from China again? I don't know." Lynne found herself in the ultimate maternal double-bind.

After learning about the trafficking scandal linked to their daughter's orphanage, Lynne and Mike continued to research Chinese adoptions and international adoption more generally. Mike in particular immersed himself in the economic and political aspects of international adoption as an institution, looking for patterns and further clues to his daughter's story in the media coverage he devoured. Telling me where his research had led him, he explained,

> The coverage, especially in China—all the child trafficking, women being given cash for their babies—it feels bad to be part that. A very high proportion of the children in China who are up for international adoption have been trafficked. That doesn't mean they're kidnapped, but there are payments along the way. It's very commonplace there. And I think people recognize that there is a great degree of corruption in the system, but [they think] that it stems from the one-child policy and the other corruption that's endemic in the system. So maybe people feel a little bit bad about perpetuating this, but they feel much better about providing a good home for a child who needs one.

Mike clearly articulates the complexity behind reports of child trafficking, but he just as clearly uses that complexity to rationalize his own actions, as an adoptive father, as the lesser of evils. Again referencing Guatemala, Mike continued, "You have to understand that you're part of a whole process, whether it's a war orphan or a trafficked baby, that you're part of a process." Throughout the first half of our interview, in which we discussed the nuts and bolts of their adoption process, their motivations for adopting, and their daughter's adjustment to the family postadoption, Mike deferred to his wife and remained practically silent. But when allegations of fraud and corruption came up, Mike dominated the conversation. He was proud of the research he had done and stood behind his solution to the complicated political and intellectual puzzle that he felt he had solved.

Lynne and Mike sought out China's adoption program for its "clean" reputation but nonetheless found themselves implicated in serious allegations of child trafficking. Where Mike hewed to a masculine rationality, Lynne proceeded on (wholly secular) faith, his "rationality" and her "irrationality" clearly following gendered norms.[7] As Lynne explained, "You have to go into it with good faith, you have to hope that these countries, these agencies, are transparent, [but] you really don't know. You kinda have to trust that it's transparent, that it's not totally corrupt. But for any country that's allowing so many adoptions out of its borders, looking back, my guess is that there's some level of corruption going on; where are they getting all these babies? How are they allowing so many to be placed?" Lynne and Mike went into their adoption process trusting China's program and placing good faith in the parties responsible for bringing their adoption to fruition. They brought their daughter home without incident. Years later, when they began to read about corruption in the system, they were forced to reckon with the moral weight of their actions. Both Lynne and Mike expressed sadness and regret as well as uncertainty and deep ambivalence. Their bottom line, however, was clear: as Mike explained, "You have to do a fair amount of reading to really understand the nature of the problem. But all I can say is, just look at the result.

We're happy, she's happy." Responding to her husband, Lynne added, "She has a *fabulous* life. We can't go back and do anything about it, it is what it is, we move forward."

"We Trusted Our Agency"

While Lynne and Mike learned about adoption irregularities after the fact, many other adoptive parents saw red flags early in their adoption processes. Alyssa and Keith, introduced in the previous chapter, are a white married couple with a young daughter, Isabella, whom they adopted from the Democratic Republic of the Congo. Alyssa and Keith's top priorities in adopting were a quick referral time and a young infant, which left them with few choices of sending nations at the time they began their adoption process. They elected to adopt from the Congo because, as Alyssa explained, "We found out about a new program in the Congo, fast referral times. Our [first] referral came three weeks after we had USCIS approval." But, Alyssa continued, "we got our first match, and it fell through after a month. I don't know if our agency rep had all the information either, because they're working with a Congolese attorney, and a lot gets lost in the communication. But we were told that when our agency went into the orphanage to move [the referred child] to foster care, they found out that there was a bidding war going on [between agencies over that child]. So they backed out because they don't participate in, you know, child trafficking and buying children." Rather than being alarmed, Alyssa took comfort in the fact that her own agency had pulled out of this type of illicit activity. Ignoring this first clue, Alyssa, like Lynne and Mike, did not begin to seriously consider improprieties in Congolese adoptions until a year after her own daughter came to the United States and the Congo shut down its international adoption program entirely, denying exit visas to a number of children who had already been legally adopted and granted visas to enter the United States (Chiaramonte 2014; Graff 2014; Ligtvoet 2014; Pham 2015; USCIS 2015). Alyssa then acknowledged, "We trusted our agency, maybe a little too much in some ways."

Jen is mother to two daughters, Ruby and Eva, who are biological sisters adopted from Ethiopia. Jen told me a similar story about how she was initially matched with a set of twin boys, yet the match was quickly dissolved. As she explained, "It was found out that they had living parents. The parents were arrested, the boys were taken out of the adoption process, and that fell through." Jen was then matched with another set of siblings. Their story, though not caught early on, proved to be quite similar. She recounted, "Supposedly the mother had died in '08 and the father could no longer care for them. When they learned English, the story came out that the mother was living, they have grandparents, [and they told] us that they also have an older sister. I called the agency and said, 'You have to red flag [these sibling groups].' I said, 'You need to investigate this further than you're doing, because to have two situations this similar makes me question what you're doing.'" Much like Alyssa, Jen did not feel the need to suspend her plans to adopt because her agency had uncovered an irregularity in her first match; rather, Jen saw this incident as evidence that her agency was doing their job. But once her daughters were able to fully communicate with her, Jen saw the entire enterprise as a cover-up.

While many parents bemoaned the sensationalized nature of negative media reports on international adoption, the language of those reports—of "finders," "harvesting," and "trafficking"—found its way into their narratives. A few of the parents I interviewed pushed back against the use of such language, and I highlight the most vocal opponent of what she called "antiadoption rhetoric" at the end of this chapter. However, such opposition was a rare exception. The majority of the parents with whom I spoke reported seeing—in the words of Ivy, who adopted her son from Nepal—"one red flag after another." Indeed, the majority of the parents I interviewed developed a highly nuanced perspective on how their child(ren) came into their family. But for most parents, much like Mike and Lynne, the murkiness, the lack of transparency, the ethical ambiguity, and in many cases, the unknowableness of their children's stories were balanced by the "better"—or even "fabulous"—life that they had in the United States.

"My Mama Gut Told Me"

While fraud and corruption remained abstract for some parents in my sample, this was far from the case for other mothers with whom I spoke. The evidence of corruption and fraud was, for some mothers, inescapable and permanently visible on their children's bodies. These mothers expressed utter horror at what had happened to their children individually and profound discomfort with international adoption as a system. Two of these mothers in particular, Ivy and Emily, illustrate the ways that an intensive commitment to motherhood mediated the cognitive and emotional dissonance that they experienced with respect to international adoption, something that they found extremely problematic despite the fact that they themselves had participated in it. Ivy and Emily both talked about a "gray scale" of ethical considerations in international adoption as a way to rationalize their own imperfect actions, and they both spoke of their "maternal instincts" or "mama gut" as a way to frame their responses to corrupt or fraudulent activities.

Ivy, the professor whose story of facing the commercial side of international adoption I told in chapter 2, was caught in the middle of the U.S. Department of State's shutdown of adoptions from Nepal. Ivy explained to me that she and her husband, Paul, had been concerned about allegations of corruption and trafficking in international adoption from the outset, which is how they ended up choosing Nepal as a sending nation. Ivy explained that they had quickly ruled out adopting from Guatemala, telling me, "I did not want to be part of that system.... I knew about the *coyotes*; I knew about the selling. I knew there were people here in the United States who had already been prosecuted for trafficking. I was just totally queasy." Reeling from the confusion and pain of secondary infertility, she and Paul elected to pursue an adoption from South Asia. She told me how she felt that the "need" of the children outweighed other ethical considerations, explaining, "India emerged as, there's no question they need help. Millions of children not in families, it's clear they need help, as opposed to other countries where the child trafficking situation may have been more overt. So we felt that India, on the gray scale, was more ethical than some other places." Much like the mothers whose stories I told in chapter 2, who sought a "win-win" situation in adopting their children, Ivy implied that if she adopted a child who "needed help," she could outweigh the ethical problem of adopting a child internationally at all. Framing India as "more ethical than some other places" on a "gray scale," Ivy acknowledged the underlying danger of child trafficking and the corruption that may be more or less "overt" in different contexts. Ultimately, Ivy's adoption agency steered her to adopt from Nepal, a decision that she described as "irrational," but she took "a leap of faith" and followed the lead of her agency.

Ivy explained to me about how she had organized, managed, and then "begged" for more unpaid leave from her job; how she had coordinated care for her biological son, then-seven-year-old Josh; and how ultimately she was left to care for a very sick baby girl. Recalling Becca's first weeks at home with the family, Ivy related,

> She was [in the orphanage] way too long, so she had a cross-eye problem from being in a crib for eighteen hours a day. She also had persistent giardia, persistent parasites in the gut, the worst smelling diarrhea you have ever smelled in your life. It's also extremely contagious and when we got home we were contacted by the public health department because we had a child with contagious giardia. You have to be really careful how you dispose of the diapers; the caretakers could also get it. But I mean, we were really lucky. She did not have hepatitis, she didn't . . . I mean, once we brought her home, I went into panic mode: What if she has epilepsy? What if she has HIV? You know? Because all we had [when we adopted her] was height, head circumference, and weight. And three pictures of her crying. And we thought, yeah, let's bring that little girl home. We'll fix her up, a loving American family.

It was after coming home, resuming normal work routines, battling major post-adoption depression, and "sorting through all this for years in therapy" that Ivy, in retrospect, wonders why she ignored the very warning signs of corruption that she had initially set out to avoid and why she had so wholeheartedly bought into a triumphal narrative whereby a "loving American family" was all that mattered.

Ivy's story toggled through sadness, bitterness, exhaustion, and guilt. The trauma of bringing Becca into her family fundamentally ruptured any triumphal narrative of international adoption.

Ivy explained to me that despite seeing red flags along the way, she ignored them in pursuit of bringing a child into her family, and her critical perspective on international adoption did not begin to deepen until some time had passed after bringing Becca to the United States. Similarly, Bridget, a single mother of an older son by birth and a daughter adopted from Guatemala, told me that thoughts of corruption and fraud had only crossed her mind several years after she brought her daughter home. I asked her, "Even with all the coverage in the media?" And she said, "Honestly, I was too busy taking her to doctors' appointments and changing diapers to pay much attention." Beth, a single mother of a daughter adopted from Russia, similarly explained, "I was too focused on taking care of my daughter to get wrapped up in all that. The media sensationalizes everything anyway." Like Gail, the mother who adopted from Ethiopia quoted at the head of this chapter, Ivy said that she "didn't want to know" about the potential for fraud and corruption in Nepal. In retrospect, Ivy mused, "Who knows? Supposedly [Becca] was found at a public water tap. That's a common story, which is why the embassy shut these down—because it's a generic story. Some poor woman, whether she was a sex worker, a circus performer, a servant, a maid, whoever this person was—it's illegal for a woman in Nepal to relinquish a child. A male relative, however distant, has legal authority over that child; a woman cannot relinquish her child. So they bribed a policeman. I feel like I was an idiot in a way, to overlook it." Ivy accepted the fact that Becca's story was generic, uncertain, and likely problematic, and Ivy rejected a triumphal narrative on an abstract level. But Ivy continued, throughout our interview, to toggle back and forth between a critical view of international adoption and a sense that she had, on an individual level, done something positive for her daughter.

In Nepal, Ivy and Paul had hired a private driver who, according to Ivy, "did everything." Ivy described their driver as "something of a fixer, which means he'll never get a visa to America because they think of him as a child trafficker." Yet he "fixed" Ivy's adoption problems, allowing her to bring Becca to the United States quickly, without getting "stuck" in the delays that faced other families involved in the Nepal shutdown. Becca was acutely sick at the time and faced chronic malnutrition as well. Ivy explained, "Her twelve-year molars are erupting, [but] she just celebrated her eleventh birthday. She's menstruating. She was probably a year older than they told us. I can't even let myself go to the place of understanding the malnutrition, the lack of care, the lack of stimulation, for her to be that small and to have been a year older [than we were told]. Because when we brought her home, we were told she was small for the age we were told she was." Ivy tells a story in which she saved her daughter from poverty and neglect on an individual level, despite the problematic nature of a broader triumphal narrative.

In addition to the fracture of a triumphal narrative, Ivy's story also illuminates profoundly unequal gendered family arrangements. It was Ivy, not her husband Paul (also a tenured university professor), who pleaded with her department chair for an extra semester of unpaid leave. Ivy drove Becca to appointments with medical specialists all over town. Ivy dealt with the bureaucratic fallout of the inquest from the public health department. Ivy showed up at PTA meetings and school performances for her son, Josh, brought Josh to his chess lessons, and generally functioned as the primary parent. And then Ivy, not her husband, spent "years in therapy" working through the emotional and ethical implications of her own blinding commitment to mothering. Not only was Paul absent in our interview, but he was absent in Ivy's narrative. In his absence, it was Ivy's "mother's instinct" that legitimized Becca's adoption. Continuing to explain the neglect that Becca faced in her orphanage, Ivy related to me, "We were told that she had been born [birth date redacted]. We had height, weight, head circumference, and *nothing* else. Now, look at those feet [showing me Becca's referral photo on her tablet]. The first thing I thought was *If she's only a year old, those feet are too big*. My mother's instinct—I knew those feet were too big." For Ivy, the politically engaged and highly critical professor, it was ultimately an essentialist take on motherhood that justified her participation in a "gray scale" of ethical (and unethical) actions.

Emily's story, like Ivy's, illustrates how a commitment to intensive mothering as a distinct gender ideology can insulate mothers from the full emotional effect of the double-bind in which fraught international adoption processes place them. A single mother in her late thirties, Emily decided to pursue an adoption from Ethiopia in part because of her political and professional interest in the region, which stemmed from working on public health projects related to both HIV/AIDS education and public water systems in several African nations. Emily had traveled widely in central and southern Africa, and Ethiopia was her first choice of sending nations from which to adopt. Emily and her daughter, Mara, live in a modest home in a suburban neighborhood, where Emily had settled down when she chose to adopt. At the time of our interview, Emily had made the decision to take some time off of work in order to fully support Mara's social-emotional and educational needs and was living off a combination of savings and her parents' support. In addition to telling me about Mara's struggles in school, Emily also shared a story with me of such deep corruption in the agency she used that the agency, according to Emily, "went belly up" only weeks prior to our interview. Explaining the situation that Mara had faced in that agency's orphanage, Emily said, "[Mara] arrived in care heavy, pudgy even. She was an extremely well-cared-for baby before she came into the care of the agency. During the period that she was in care, a number of babies died of protein-energy malnutrition because of an insufficient supply of formula and because the nannies were not appropriately trained to administer the formula. And the reason that she was so tiny [when I gained custody] was the direct result of that." In this case, Emily alleges, children died as the direct result of a corrupt agency, whose in-country director for Ethiopia, according to Emily, "was making over two hundred thousand dollars per year. And she was the person who brushed off the volunteers who were trying to help and, for whatever reason, chose not to bring in sufficient formula to feed the children or train the nannies to administer it."

Emily continued, "At the time I accepted [Mara's] referral, I was told she was abandoned. I received a report with the name of the person who supposedly found her and the location in which she was supposedly found. All of that is, at this point, highly questionable and probably not true." But Emily sees the consequences of that "untruth" as particularly immediate. Less concerned with abstract ethical debates than with her daughter's health and development, Emily explained,

> I've had my child's case referred to as "benign fraud," but there's no such thing. It's abundantly clear that my child is older than I was told. She's six years old on paper, but she's not six years old. Her birthday is probably six to eight months off. But that meant that she was referred to me as an "infant girl" when she was actually a young toddler. But the demand was for infant girls, so they made her an infant girl. Well, the problem is that when I brought her home, she weighed thirteen pounds, and she was supposed to be thirteen months old. Well, that would be bad enough, but she was actually eighteen to twenty months old. And she weighed thirteen pounds. The pediatrician apologized that she didn't realize the discrepancy, but it was so hard to fathom that she was so tiny, much less that she was even older than we thought. Thank God, she's fine. The pediatrician said, though, that if she had known that [my daughter] weighed thirteen pounds at eighteen months, she would have sent us out the door and straight to the hospital, and that would have been bad for our bonding. Thank God, she's fine, but she might not have been fine.

For Emily, the prospect of what might have been is too much to bear, and her anger and frustration at the danger her daughter faced were palpable throughout our interview.

Emily described her commitment to her daughter as "fierce" and, indeed, had quit the workforce to devote herself to Mara's academic and social-emotional development. A proponent of attachment parenting, Emily described wearing Mara in a baby sling for most waking hours following Mara's arrival in the United States. Emily initially shared a bed with Mara to promote bonding and, from the beginning of their relationship, had devoted tremendous amounts of time to one-on-one interaction and play. But while Emily's intensive efforts were fruitful at home, they did not prevent Mara from experiencing tremendous difficulties in elementary school, with reading in particular. It was Mara's diagnosis of multiple learning disabilities that led Emily to quit work, become more involved in Mara's school, and fill Mara's life with other kinds of enriching activities—dance, gymnastics, music, art—that, in Emily's assessment, made Mara "feel good about herself." Meanwhile, Emily has been left wondering if Mara's experiences in her orphanage may have led to her academic difficulties. Emily insists that if Mara's issues are related to adoption, they were not due to abuse or neglect in her birth family but rather caused by a corrupt orphanage and a system that was more concerned, as Mara put it, with "expediency" than child welfare.

In addition to uncertainty about Mara's intellectual development, Emily is also left to navigate the ethical uncertainty of Mara's adoption in the first place. Like many of the mothers I interviewed, Emily came to see international adoption as a system as not wholly benign or wholly corrupt but a complicated tangle of interests and a "gray"—rather than "black"—reproductive market. At the end of our interview, Emily explained,

> I don't know if it was pure corruption, like she was trafficked or purchased or harvested, or if someone was coerced, or if it really was that the person who truly had the power to make that decision—her birth mother or birth father or a grandparent—hadn't actually died but made that choice. And then someone erased her history to make it easier for her to be adopted. Or whether it is truly harvesting and trafficking, I don't know. But I know that the story that she was left at an animal market, it's bullshit. My suspicion is that it's not flat-out trafficking, but it's obvious, now that people are sharing their stories, that there's no way in hell there were that many abandoned infants from the place where my daughter's from in an extremely short period of time. For that to be true, there would have to have been babies falling from the sky. There was probably some heavy recruiting and then erasing the trail back to families.

Emily points to three distinct aspects of the "gray" side of the international adoption market that have come to light over the past fifteen years. First, like many of the adoptive parents with whom I spoke, Emily adopts the language of "trafficking" and "harvesting" with respect to her adopted daughter, taking on some degree of complicity in a system that she has come to understand as ethically problematic. Second, Emily acknowledges the possibility that Mara's birth mother (or father, or grandparent) may have made a conscious—if forced—choice to place Mara for adoption. This possibility, of course, is in tension with the possibility of trafficking, and this tension creates more, rather than less, ambiguity for the adoptive mothers I interviewed. Finally, Emily very clearly identifies the fact that patterns of fraud and corruption could never have come to light without people "sharing their stories"—something that, thanks to social media, is much easier and much more efficient today than it was only fifteen years ago. Emily herself spoke of her active participation in many social media groups that are highly critical of international adoption.

Ultimately, both Ivy and Emily turned to essentialist ideals of mothering as a way to negotiate through their circumstances. Emily concluded, "Looking back on what the agency did to her for money and for expediency to get that money, I can't believe it. I just can't believe it. The majority of the issues she struggles with are related to how her adoption was processed, not to the reason she was adopted. The research I've done and my mama gut tell me that my daughter has a history. I know my child was not abandoned. But for expediency, someone chose to erase why she got to where she was." Ivy's and Emily's experiences and self-reflection illustrate the particular double-bind in which adoptive mothers find themselves. They both settle into the unavoidable contradictions presented by their daughters' stories. On the one hand, as adoptive mothers, Ivy and Emily are suspect: if their daughters' adoptions were fraudulent, then they are implicated as selfish, uncaring antimothers who stole and trafficked their children. On the other hand, their "fierce" exercise of maternal obligation simultaneously saved their children: in Ivy's daughter's case, from the life of sex work or indentured servitude that Ivy envisioned; and in Emily's daughter's case, from dangerous malnutrition and likely death.

Maternal Femininity and Paternal Masculinity in the Face of Fraud

Like Ivy and Emily, Kate embodied an ideal of intensive mothering as a response to her child's needs. Kate, whose feelings about domestic adoption were highlighted in a previous chapter, describes how her family uncovered the truth of her son Jonah's adoption story. Kate told me that Jonah experienced a particularly difficult adjustment in joining the family; alternating between sullenness and anger, Jonah was both hard to manage and hard to reach. When he was in kindergarten, about a year after coming to the United States, he ran away from home one night. Kate's husband found him standing in the middle of the highway on-ramp a few blocks from the house. Jonah reported that he was going to the airport so he could go back to Ethiopia. This was a wake-up call for Kate and her husband, who immediately entered family therapy with their son. Kate also put a tremendous amount of research into finding an individual psychotherapist for Jonah, ultimately selecting a renowned expert in attachment in internationally adopted children. Kate stopped full-time work and would bring Jonah to appointments, almost three hours away from home, every other week. Kate's husband, meanwhile, continued working the long hours that the financial sector demands, and Kate took on the bulk of the new family work that grew out of Jonah's struggles (see Blum 2015).

Kate told me that the family had been planning to return to visit Ethiopia at some point in the future but that in response to Jonah's behavior, the new therapist said, "Jonah is clearly telling you that he needs to go now." Kate set about planning a trip to Ethiopia, and she contacted her adoption agency to let them know. The agency contacted Jonah's birth family, and the true story of Jonah's birth parents came out. She explained,

> The Ethiopian social worker on the ground there went multiple times and the whole story came out. She was alive. He was alive. They were young. He left her as soon as he found out that she was pregnant. The parents couldn't support that. I think there was some shaming there. And so that's what happened. The mom was living with her aunt, our son's great-aunt, who was only a couple of years older than his mom. And we met the aunt when we adopted him. So the two of them sort of created this story based on a friend of theirs in the village who said, you know, I know about these orphanages. If you want to get him in there, you need to say that everyone died.

And so, beyond assuming responsibility for managing both her son's psychotherapy and her family's travel arrangements, Kate also assumed the emotional labor of legitimizing the lies that had brought her family together. And this made new work for her: keeping her family together and well in the face of those lies. She told me,

> Personally, I know my role in his life, so I never had any feelings that I was competing with someone. I was concerned about him, about how he was going to handle it. He would cry and cry and really mourn the loss of these people. His birthdays have always been hard, he just gets very reflective on his birthday. I just didn't want him to feel rejected. And honestly, I felt sad that she had to create this story to make a plan for herself and her son. I felt really sad that she had no other choice. When we found out, it was about six weeks before our trip. We had a few more therapy sessions, which was really helpful. I will say, though, our son was just happy and so excited to get to meet her.

Like Ivy's husband, Paul, Kate's husband is absent in her narrative. In assuming the day-to-day responsibility for Jonah's care, as well as the emotional responsibility for his adjustment, Kate reproduces stereotypically gendered family arrangements. And Kate embraces normative (intensive) maternal femininity as a response to both her son's individual trauma as well as the broader implications of the fraudulent circumstances of his adoption.

Deirdre and Thomas are a white married couple in their early fifties with two sons, biological brothers who were adopted from Ethiopia. The family lives in a close-knit neighborhood in a rural New England town. In my sample, Thomas was exceptional—one of only five fathers to participate in an interview, he stood out as highly involved at all stages of he and Deirdre's decision-making. But most strikingly, whereas other fathers spoke matter-of-factly about completing paperwork, home studies, and travel arrangements, or intellectually about the politics of international adoption (like Mike, above), Thomas spoke emotionally and relationally about his experiences as a father. A devout Christian, Thomas spoke movingly about his love for his children and his wife, as well as about the relationships that he was able to forge with his sons' birth relatives—fellow Christians—in Ethiopia. Yet in his deep involvement in family relationships, family work, and family decision-making, Thomas nonetheless represents an idealized paternal masculinity in the way that he, ultimately, processed the news that his children's adoption paperwork had been fraudulent.

Deirdre and Thomas's story, in many ways, follows a predictable trajectory: Deirdre and Thomas couldn't conceive, they pursued fertility treatments, then moved on to domestic adoption, and finally arrived at international adoption after exhausting most other options. Deirdre and Thomas even described Ethiopia as their "final option" among potential countries from which to adopt. However, Deirdre and Thomas quite exceptionally describe a steadfast ethical commitment to and profound empathy for the birth mothers and families with whom they became intertwined throughout their long process of adopting. Deirdre and Thomas told me how they had pursued private domestic adoption but elected to adopt from Ethiopia after a failed placement in which the birth mother pulled out at the last minute. Deirdre told me that at the time, she was disappointed but ultimately "happy for the mother" who decided to raise her child after all. When Deirdre and Thomas decided to pursue an adoption from Ethiopia, they were matched quickly with their sons, who were two and a half and almost one at the time. Initially, Deirdre and Thomas were told that the boys' birth father had passed away while the mother was pregnant with the younger boy and that they had four older biological siblings. Deirdre's response to the family's circumstances was reflective: "I was surprised that they had a [living] birth mother. In my mind, I had it that they would be orphans. I had a bit of an internal struggle, of 'is this the right thing to do?' when the only reason she was making this decision was because of her financial circumstances. But then I thought, [having considered domestic adoption,] why would I put a different set of standards on her than I would on someone domestically?" Deirdre suggests that living birth mothers in Africa could be making conscious choices, however "forced," to place their children for international adoption. Given her experience with a failed domestic placement, Deirdre decided to proceed with the match from Ethiopia after deciding not to apply a double standard to Ethiopian birth mothers.

After accepting the match, Deirdre and Thomas set about preparing for their boys' arrival. When they received clearance to travel to Ethiopia, they quickly put the final touches on the boys' room, made a last-minute trip to Walmart, and packed their bags. Deirdre described going immediately from the airport in Addis Ababa to meet the boys, then hesitantly saying good-bye in order to sleep for the first time in several nights. On their second day in Ethiopia, Deirdre and Thomas set out with another adoptive couple on a five-hour Jeep ride to visit their children's natal villages. Deirdre described the journey, which would ultimately span years and continents, leading to the truth about her boys' story. For Deirdre, it began somewhat serendipitously:

> We got a flat tire. So the driver told us to go and have some coffee while he fixed the tire. The other couple were reading to us out of the *Lonely Planet* guide about the town we're in, and they call it the armpit of Ethiopia. Just then, we were approached by two men: one of them is the social worker from [our agency] who lives in Ethiopia and the other, I didn't get it at first, but he was the birth uncle of our boys. He was their birth father's brother. So they sat down with us, and once I realized who it was, I remember thinking, "I have to remember everything for my children for when they get older." He was there to help show how to get to our family. So we pile into the Jeep, we drive another hour, we get on a dirt road, and then they stop and they're like, "OK, it's your birth family."

Speaking for Thomas and for herself, Deirdre recalled their visit with the boys' birth family as an overwhelmingly positive experience. She was surprised not only by the family's hospitality but also by her own reaction to the meeting, telling me, "We had a wonderful, amazing, positive visit. I was prepared for sadness, tears, but I was the only one who cried. When we got in there, they brought out each of their brothers and sisters and introduced them, and we hugged them, and we met their birth mother. The hospitality that she had was amazing."

Deirdre was also not prepared for the idea that her sons' biological family might continue to play a role in their lives—and in hers. In fact, she was startled by the extended family connections that began to emerge. Continuing her story, she recounted,

> Driving back [to Addis Ababa with the other adoptive couple], the uncle says to [all four of] us, "You have to stay in close touch, because your children are from the same tribe." And I have no idea what that means. So we were nodding, like, "Yeah, we'll keep in touch." Well, about six months later, the birth uncle won the immigration lottery to come to America, and he calls us, and it was at that point that he told us that the twins [adopted by the other couple] were the boys' first cousins. Their birth mother was [our] boys' birth father's sister. [Remember,] we're told at that point that our boys' birth father died. So the birth uncle, he wins the lottery to come to the U.S. But it's 2008, the recession hits, he's not able to make a go of it, so he joins the army. He marries his girlfriend from Ethiopia, brings her over.

Deirdre and Thomas kept in touch with the boys' uncle, and the boys developed a relationship with him and his wife. When Deirdre and Thomas decided to bring the boys to Ethiopia for a visit, she let their uncle know, explaining, "I'd said to him, a couple years ago, 'I'd like to go back to Ethiopia and visit the birth family,' and he said, 'Well, if you do, let me know, I'd like to go with you.' So last year, we decided to go back to Ethiopia, and last August, we went, and he, true to his word, he went with us." But Deirdre and Thomas also contacted their adoption agency, which sent a social worker to visit the boys' birth family's village. That visit led to Deirdre and Thomas's discovery that the story they had been told about their children's adoption was not wholly true and that the uncle with whom they'd been in contact had been lying to them as well. Deirdre related, "We found out that the birth family had lied, that the birth father had not passed away, but that [the birth parents] knew [an orphanage] would not take the children if both parents were alive. So they fabricated this story, and the birth father is alive. He's so alive that they've had two children since then."

Through a combination of global flows, cellular phones, and the luck of the draw in the green card lottery, Deirdre and Thomas came face-to-face with the truth of their sons' adoption story. I asked Deirdre how she reacted when she found out that her sons' birth mother had lied and that their birth father was alive. Like Kate, she responded with startling empathy, explaining, "For me, I was just—I guess I had the same reaction the boys did: dead is bad, alive is good. So great, we have a birth father too. I'm not walking in her shoes, or his shoes. If I can't feed or clothe my children, I might lie too. I didn't have any judgment for them, I was fine with it." Deirdre went on to describe her sons' reunion with their birth father as "joyful" and—like Kate, whose family ultimately met Jonah's birth family—"healing." She told me that upon meeting the boys' birth father, he said, "'I want for the boys, that when you get older and they get older, I want them to take care of you. They owe us nothing, and they owe you everything.' Because in Ethiopia, when [your] parents get older, you take care of your parents. So that was him saying, 'We're not their parents; you are their parents.'"

Thomas also developed a relationship with the boys' birth family and, in particular, with the boys' uncle. Thomas felt that he bonded with the boys' uncle, as well as with the boys' birth father, over their shared Christian faith and that he was able to forgive them for their dishonesty on those grounds, explaining,

> While we were in Addis, their uncle came there. And he left a little before we did. But he came to talk with us, and I could tell something was really on his mind. I walked him out, because I could tell something was really, really bothering him. So I walked him out into the hallway, and that's when he told me about the decision they'd made to give the boys up. And he said, "They didn't come about that easily." It was aunts and uncles, they all got around and talked about it and discussed. It's not something they did lightly. And after they did

do it, they agonized about it, because they weren't being truthful. And that had been eating on them for years; it had been six years up to that point. So when they knew we were coming back for a visit, he wanted to just let me know how they felt. He was emotional when he was telling me. He said, "They just want you to forgive them for not being truthful." I'm getting teary eyed now, talking about it. But I said, "Well, you know, I can't throw stones at you for this. You just let them know that I don't hold anything against them for that. I forgive them for that." So anyway, it was pretty emotional.

Thomas even told me that because he and the boys' uncle were both Christians, he felt like they were "speaking the same language" and could communicate on a level that transcended their cultural differences.

For Thomas and Deirdre, as well as for Kate, "knowing" that their children's birth parents had "chosen" to place their children for international adoption allows them, as adoptive parents, to understand their adoption as ultimately beneficial to their children. They echo Alyssa, who was able to proceed in good faith with adopting from the Congo because her agency caught an initial case of impropriety. They also echo Lynne and Mike, who insist that despite compelling evidence that their daughter was trafficked, "she has a *fabulous* life." In the context of the notion that China's one-child policy led to a large-scale abandonment of baby girls, Mike says, "So maybe people feel a little bit bad about perpetuating this, but they feel much better about providing a good home for a child who needs one." Kate also addresses this ethical trade-off in her understanding of Jonah's adoption story. About Jonah's birth mother, Kate says, "I felt really sad that she had no other choice," yet she ultimately concludes, "I know my role in his life." For Kate, Deirdre, and Thomas, understanding that their children were not "true" orphans is ironically what allowed them to cling to a shred of an otherwise discredited triumphal narrative of international adoption. Kate, along with the other mothers presented in this chapter, filters this understanding through a commitment to the prevailing ideologies of maternal femininity, and Thomas, though in many ways exceptional, nonetheless filters his understanding of his children's adoption through his commitment to normative paternal (and patriarchal) masculinity.

Mothers as Activists

Anna and Dan are a white married couple in their midforties with a seven-year-old son, Jacob, whom they adopted from Nepal. They live in a single family home in an affluent suburb and are both employed full time. Anna and Dan decided to pursue adoption after several years of unsuccessful fertility treatments. Eighteen months after submitting paperwork to their adoption agency, they were matched with their son, Jacob. They left for Kathmandu shortly afterward and, upon landing, headed straight to Jacob's orphanage. The first meeting went well, and the couple began to bond with their son over Goldfish crackers and soap bubbles. Leaving Jacob that first night, they anticipated appearing in Nepali court the next day in order to take temporary custody pending their final adoption decree, a process that they were told would take about five days. But the next morning, Anna explained, "[We were] on our way to the orphanage. The State Department called us and said, 'We want to talk to you before you sign the decree.'" So they asked their driver to turn the car around, and instead of meeting Jacob, they headed to the U.S. embassy. At the embassy, Anna and Dan were told that the U.S. Department of State had frozen all adoptions of children in Nepal due to evidence of fraud and corruption both at the level of the Nepali government and within individual orphanages. They were told that their son's adoption story may be false, that his parents may not have relinquished him, that he may have been stolen or sold. Like all other U.S. families in the middle of an adoption process in Nepal, Anna and Dan would have to positively prove that their son's documents and adoption story were not fraudulent.

Caught in the middle of this 2010 shutdown of adoptions in Nepal, Anna felt like she was acting on "impulse"—a maternal impulse to protect her child. She explained her and Dan's decision-making process: "So we say, 'What do we do?' So, 'Well, let's go ahead with what we're doing here, and we're just going to have to figure out along the way what's happening. We can't cancel this on something that may or may not be accurate. If it is accurate, then we have to find his birth parents and rectify what's happened. If it isn't accurate, we can't risk that he's growing up in an orphanage for nothing.' And so we went to the ministry, we signed the papers." Anna and Dan took Jacob back to their hotel and prepared to wait out the situation. Two days later, Anna, Dan, and Jacob came down to their hotel lobby and were met by a representative of their adoption agency who told them, "You can't leave the hotel, you'll be swamped by journalists—they shut down the program."

Anna and Dan were then invited to a meeting at the U.S. embassy, in which they were told, according to Anna, "We don't know if we can trust [your child's] documents. You can leave [Nepal] at any time, but you can't bring your child." Anna asked, "What would you recommend that we do?" and reports that she was told, "Well, you can annul the adoption and return him to the orphanage. If you stay, you could be here for up to two years." Anna's response was swift and decisive: "So, then we'll be here for two years." Anna had, indeed, wholeheartedly donned the mantle of maternal responsibility and adopted the most central, normative assumption we hold about motherhood: that a mother does not abandon her child. She was instantly determined to uproot her life and live in Nepal, waiting for her child's adoption to be finalized. Anna and Dan's next step was to contact an immigration attorney in the United States, who drafted a letter to the U.S.

embassy in Nepal. As Anna explained, "Apparently adoption law is pretty clear; if the child is most likely an orphan, then the child is considered an orphan. But the response [to the attorney's letter] was, 'We're the U.S. State Department, we don't have to follow the law.'" Anna's take on the State Department's position was pragmatic. She explained, "I think [the embassy] assumed that people would just go home. But that was a weird assumption. They didn't understand that people who adopt are just as attached to their children as anyone else." Indeed, Anna explained that she had been "waiting for [Jacob] for so long, there was no way I was giving up on him."

Anna and Dan were told that in order to secure a visa for Jacob to enter the United States, they would have to hire a private investigator to confirm that Jacob was, indeed, an orphan. So Anna and Dan hired a private investigator, and Dan returned to the United States to work while Anna and Jacob moved into a rental apartment in Kathmandu. Thrust into "survival mode," as Anna put it, she spent the days caring for Jacob and the nights ("until four o'clock every morning") searching the internet, corresponding with lawyers, doing whatever she could to contribute to her case. The investigator's 120-page report ultimately confirmed the story that Anna and Dan had been told—that Jacob had been abandoned on a riverbank, with no way to trace biological kin. Anna's story provides a clear illustration of how a disruption to her international adoption process drew out her total commitment to intensive mothering. Anna abandoned her job, her home, and her spouse in order to wholly devote her intellectual, emotional, and financial resources to bringing Jacob to the United States. Anna went up against the United States government and, in her mind, emerged victorious, with moral certainty that her son's adoption was not only legitimate but also ultimately benevolent.

Anna's narrative brings together an ideological commitment to intensive mothering and a parallel ideological commitment to a triumphal narrative of international adoption. But Anna also fits Pamela Stone's (2007) description of the "professionalization of motherhood" whereby highly educated, professional women, pressured or forced out of the workforce, channel their professional skills into intensive mothering. While the mothers in Stone's study are driven out of the workforce by their generally ordinary circumstances of inflexible bosses and commitments to intensive engagement with their children, Anna was forced into an advocacy role by the extraordinary circumstances of her son's adoption. Yet the mothers in both cases "professionalize" motherhood at an intersection of ideological commitment to intensive mothering and structural gender inequality. Indeed, while Anna's husband continued to work full time after Jacob's adoption, Anna went back to work part time, devoting herself not only to mothering Jacob but to substantial public activism. Anna frequently traveled to meet with U.S. senators and congressional representatives as part of a lobbying effort to reopen adoptions with Nepal, and she told me that she was actively pursuing an independent legal case that would allow her and her husband to adopt a second child from Nepal. In this sense, Anna's story—as well as those of Leslie and Arden, two other "activist" mothers—illustrates the ways that intensive mothering exists alongside a neoliberal turn toward self-sufficiency and the privatization of care work. The closing and reorganizing of international adoption programs across the globe, as well as the fracture of a wholly triumphal narrative of international adoption, left mothers to struggle on their own. It was within this void of public, institutional, and often familial or spousal support that some mothers fashioned themselves into activists for their children. Though writing in the context of Clinton-era welfare reform, Hays points out a fundamental contradiction facing U.S. families, including many of those that participated in this project: "Our nation is simultaneously celebrating the importance of children, holding high an ethic of care and commitment to others, while at the same time demanding that all Americans be completely self-reliant" (2004: 232). In the stories of these activist mothers, self-reliance and professionalized, intensive mothering are deployed to resolve their children's disrupted adoptions and, in the process, preserve a final shred of the triumphal narrative whereby a mother's love and U.S. exceptionalism ultimately justify their actions.

Arden, another activist mother, was the singular voice in my sample who spoke consistently and forcefully against what she called an "antiadoption" position. Arden and her husband, Michael, a widower, are both affluent, highly educated professionals raising two teenage biological sons from Michael's first marriage as well as a preschool-aged daughter born about a year after their marriage. Arden and Michael are also the legal parents of Chloe, a two-year-old girl whom they adopted in the Democratic Republic of the Congo. However, despite an adoption decree naming Arden and Michael as parents, Chloe was "stuck" in the Congo at the time of our interview. As Arden explained,

> It got rocky when the Congo stopped issuing exit visas [to Congolese citizens] after we had already adopted her. We signed the adoption decree, so we're legally her parents. In January 2013, the U.S. embassy announced that they would be implementing a mandatory three- to six-month investigation of each and every orphan petition in the Congo, which would begin only after we had signed all the paperwork and had legally adopted our children. So that was the next step, to begin that clock. Then you would get the U.S. visa. We have still not gotten the U.S. visa; it's been more like six to twelve months. But then, after you get the U.S. visa, you have to apply to Congo for the exit visa. Exit visas are not normal; they're probably illegal under international law, but countries like the Congo restrict the movement of their citizens. [In any case,] they suspended issuing exit visas.

I asked Arden what she expected—and what she hoped—would happen next. She quickly replied, "The U.S. government needs to pay [the Congolese government] off. So they release the pipeline kids."

A few months into this ordeal, Arden quit her job and immersed herself full time in lobbying Congress, attending congressional hearings, and participating in rallies and other campaigns that have grown around the shutdowns of international adoption in several countries, including the Congo. She made contacts at the Department of State and at various nongovernmental adoption advocacy organizations, and she filed multiple Freedom of Information Act requests in an attempt to publicize what she sees as gross incompetence and mismanagement at the U.S. Department of State. Arden, a licensed attorney, truly channeled all her professional energy and expertise into the project of mothering—in her case, doing everything necessary to get her daughter out of the Congo and into the United States. Indeed, Arden framed her activities in terms of both a commitment to mothering and a steadfast belief that international adoptees would be better off in the United States.

Arden harshly criticized the U.S. Department of State for, in her view, creating a diplomatic climate that is fundamentally hostile to international adoption, insisting,

> [The State Department] has the antiadoption language going, [questioning] the motives of parents who decide to adopt internationally. The State Department has this attitude that [adoptive parents] are all a little corrupt, a little shady. A lot of the consular officers are just doing their job. They don't have a mandate to treat orphan petitions as anything but an immigration matter, and children's best interests don't come into the equation, [so they] end up in a spitting match, and children wind up in limbo. . . . It's not the State Department's intention that tens of thousands of children be left behind and have their lives destroyed in institutions; their intention is to increase transparency and accountability. But the result is that tens of thousands of children's lives are being destroyed to root out what may be a couple more cases of fraud. I don't think the intention justifies what we have as the result here.

In our interview, Arden clearly advocated for less bureaucracy and oversight in international adoption processes.

In a similar vein, Arden went on to characterize the disruptions to a variety of international adoption programs as purely politically motivated:

> Just like Russia used the excuse of abuse in families in the U.S. to shut down adoptions when everybody knew that's not what it was really about, Congo used the excuse of the Reuters "rehoming report," which did not actually involve any children from the Congo. But it's bullshit, and everybody knows it's

bullshit. What I do know, what everybody knows, what I know from contacts in [the Congolese] government, is that the DRC has put trade on the table, it's just a shakedown. Pure and simple, it's a shakedown. Some people think it has to do with Congo being declared a Tier 3 Human Rights Violator [by the U.S. Department of State] for the third year in a row, which automatically starts funding cuts. So these children are hostages, basically, while the Congo shakes down the [U.S.] government. Congo is the poorest country in the world, and it's shaking us down.

Here, Arden handily dismisses well-researched journalism as "bullshit," suggesting that any discussion of misconduct among adoptive parents—and any systemic problems with international adoption that such a discussion might suggest—is inappropriate and irrelevant. She alleges that the Congo refused to release adopted children to the United States as a way to get the United States to restore humanitarian aid and other types of governmental funding. Arden's suggestion that governments lean on the rhetoric of "the best interests of children" to justify diplomatic, political, and economic positions and activities that have little to do with children's welfare echoes well-established academic arguments.

While Arden was exceptional in the ferocity with which she clung to a triumphal narrative, she was not alone in the view that international adoptions should be easier, because, in terms of child welfare, the benefit of living in a family outweighed the damage of living in an institution. Leslie took this position strongly. A married mother of a daughter adopted from Nepal, Leslie was the only participant in the study who was part of a same-sex couple, and one of only two participants who identified as gay or lesbian. Indeed, Leslie understood her position vis-à-vis international adoption as deeply rooted a lifetime of feminist activism. When Leslie's daughter, Judy, was "stuck" in Nepal at the same time as Anna's son, Jacob, Leslie was unable to leave her job and her older children to stay in Nepal with Judy. From her suburban home office, Leslie dedicated herself to organizing a campaign to "bring home" the handful of "pipeline" children in Nepal, whose adoption processes had begun but had not been finalized before the State Department shut down the program.

Leslie drew a hard line when it came to keeping international adoption programs open, but she was nonetheless circumspect about allegations of fraud, corruption, and trafficking. Quite unlike Arden, Leslie pointed to the difficulty of identifying the "truth." She explained, "I think that [allegations of corruption and fraud in international adoption are] so complicated that no one is telling a whole, balanced, fair, appropriate story. Because it's impossible to do it. You have the big camps—proadoption and antiadoption—with all the little camps underneath [them], not always clearly defined to themselves. There's too many perspectives. It's too complicated to tell a clear story. You can't; these countries aren't the same, all with their own political systems, their own understanding of personhood. It's too complicated." Wholly certain in her position on a policy level, she nonetheless lives with a degree of uncertainty. Leslie explained that despite the complexity inherent in international adoption, she firmly believed that children were universally better off living in loving families than in institutions. She was unable to uncover any information about her own daughter's history, yet remained steadfast in her belief that adoption saved her daughter from a life of poverty, dislocation, and likely sexual or domestic servitude. I asked Leslie how she lived with the cognitive dissonance of "knowing" she'd "saved" her daughter, despite not fully knowing her "true" story. She replied, "I'm queer. Cognitive dissonance doesn't bother me." Like Ivy, who sees the ethics of international adoption on a "gray scale," Leslie holds on to a triumphal narrative of international adoption by accepting the complex, contradictory, and dissonant nature of a position that discriminates between the lesser of evils.

Beyond the ways that the mothers with whom I spoke continued to express a triumphal narrative of international adoption, they also described a tremendous commitment to private action in pursuit of disrupted adoptions. International adoption is widely acknowledged to lack standardization, to be largely unregulated, and to transpire extragovernmentally, if not extralegally. But it is particularly striking that in some of these cases, it was the U.S. Department of State that ultimately told U.S. citizens to step outside protocol, outside procedure, and outside the law or else abandon the children that they had already legally adopted. Ivy hired a driver, Anna hired a private investigator, Arden quit her job to become an unpaid lobbyist in a one-woman shop. The extreme nature of their actions begs the question: motherhood at what cost? Motherhood against all odds? Motherhood against the will of the U.S. government? A compulsion toward all-encompassing, totalizing, intensive motherhood led to tremendous upheaval in their lives. Even mothers whose children were not "stuck" and who did not take on public activism described intensive efforts to uncover their children's full histories. In so doing, they found a way to cling to the shreds of a triumphal narrative.

"Lucky" Babies

Standing on a street corner in Antigua, Guatemala, I once overheard a conversation between two sets of U.S. adoptive parents, strangers to one another, both vacationing in Guatemala with their Guatemalan adopted children. One mother, of two preteens, said to the other, who was pushing a stroller, "She's one of the lucky ones." The mother of the younger child replied, "No, we are." In a reference to the shutdown of Guatemalan adoptions, the first mother suggests that the child in the stroller was "lucky" to get out of Guatemala before the 2010 adoption freeze, while the mother of the younger child sounded a note often heard among adoptive parents—that adoptive parents are the ones who truly benefit from the adoption of their child. Across Africa, Asia, and Latin America, the phrase *lucky baby* reverberated in the ears of the adoptive parents I interviewed. In China in particular, adoptive parents I interviewed visited zoos, palaces, and the Great Wall, followed by a veritable chorus of local residents calling out, "Lucky baby. Lucky baby." But the political and ethical complexity surrounding the systemic movement of children via international adoption problematizes the notion of a straightforwardly "lucky" baby. Jackie's story makes this painfully clear.

A single mother in her early fifties, Jackie holds a prestigious professional degree and is employed full time in a highly demanding field. She has two adopted daughters. Jackie's first daughter, Ana, died while in foster care in Guatemala. Though Ana had been legally adopted in Guatemala, she was in foster care waiting to join Jackie in the United States, her paperwork indefinitely delayed because of the adoption freeze in that country. A few years after Ana's death, Jackie adopted a second daughter, Zhara, from Ethiopia. When Jackie had set out to adopt Ana, adoptions in Guatemala were, from her U.S. perspective, relatively straightforward and moving relatively quickly. Jackie had several friends who had adopted children from Guatemala with relative ease before the country experienced multiple shutdowns. But almost immediately after Jackie flew to Guatemala to legally adopt Ana, adoptions in Guatemala were frozen, and while Jackie could have stayed in Guatemala and parented Ana, she had to return to the United States to work. For many months, she visited Ana in her foster home every few weeks, flying in for the weekend whenever she could. Over the course of those months, Jackie helplessly watched as Ana's health deteriorated. On her final visit, Jackie took Ana to the hospital, where she passed away as a result, Jackie finally discovered, of abuse and neglect that she was subject to in her foster placement. Jackie mourned the loss of her daughter alone and with little of the traditional support that might coalesce around the loss of a child. About two years later, when Jackie felt ready to begin a new process of adoption, Ethiopia was one of the only options available to her as a single woman. She said Ethiopia was an attractive option because "[she] was so traumatized, [she] just wanted as quick a process as possible." Ana would have been "lucky" to get a visa before she died, but does her death (or Jackie's suffering) justify the ethical ambiguity of new adoption process that's "as quick as possible"?

Many of the mothers whom I interviewed worked fiercely to uncover the truth about the circumstances of their children's adoptions, and many were successful. Either way, the process of investigating their children's adoptions brought them face-to-face with ethical ambiguity and emotional uncertainty. International adoptive mothers are complicit in an ethically complicated system, and some of the mothers I interviewed uncovered direct evidence of their own complicity in outright fraud. Mothers with differing appetites for uncertainty in their individual stories, as well as differing views on the ethics of international adoption more generally, still coalesced around the idea that the adoption of their child was the best of possible outcomes because it elevated the "best interests" of their individual child over other concerns. Nobody in my sample, though, was as committed to a purely triumphal narrative as Arden, the mother whose adoption from the Congo was still in process at the time of our interview. Arden explained to me that she is supportive of "social justice and poverty alleviation and all that, but international adoption is treated like the scapegoat. There are all these children who, because of poverty, in large part, need parents." Arden held the firm belief that international adoption was an appropriate and benevolent means of poverty alleviation that only benefitted children who would otherwise be deprived of a loving family and the chance for a fulfilling life. Quite unlike Arden, though, most mothers I spoke with expressed some degree of ambivalence and sensitivity to the complex tangle of interests at stake in international adoption. Leslie—who adopted her daughter, Judy, from Nepal—echoed a widely understood argument in the scholarly literature on international adoption, declaring that "the fight is over the United States' relationships with sending nations"—not over the well-being of the children on the ground. She explained that she understood this position, but that it didn't change her committed belief that her daughter belonged in her family. Donna—who adopted her son, Hunter, from Ethiopia—said, "it's not really in the best interests of the [sending] countries to send kids away, and so I ask myself if [adoption] is really helpful long term." She went on to describe how her son was thriving, but in a personal yearning for resolution, she continued, "If we could make contact with the [birth] family, I would feel better about it."

In the context of a changing discourse in politics and the media surrounding international adoption, the narratives in this chapter suggest that lifting the veil on a triumphal narrative of international adoption disrupts not only international adoption on a practical level but also a broader narrative of intensive mothering as noble, selfless, and "natural." The mothers I interviewed described a growing awareness of the structural inequality, the commercial organization, and the consequent corruption and fraud that defined many of their experiences with international adoption. These mothers mobilized their resources to extract their children from orphanages, to push through paperwork, to outmaneuver governments. They hired private investigators, they lobbied Congress, they formed advocacy groups. And this adherence to normative expectations of intensive mothering invited the accusation that they had trafficked their children. In the course of their investigations, they glimpsed the possibility—or sometimes shook hands with the actual living, breathing evidence—that their children's adoption paperwork was fraudulent. Faced with this new and complicated awareness, the mothers I interviewed were called to reckon with what much of the media, many foreign governments, the United Nations, and even the U.S. Department of State have placed somewhere on a continuum between ethically complicated and politically incorrect. Despite a range of political opinions, the mothers I interviewed clung to two things: their intensive commitment to mothering and, though to varying degrees, their belief in a triumphal, redemptive narrative regarding their individual children's adoptions into their American homes. This is how they defended their families' legitimacy.

Conclusion

THE REPRODUCTIVE POLITICS OF
INTERNATIONAL ADOPTION

"While we were in Nepal," Ivy told me over coffee, "there were riots in the streets, there were police with guns. Students were rioting in the university and throwing firebombs in the university." She laughed and continued, "So you know, I really didn't have time to think about the big picture. I was worried, 'Are we going to get home before curfew tonight? Will a policeman stop us on the road with a semiautomatic rifle?' I'm not kidding, I lost twenty pounds in three weeks. Best diet ever. I couldn't eat [because of] the terror that took up residence in my gut." The greatest surprise Ivy encountered in Nepal, though, was not student protests or political instability. It was not even the bureaucratic delays that copped up in the adoption of her daughter, Becca. Rather, it was the response that she and her husband, Paul, received from average Nepalis who saw them with their new daughter. As Ivy told me, "When we did go out [with Becca in Kathmandu], everybody took one look at us and said, 'Nepali baby? How much did you pay?' That was the immediate question, every single time. Or, people said, 'Lucky baby. How much did you pay?' So I knew." Ivy knew—or quickly learned—that her view of international adoption as a wholly benevolent transaction was not universally shared. Elaborating on what she came to perceive from the Nepalis she encountered on her trip, she told me, "Nobody smiled; everybody looked very grim. Nobody said, 'Oh, how nice for you.' Or, 'How nice for her.' And it's in the newspapers there constantly, that Westerners come to take their children, to harvest their organs, to turn them into servants—that it's baby selling, trafficking . . . Sometimes, in a clumsy way, I would try to say the money helps all the children in the orphanage. At least, I hope that's true. Although I suspect the people who run it have nice villas and nice cars, I don't know." Sipping her coffee, Ivy shook her head and summed up, "It was like I was the criminal; I was just trying to help."

Ivy entered into her process of international adoption naive, perhaps, but with the intention that her mothering, a good in itself, would also help and provide opportunity to a girl in tremendous need of support. Ivy's story exemplifies not only a triumphal narrative of international adoption but also its rupture.[1] Despite persistent challenges and mounting red flags and weeks stuck in Kathmandu awaiting a decision after the U.S. Department of State challenged Becca's availability for adoption, Ivy's individual moment of narrative rupture came hard and fast and when she least expected it. A few weeks after returning from Nepal with Becca, Ivy described walking into an evening parents' meeting for her older son, Josh, at his school. When Ivy entered the room, the speaker stopped midsentence, and the whole room rose to their feet and broke into applause. Ivy was not grateful, or honored, or proud. She was exhausted, and she was angry. This display broke Ivy down. After confronting not only Nepal's extreme poverty but also student riots, paramilitary police, accusations of child trafficking, and Becca's severe illness upon returning to the United States, Ivy saw the absurdity of a wholly triumphal narrative reflected back to her in the naivete of her neighbors' applause.

Erin, a married mother of a son adopted from Ethiopia, understood and expressed her family's story of international adoption very differently from Ivy. She described to me how it was particularly difficult when she and her husband, Scott, arrived in Ethiopia because their son, Dominic, was very ill when they met him at the orphanage. Though the orphanage staff said it was "just a cold," Dominic was also reported to be eight months old but weighed only nine pounds. Erin told me that the orphanage staff referred to Dominic's weight as "mild malnourishment." Over the first few days that they were in Ethiopia, Erin and Scott advocated that Dominic be taken to the hospital, where doctors found that he was suffering from severe dehydration, pneumonia, a high fever, and a double ear infection. Dominic's hospitalization turned out to be the first of many, as well as a particularly painful ordeal for Erin because she had not yet been granted custody and therefore could not communicate with Dominic's doctors and nurses nor remain with him outside of a few short visits. When Dominic was released from the hospital, his adoption was finalized, and the family was cleared to fly back to the United States, Erin cut her ties with the orphanage because, as she explained to me, "We suspected they had more information on him medically that we've never been given." When I asked, "What makes you suspect that?" Erin continued, "He has something called schizencephaly, so he was born without his [brain's] right parietal lobe; from your frontal lobe all the way back to where your eyes are, it never formed. He was diagnosed here when he was fourteen months old, they found it on an MRI." Erin teared up, and then continued, "He was so sick, and he was so small, and he was in care for three months before he was cleared to be 'healthy' for a referral, so we just feel that we're missing some information." When Erin contacted her adoption agency to try to find more information on Dominic's health history, she was told that they had given her everything they had.

Erin went on to explain how, upon returning the United States, Dominic, who was five years old at the time of our interview, was diagnosed with a neurological condition: "We were seeing every doctor under the sun. We had weekly visits to the pediatrician for weight checks, we went to the international adoption clinic, we had hearing tests, eye tests, neurology, stool samples, blood draws. We had already called Early Intervention, because we just assumed, [based on his] time in institutionalized care, he would be behind. So they came pretty quickly after he came home." Initially, as Erin explained, Dominic was healthy. She recalled,

His right side of his body was developing really well. But I had worked with stroke patients in the past, and I said to my husband, "He doesn't know he has a left side of his body." And my husband would say, "Yes he does, it's just not his strong side." But he had no idea, no idea that he had a left hand, a left leg. I thought he'd had a stroke. So I took him to the pediatrician and the pediatrician said, "Looks like he had a stroke." So I didn't feel crazy. Our initial neurologist didn't want to do an MRI. We're not with him anymore. But was like, "I *guess*, if you feel we *need* to do an MRI." And that's how we discovered the brain malformation. It's a gaping spot in his brain that's just not there.

When I asked Erin if she could tell me more about what Dominic's condition meant for him—and for her and Scott—on a day-to-day basis, she explained,

He has a left-sided paresis, so he uses a wheelchair for long distances, a walker for shorter distances, or holds your hand. He has a speech-language delay, so he uses some sign language, and then they're working on a communication system for him. He has epilepsy, he's legally blind, and he has a mild hearing loss. But he's a hot ticket; I wish I could have brought him with me. When you look at him, you see that he has physical limitations, and when he talks it's hard to understand, but he just doesn't carry himself as someone who's facing the challenges he's facing. He is a people person; he loves people . . . loves to be in the middle of everything.

Dominic's disability presented real logistical and emotional challenges for Scott and Erin, which they tackled with the help of a strong social network and support from each of their large families. Raising a child with a severe disability was unexpected, and Scott, an athletic trainer, particularly struggled to let go of his dreams of sports, coaching, and competition alongside his son. Erin, a special education teacher in the local public school district, threw herself into coordinating Dominic's medical care and educational interventions, cementing her identity in the work of mothering a child with special needs. It was from this vantage point that Erin spoke about the ethical context of Dominic's adoption:

When we met his birth mom, she cried because she adored him. She kept him with her for three months, but she just couldn't provide for him. We question whether she knew. People assume that if he was adopted, then his mother must have been addicted to drugs or an unfit mother. Something that they're used to here in the U.S. But I truly don't think was the case. She truly lived in poverty and couldn't provide for him. I know in Ethiopia there were ethical questions, a lot of [adoptive parents] joined the program, and then [the program] had a lot of pressure to find them healthy babies because that's what people wanted. People say they know families who had their cases searched, and researched independently and that they found that their child wasn't a true orphan, and they found the birth family, so I don't know. I think there certainly is a possibility that they were creating orphans for them, but for us, in our case, we've never questioned whether or not it was truly an ethical decision for his family.

Because of Dominic's severe disabilities, Erin and Scott were able to maintain a view of Dominic's adoption not only as ethical but as a triumph that saved his life.

The End of International Adoption?

The narratives in this book reflect a particular historical moment and a distinct cohort of international adoptive mothers. The mothers I interviewed for this project, by virtue of their timing, found the entire system of international adoption shifting under their feet. In a previous era, adoption records were sealed and birth mothers remained anonymous and invisible across oceans, languages, and unabating poverty. But every single mother I interviewed who adopted from Ethiopia was taken, by their adoption agency, on an excursion from Addis Ababa to their child's natal village, where they met their child's biological kin. More than once, their child's reputedly deceased birth parents stood to the side and watched as cousins, aunts, uncles, and grandparents posed for photographs with the U.S. adopting couple. And they kept in touch. More than one adoptive mother I interviewed exclaimed with (perhaps misplaced) surprise, "Everyone in Ethiopia has a cell phone!" The travel, communication, and overall interconnectedness of our globalized world allowed, in many cases, for the truth of individual children's adoption stories to come to light.

Social media has played a tremendous role in many adoptive mothers' narratives of reckoning with the institutional shifts that have in many ways ended international adoption as we knew it. Today, more than 20 percent of the global population has a Facebook profile; at the height of international adoption in 2004, the social media platform was the exclusive domain of a few elite American college students. All kinds of members of the adoption community—adoptive parents, adoptees, and their biological parents, grandparents, and siblings—have flocked to social media for community and support at precisely the same time that critical media coverage of international adoption has increased. Online adoption groups share articles, links, blogs, and all manner of conversational topics, many highly critical of international adoption. The parents I interviewed relied on these groups and, alongside the simultaneous increase in conventional media coverage on the subject, bore witness to the cracking of the ideological facade surrounding international adoption in the United States—the rupture of a triumphal narrative. While many parents I spoke with uncovered direct evidence of problems with their children's adoption stories, even the parents I interviewed whose individual adoption processes did not come under direct scrutiny had been forced to confront emerging evidence of corruption in their children's countries of birth as well as in international adoption more generally.

Entering into their adoption processes between 2004 and 2014, the mothers interviewed for this project lived through a fundamental shift in international adoption as an institution. Both programmatic changes and political volatility delayed and threatened many of their adoptions. The bureaucratic challenges, as well as the diplomatic and political debates that they encountered, exposed them to the structural forces that underlie international adoption and that keep the adoption marketplace supplied with children. Previous to the changes to international adoption at the beginning of the twenty-first century, all adoptive parents traveling to their child's birth country would have encountered poverty. But due to fractures in the system, the adoptive mothers whom I interviewed spent more time in those countries, likely gave more thought to the operation of those countries, and often encountered far more than poverty. Like Ivy, terrified in the streets of Kathmandu, they faced the most profound kinds of social and economic dislocation. Brought face-to-face with the underlying structural apparatus of the international adoption market, many of their individual triumphal narratives broke, and during the time period captured in their stories, much of our larger societal narrative did too.

How the triumphal narrative of international adoption ruptured and what the break in that narrative reveals is a story about reproductive politics in twenty-first-century America. International adoptions in the United States began as a trickle of families responding to the humanitarian aftermath of World War II and the Korean and Vietnam Wars. As highly educated professional women and men increasingly delayed marriage and childbearing over the last decades of the twentieth century, international adoption became a full-fledged and demand-driven reproductive marketplace. As the number of international adoptions to the United States climbed in the 1990s and early 2000s, a triumphal narrative reigned. Wave after wave of international adoptions—from Romania, China, Guatemala, Ethiopia—all conformed to a narrative wherein U.S. parents "save" orphans at the same time that they add a child to their families. International adoptive families have been a highly visible representation of America's noblest aspirations toward multiculturalism, postcolonialism, and the universalism of our own brand of democracy. This narrative also says something about the

American family: that its unity is stronger than the differences within it. When international adoptive families show that the private provision of love and care can heal trauma and erase difference, the family—and, of course, mothers in particular—do the work of the nation.

Beginning in the early 2000s, evidence—primarily journalistic—began to emerge surrounding patterns of corruption in international adoption programs around the world. At the same time, scholarly literature in the social sciences and the law began to analyze those patterns in terms of systemic global inequalities. The U.S. Department of State responded, shuttering programs in Cambodia, Nepal, and the Democratic Republic of the Congo while exercising increased scrutiny in a variety of other contexts. Likewise, sending nations Guatemala, Ethiopia, China, Russia, and others closed or substantially curtailed their own programs. Today the number of international adoptions each year has decreased by more than 75 percent from its peak in 2004. Equally significantly, the average age of children at adoption has increased dramatically: fewer than one in twenty international adoptees are currently adopted as infants, compared to 40 percent in 2004 (Bureau of Consular Affairs 2016). Beyond reflecting a significant change in adoption policies and practices, the dramatic changes in these numbers signal new questions and contradictions within our contemporary reproductive politics.

Sometimes the moment of a narrative's breakdown is rooted in the dynamics of the marketplace. Pat and Rich were an older couple who wanted to be parents; Pat had worked with Guatemalan refugee women in Mexico during the armed conflict in Guatemala in the 1990s, and Rich, a former labor organizer, described himself as "part of the global working class." While they were clear that their primary motivation for adopting was to have children, they believed, like most of the parents I interviewed, that international adoption was also beneficial for the children who came to the United States. Pat and Rich did not subscribe to a triumphal narrative because of their international experience or their progressive politics; among adoptive parents, commitment to a triumphal narrative cut across lines of politics and class. Their progressive politics did not insulate them from complicity in a corrupted adoption process. When Pat and Rich elected to adopt from Guatemala, adoption processes were moving quickly and seemingly smoothly. Pat acknowledged that they should have done more due diligence when they accepted a match with a baby girl, Elsa, before even submitting a complete application to the adoption agency that reached out to them. As Pat explained, she was very eager to become a mother. When Pat and Rich discovered that the adoption agency had lied to them, hiding Elsa's severe cerebral palsy, Pat and Rich backed out of the adoption. Pat and Rich's story clearly illustrates a straightforward ethical dilemma that accompanies international adoption, one that has always accompanied all kinds of adoption, in terms of which children are deemed "adoptable" and which, for any number of reasons, are not. Pat and

Rich's story also illuminates the market dynamics that underlie international adoption: because it's a market, adoptive parents hold the cards. Pat and Rich, victimized by fraud, were able to clearly see the commercial nature of international adoption, and it was through their ultimate choice not to adopt Elsa that they confronted their function as consumers in a marketplace.

Many of the mothers I interviewed told me that they ruled out domestic adoption because they felt that in pursuing international adoption, they maintained more agency and control over the process. In private domestic adoption, where birth mothers select their babies' adoptive parent(s), the adoptive mothers I spoke with balked at having to "be chosen." These mothers are clearly aware of their positionality vis-à-vis the market; they act, correctly or incorrectly, to maintain their own interests. Many of them express a deep discomfort with the commercial nature of international adoption and the fact that they became mothers through participation in a commercial enterprise, and their ethical ambivalence is well placed. As the historian of adoption Ellen Herman notes, "adoption commerce has always been a significant dimension of adoption history" and is "deeply disturbing because of its implication that children are bought and sold as commodities. This practice echoes slavery, negates the pricelessness of modern childhood, and mocks the human values that modern social welfare supposedly represents" (2008: 295). Viviana Zelizer (2010) argues that the best way to mediate both the material inequities and the ethical problems that plague reproductive marketplaces (including domestic and international adoption) is to create the possibility for open, transparent, and well-regulated economic exchanges. At this moment of narrative rupture, when we have the opportunity to interrogate the workings of our cultural scripts, it's worth asking what Zelizer's vision of an efficient and transparent market could have done in Pat and Rich's case. Pat and Rich would never have been matched with a child they were unwilling to adopt, and they would have been spared the emotional turmoil of making that decision after the fact. But nothing would have changed for Elsa at all.

In theory, economic actors behave rationally, and the mothers I interviewed describe making a series of rational (or rational-seeming) choices surrounding the attributes that they would like their future children to possess. While distasteful to some, the decision not to adopt a child with severe disabilities can be understood as a rational one. We know from the body of work on reproductive markets that prospective parents will pay a premium for what they consider to be the "best" genetic material for their future children and that egg and sperm "donors" are differentially compensated based on their height, weight, eye color, SAT scores, and the like. Ultimately, little about the desire to mother is rational, as the mothers in this study who faced contested adoptions clearly illustrated through their sometimes extreme actions. Zelizer's call for a well-regulated adoption marketplace may adequately address the needs of adoptive mothers who already see themselves as autonomous economic actors, but the crack in our society's story reveals some questions that have not yet been fully answered. What about birth mothers, whom investigative journalists and critical scholars have framed as "subterranean women" facing extreme social and economic dislocation? What about the complexity of what constitutes the "best interests" of children in a way that respects children's full personhood? Most centrally, when reproductive markets mean that some children are so much more likely than others to be passed over or left behind, we, as Barbara Katz Rothman writes, "are forced to confront, in no subtle way, what makes for worth in human beings" (1989: 175). These are the reproductive politics revealed by the breakdown in our narrative of international adoption as a social and cultural triumph.

Mothering Work in the Face of Fraud

The women I interviewed for this project were, on the whole, primarily motivated to enter into processes of international adoption by a desire to mother a child. But particularly in the cases of those mothers who took extreme actions to pursue politically and legally challenged adoptions, what other factors were at work? Why would the mothers I interviewed—without exception intelligent, well informed, well educated, and professional—enter into an unstable international adoption program when so much information about that programmatic and political turmoil was available through a quick Google search? More significantly, what drove these mothers to persevere in the face of the daunting legal, financial, and emotional hurdles that they faced, once their individual adoption processes became challenged? Thinking about the workings of a "compulsory" side of motherhood and maternal responsibility could be helpful. As Angela Davis writes, "Motherhood lies just beyond the next technology," and the result of ever-increasing technologies—in the broadest sense of the word—is, as Davis and others argue, an "ideological compulsion" to mother (1993: 360). The mothers I interviewed displayed both a firm commitment to an ideology of intensive motherhood and, as they fought for their cases to be resolved, an abiding belief in a triumphal narrative of international adoption, despite the ways in which that narrative was crumbling around them.

When Sharon Hays develops the concept of "intensive motherhood" (in *The Cultural Contradictions of Motherhood*, 1996), she demonstrates that it is a distinctly gendered phenomenon operating within our society's broader contradictory ideologies surrounding family work and emotion at a time of increasing egalitarianism in both public and private life. In the context of the mothers interviewed for this project, we know that mothers generally assume the majority of both household management tasks and "fertility work." Many endured challenged adoptions and allegations of fraud and corruption that exacerbated the gendered inequality of their family arrangements. Bureaucratic delays created more work on an administrative level; multiple visits to courts, doctors, and U.S.

government offices to get new or additional documents were common. As one mother who reported being inundated with paperwork quipped, "You wouldn't think fingerprints could expire." But they did, and it was she, not her husband, who twice brought her older biological children on daylong expeditions for new FBI-certified fingerprints.

Allegations of fraud and corruption created even more bureaucratic hurdles, which led to more pronounced gendered dynamics both pragmatically and emotionally. Anna, the adoptive mother who stayed in Kathmandu with her Nepali son for several months, became his sole caretaker and primary legal advocate so that her husband could return to his job in the United States. Arden, the Congolese adoptive mother who quit her law practice, likewise embodies a total and intensive commitment to motherhood, as well as the "professionalization" of motherhood among highly educated mothers who leave the labor force in order to fully dedicate themselves to mothering work (see, in particular, Stone 2007). Additionally, the adjustment issues and other special needs that adopted children—particularly older adoptees—can face led other mothers to scale back their professional commitments. Emily, a single mother working in the nonprofit world, quit her job in order to help her academically struggling daughter thrive. Kate, an attorney, cut back to part-time work in order to drive her son to therapy appointments with a specialist located 150 miles from their home, and when new kinds of family work emerged surrounding her son's difficulties, Kate assumed full responsibility. When families are stressed, mothers pick up the slack. As Arlie Hochschild (1989) argues with respect to "emotion work" and Hays (1996) echoes in terms of "ideological work," disproportional responsibility for family labor and its increasing demands require that mothers re-up their commitment to "traditional" gender and family arrangements.

Beyond the pragmatic aspects of organizing family work, allegations of fraud and evidence of corruption also demanded from mothers a particular kind of emotional and ideological work. As Ivy reported about outings in Kathmandu immediately after assuming custody of her daughter, Becca, "Everybody took one look at us and said, 'Nepali baby? How much did you pay?' . . . That was the immediate question, every single time . . . so, I knew." Ivy came to "know" that adopting her daughter was a fundamentally commercial transaction and, therefore to her mind, an ethically compromised one. Ivy saw that Nepalis on the street were "very grim" about international adoption, and she truly felt on a certain level that, as she said, she "was the criminal." But Ivy also "knew" that she was "just trying to help." Good mothers, by definition, are not criminals; good mothers do not place their desires over the best interests of their children. The ethical dilemma that Ivy faced called into question her family's legitimacy and her legitimacy as a mother. Just as the mothers that Hochschild interviewed thirty years ago had to adjust their feelings about unequal family work— and about motherhood—to align with prevailing ideologies about gender and families, and just as Hays suggests that mothers must work to align their ideologies about mothering to support the reality of their lives, the mothers in this study had to wrestle with reproductive injustice in order to preserve the legitimacy of their families.

Different mothers did this in different ways. Anna, the mother who spent several months living in Kathmandu with her adopted son, accused the U.S. Department of State of acting outside of Nepali children's best interests, pronouncing, "Humans are the only species that hold their own children hostage for political reasons." Anna's implication is that the children's welfare is far from our top priority when we craft the programs that are charged with ensuring their welfare. Anna considered the shutdown of adoptions in Nepal an "overcorrection" to the problems of fraud, corruption, and child trafficking that, in her words, "probably existed" in other sending nations. But Anna remained adamant that her son, as well as the other children in Nepali orphanages, were "innocent victims" of both extreme poverty and the political battles being waged around them. Arden, who quit work as an attorney to advocate full time for the lifting of restrictions on international adoption, acknowledged that corruption exists but suggested, as a remedy, that international adoption should be treated more like a marketplace, not less. She explained, "I think the reason people don't want a commercial approach to international adoption is because of inequality ... [but] I spent time abroad, studying financial fraud. I do not expect adoption to be the exception to the rule in countries that struggle with corruption, but that seems to be the expectation in the Department of State. If there's a plane crash, do we ban airline flights? No, we deal with it." Arden also insisted that birth mothers, however constrained their choices may be, are aware of what they're doing when placing their children in orphanages, and she clarified that she finds it "patronizing" to suggest otherwise. As she quite bluntly put it, "I don't think poor people are as stupid as we make them out to be." In this, Arden maintains a tension between two seemingly opposing positions. On the one hand, she does not seem to think that birth mothers in the developing worlds should be afforded any particular protections. At the same time that she stakes out a neoliberal argument, though, she clearly argues that poor women in sending nations are capable of—and should be empowered in—making their own decisions about their reproductive and family lives.

Like Anna, Arden aligns herself with the position that supporting international adoption promotes children's right to live in a family, as well as their interests overall. Arden sees the U.S. Department of State's intervention into international adoption programs as harmful to children's interests, explaining, "It's not the State Department's intention that tens of thousands of children be left behind and have their lives destroyed in institutions, their intention is to increase transparency and accountability. But the result is that tens of thousands of children's lives are being destroyed to root out what may be a couple more cases of fraud. I don't think the intention justifies what we have as the result here." But Arden's argument for deregulation flies in the face of evidence that illicit activity would flourish without stringent oversight, that birth mothers' rights would be trampled on, and that children would be baldly bought and sold as commodities irrespective of their "best interests." By this measure, the "*fabulous* life" that international adoptees may have in the United States makes up for the possibility of illicit activity. In assuming this antiregulation stance, Anna and Arden show how an ongoing triumphal narrative relies on applying co-opted neoliberal claims of freedom and choice.

While Arden and Anna expressed very little ambivalence around these emotional, ethical, and political contradictions, other mothers clung to pieces of a triumphal narrative without subscribing to it wholeheartedly. These mothers turned to an ideology of intensive motherhood and the consequently unequal division of family work in order to persevere through challenged adoptions, but they also relied on a triumphal narrative of international adoption in order to justify fighting for the resolution of their adoption processes. For some mothers, commitment to a triumphal narrative was fundamentally at odds with their vision of reproductive politics. Emily, a single mother of a daughter adopted from Ethiopia, came to see her daughter's adoption records as "a total lie," telling me that her daughter should never have been separated from her birth mother and that she believed the adoption system alone was responsible for her daughter's presence in an orphanage, as well as the developmental challenges that her daughter faces as a result of neglect in that orphanage. Marty, a mother of five biological siblings from Ethiopia, adopted one after the other when she learned through the daughter she adopted first that her records had been falsified and her siblings remained in Ethiopia. In our interview, Marty told me that if her politics had driven her to adopt the first of her Ethiopian children, then her politics demanded that she follow through, given the corrupt circumstances under which they came to be living without their parents. Danielle, a married mother of an older daughter by birth and a younger daughter adopted from China, explained that while she and her husband had been unable to uncover direct evidence of fraud in the case of her daughter's adoption, it was clear that the "system was corrupt" in the province where her daughter had been in orphanage care. Danielle told me, point blank, "If I'd known then what I know now, I wouldn't do it again."

For other mothers, politics were more complicated. A married lesbian mother and self-described "progressive feminist committed to child welfare" who adopted a daughter from Nepal, Leslie applauds the United Nations in many of its efforts but abhors the United Nations International Children's Emergency Fund (UNICEF) in its insistence that children should live in institutions in their natal countries rather than in families who want to adopt them abroad. "Children belong in families," Leslie believes. Describing the complexity of the political positions surrounding international adoption, Leslie explained, "You could make a chart [of] the Evangelicals teaming up with the liberal, pro-choice people while antagonizing each other but fighting together." About this internally contradictory tangle of interests, Leslie said, "I feel frustrated most of the time." This individual-level frustration and the ambivalence of the mothers with whom I spoke corresponds to larger contradictions in our political thinking about international adoption. When UNICEF and others on the left argue that children belong in their natal countries, they're doing so in the name of preserving cultural patrimony and serving the long-term interests of sending nations. Yet in so doing, they're also making an essentialist argument about where people "belong" that's based in a fundamentally conservative notion of immutable difference.

A triumphal narrative has validated U.S. colonialist-style extraction of children from poor nations and, in a context of poor regulation, has led to numerous abuses. The triumphal narrative has also told a story of an optimistic modernism, postcolonialism, and the seedlings of a more pluralistic and racially egalitarian society—speaking, in theory, to some of our most progressive aspirations. This narrative transcended political difference and continues to unite, as Leslie put it, "strange bedfellows" across social divides. To the extent that the triumphal narrative has ruptured in the face of mounting evidence of corruption and fraud, what does that rupture mean? And to what extent has the supporting narrative of international adoption reorganized itself? If international adoptees are not "better off" with adoptive parents in the United States, then what do we make of the extreme actions that so many of the mothers I interviewed undertook in order to bring their children home? If we abandon a triumphal narrative, we blame these mothers for participating in fraudulent adoptions rather than applauding them for their heroism. On a collective level, applauding these mothers for heroism erases the structural inequalities and murky or absent regulations that buttress large-scale international adoption as a system. But if, on a collective level, we demonize them, then we lay the weight of the world's civil wars, ethnic conflicts, infectious diseases, and economic injustices on their individual shoulders. This point should not absolve all international adoptive mothers everywhere of any potential wrongdoing but, rather, should probe us to ask how best to pursue reproductive justice without deepening our own culture of mother blame.

A "Healthy Baby" in the Twenty-First Century

Beyond the specific politics of international adoption, the overall reproductive decision-making of the parents I interviewed reveals broader cultural anxieties surrounding race, health, motherhood, kinship, and care. Various measures of health and "fitness" have long operated as racialized constructs within an American ethnoracial hierarchy that associates whiteness with cleanliness, respectability, and health more generally. Immigration has long challenged the black-white divide in the U.S. racial order; immigrants from Ireland, southern Europe, and Eastern Europe "became" white through upward economic mobility and assimilation into mainstream Anglo-American culture, while Chinese and other Asian immigrants morphed, in the public imagination, from a racial threat to a "model minority." As the U.S. ethnoracial landscape continues to change and the rigidity of ethnoracial hierarchies, however unevenly, continues to loosen, ideas about health and fitness are being racialized in new and evolving ways. Our economy has changed, and so today's parents' anxieties about their children's health and fitness reflect the new cognitive and social-emotional demands that we perceive to be coming from the precariousness of our new economy.

One of the clearest illustrations of this process comes from Marjorie, a married mother of three children adopted from China, who explained that she adopted children from China with "minor, correctable medical needs" instead of "significantly damaged" U.S. foster children. Framing her choices in terms of concerns about children's "health," Marjorie doesn't think her decision is about race: as she said to me, "I would have adopted three African American kids, but that would have been too much for my in-laws." Rather, setting her in-laws aside, Marjorie ruled out African American kids on her own by ruling out private domestic adoption because she did not want contact with biological kin and the foster care system because "those kids are significantly damaged." Eduardo Bonilla-Silva writes that colorblind racism functions as an "elastic wall that barricades whites from the United States' racial reality" (2006: 47), and through her own colorblindness, Marjorie is barricading herself against the racialization of her own ideas about health and fitness. Furthermore, Marjorie is clear about what she means by "damaged"—kids with atypical neurological development—telling me, "Our kids just needed surgery, and then they were fine. We could not have handled it, like, medical versus emotional issues." Indeed, she had explicitly ruled out adopting from Russia for that reason.

Marjorie ruled out damaged black kids *and* damaged white kids, both in Russia and in U.S. foster care, and she was not alone. The continued loosening of the ethnoracial order in U.S. society has led to far more fine-grained kinds of racial categorization than existed prior to the de facto achievement of legal equality that defined the mid-twentieth century. In this intersectional sense, Patricia Hill Collins argues that "skin color no longer serves as a definitive mark of racial categorization" (2004: 194), but that other factors—in the context of Collins's analysis, primarily gender and sexuality—can mediate the traditional ways in which skin color alone assigns a person to a particular racial group. In the context of the mothers I interviewed for this study, atypical neurological development loomed large as a liability in their decision-making about their future children, and adoptive parents, anxious about their children's futures, preferred to adopt a "healthy" black African child over a "damaged" child from a Russian orphanage.

That finding is at odds with the reality of antiblack racism in our society and, therefore, opens an important area for further investigation into the racialization of these African adoptees in the United States. Further, in the context of contemporary advances in medical technology, parents were far more willing to take on what Marjorie calls "minor, correctable medical needs" than they were intellectual or social-emotional disabilities, which raises parallel questions about racialization, health, and fitness in our hypercognitive society.

Today, the majority of children available for international adoption have special needs. The adoptive mothers whom I interviewed knew this because their children came home with them. Linda, a married mother of three older biological sons, described the early days of coming home with Irina and Nick, a Russian sibling pair who were in elementary school when she and her husband adopted them. Linda explained, "Suddenly I had two toddlers. They were older kids, but their behaviors were like toddlers. One day, we were driving down the highway and Nick just flung open the car door, right on the highway." Nick and Irina's paths quickly began to diverge, though. Nick adapted to his life in the United States quickly, making many friends at school and then bringing them home to play football and basketball with his older brothers. Nick needed substantial academic support but was generally emotionally stable and well behaved. Irina, meanwhile, began to steal, lie, and show other signs of reactive attachment disorder. Later, as a teen, Irina developed severe anxiety and was diagnosed with bipolar disorder. One of Linda's first clues came early—Irina was unable to use the bathroom alone. As Linda explained to me, "Later, we found out that she was horrifically abused, and that's why she needed me with her in the bathroom. It took her five years to be able to go in there by herself." Linda and her husband "drained [their] bank accounts" paying for Irina's therapy and, ultimately, residential treatment, but Linda remained adamant that international adoption is important and that she herself would do the same thing over again. She explained that she thought the benefits of international adoption to special needs children, in particular, trumped other considerations, telling me,

> Yeah, there are seven or eight kids who have died in their adoptive families in the U.S. But go and compare that to all of the Russian kids who have died in institutions because of abuse, neglect, being chained to bed—they have "laying-down rooms" where if the kid has any handicap at all, they put them in there and they die. They die from lack of nourishment, lack of nutrition, lack of attention; they die. And if you count all of those kids, it's in the thousands compared to the seven or eight who have died here. Russia has no leg to stand on. It's just a stupid thing for Putin to show how strong he is.

Likewise, Erin, Dominic's mother, advocated for international adoption to remain open on the basis of the needs of adoptive children—but for Erin, poverty alone should not determine need. She told me, "In a perfect world, you would match the families with the kids who need it, so you wouldn't have this situation of supply and demand, of long lists of families who are waiting for children, and now [the agencies] have to find 'healthy' children to give them. And then there are all these children with challenges waiting for families." Among the mothers I interviewed—in particular among those who adopted children with substantial health care needs—a redemptive narrative of international adoption hinged on a narrative of individual rescue.

ADOPTION MARKETS AND REPRODUCTIVE JUSTICE

A turn toward special needs adoption raises its own set of questions about how the triumphal narrative may live on. The motivations and experiences of international adoptive parents who consciously adopt special needs children may shed light not only on the survival of that triumphal narrative but also on broader questions about health and fitness in the new economy. Their stories would make an important contribution, given the extent to which the parents I interviewed for this project tried to avoid adopting special needs children. Do we frame international adoptees with special needs as somehow "truly" needy? Is it more understandable—or justifiable—that they would be abandoned and legitimately available for adoption? Do their special needs somehow erase—or mitigate—the broader structural issues that led to their separation from their birth families? Do we validate ourselves as Americans by continuing to "rescue" the neediest of the world's children? These shifts in a triumphal narrative of international adoption need to be investigated for what they reveal not only about motherhood and gendered approaches to altruism but also about how we understand ability and disability in a new and unstable economy. In debates about reproductive politics, as in the culture wars more generally, children become proxies for the competing value systems of the adults around them. Polarized cultural debates about adoption clearly illustrate this phenomenon. When adoptive parents team up across social and political divides to advocate for more, faster, and easier international adoptions, they are breathing air into a dying narrative about U.S. triumphalism on a global stage. Ultimately, that narrative promotes a market-based, do-it-yourself approach that, like neoliberal social and economic policies more generally, creates distinct winners and losers in a dramatically unequal world. Ongoing commitment to a triumphal narrative of international adoption purports to advance the best interests of children by means of their essential right to live in a family. While this conforms to American cultural values, civic and religious beliefs, and current trends in neuroscience and developmental psychology, it also comes with a distinct focus on decreased regulation. From legal scholar and international adoption advocate Elizabeth Bartholet to the mothers-turned-activists whom I interviewed, regulation is often framed not as a means of achieving but rather as a barrier to child welfare. This stands in stark contrast to other child welfare advocates who seek to balance complex and sometimes contradictory interests.

While the market dynamics of international adoption are undeniable, promoting an open market and placing faith in market dynamics not only commodifies children but leaves adoptive parents with a distinct advantage. Any suggestion that such arrangements equally serve the interests of birth mothers is irresponsible without substantial research into birth mothers' attitudes, motivations, hopes, and fears; at present, there is practically none. The investigative journalism that is most critical of international adoption tends to portray birth mothers as powerless, voiceless women who are robbed, duped, or otherwise coerced into relinquishing their most prized, priceless asset. A clear counterargument to this grim portrait of subaltern birth mothers emerges from the narratives of the women interviewed for this project in the form of a suggestion that poor mothers outside of the United States should be empowered to choose to place their children for adoption just as mothers in the United States are able to. Certainly, all women everywhere should be fully empowered in determining the course of their reproductive lives, but a neoliberal discourse of choice erases the structural barriers and inequalities that, in the broadest sense, force people's choices. This is particularly true in the gendered arena of reproduction, where women's invisible and unpaid work continues to define even the most straightforward of reproductive marketplace transactions. And this is even truer in the context of the profound inequalities between the upper-middle-class in the United States and poor of sending nations. In this context, it is hard to see how embracing a discourse of free choice and a transparent marketplace would lead to more equitable or just international adoption arrangements. In any case, adoptive mothers, speaking about their own experiences, cannot address birth mothers' motivations, anxieties, and interests, so further investigation is needed to bring more birth mothers' voices into a fuller conversation.

Another area ripe for further investigation is the rapidly evolving role that fertility medicine is playing in the reproductive lives of American women. At the same time that the number of both domestic and international adoptions has shrunk, the incidence of in vitro fertilization and other fertility interventions has dramatically increased. Obviously, these are not causally related phenomena, and the evolution of fertility medicine relies on political and scientific developments independent of the forces that drive adoption markets. But the attitudes and practices surrounding reproductive medicine and technology, when seen in a broader context of shifting reproductive politics, address the same questions as this story about the "ending" of international adoption. Many scholars—and families—remain committed to the idea that kinship can be forged beyond biogenetic ties. As Joshua Gamson (2015) explores, today's "brave new families" are brave in a new way, confronting the profound ethical questions that accompany their privileged participation in reproductive marketplaces. At the same time, for many families, nature is far from dead: as Linda Seligman, writing specifically about international adoption, notes, "Even as bio-relatedness recedes as the taken-for-granted criterion for constituting a family, technologies based on biological connections, and such connections themselves, continue to play central roles in how parents and children imagine their positions and activities in families in America" (2013: 7). There are obviously tremendous questions yet to be asked, let alone answered, about how ongoing advances in reproductive technology contribute to the literature on reproductive markets, motherhood, kinship, and citizenship, as well as race, health, and "fitness."

Ultimately, this book is about the ending of a system and a practice of international adoption that, for a generation, straddled contradictions between kinship and foreignness, compulsion and choice, and commerce and care. The bridging of these multiple contradictions was possible because of the widespread acceptance of international adoption as both a private and a public good. But the notion of international adoption as a triumph reveals both the most conservative and the most progressive impulses in our thinking about ourselves and our families. Adoption is progressive insofar as it proves we can transcend boundaries of race, class, and nation. Yet within a triumphal narrative, American families are simply best for kids. And a repudiation of the triumphal narrative also reveals profound political contradictions. An antiadoption position, no matter how focused on the human rights of birth mothers and adoptees, delegitimizes bonds forged by choice and essentializes "natural" family relationships. The embrace of this position feeds into a regressive commitment to heteronormative family arrangements and a biogenetic basis for determining kinship. It also harkens back to notions of eugenics, racial purity, and ugly ideas of what we mean by health and fitness. Writing not about adoption but reproductive politics in general, Laura Briggs argues that "the politics of reproduction are key to understanding our shared political life in the United States" (2017: 209). The politics of international adoption cut to the core of American reproductive politics because international adoption sits not only at the intersection of gendered family arrangements and the inequalities of reproductive markets but at a far more chaotic intersection of race, health and disability, and, perhaps, a crumbling view of American exceptionalism.

Methods and Sample Characteristics

For this project, I conducted forty-three semistructured interviews with parents who initiated an international adoption process no earlier than 2004. The primary focus of these interviews was on parents' decision-making processes leading up to the decision to adopt internationally, as well as throughout their processes of international adoption. Interviews also addressed the practical issues that families faced throughout their adoption processes and parents' responses to the media attention and political debate surrounding international adoption. Interviews were open-ended and lasted anywhere from seventy-five minutes to over three hours. In some cases, I met with an interviewee on multiple occasions. Most interviews were conducted at the interviewees' homes, others in a restaurant or coffee shop, and one in the interviewee's office. Six interviews were conducted via Skype. In several cases, I met the interviewee's children—both adopted and nonadopted—but I did not discuss any aspects of this research with them. The vast majority of the interviews were conducted in the Boston and New York metropolitan areas. I recruited participants through snowball sampling and began snowballs by posting in several local, online adoption discussion groups, as well as by reaching out through my personal network. Of the forty-three families who participated, thirty-seven of my interviews (86 percent) involved mothers alone, whether they were single or married. Of the remaining six interviews, I conducted four with both the mother and the father present, one interview with a married father without his wife present, and one interview with a single father. Thus when I refer to *mothers* throughout my writing, it is not a diminishment of the fathers who did participate in the interview process but, rather, my purposeful attention to the particular ways that the ideologies and experiences surrounding motherhood are informing this analysis on both a pragmatic and a theoretical level.

Following our conversation, each interviewee completed a short demographic survey. Of the forty-three families in the study, sixteen (37 percent) were headed by single mothers, twenty-five (58 percent) were headed by married heterosexual couples, one was headed by a married lesbian couple, and one was headed by a gay-identified single father. One of the single mothers in the sample had adopted her daughter together with her ex-husband. Several of the married adults in the sample had previously been married, but all of their divorces took place before the international adoption(s) of their children.

Altogether, these forty-three families had ninety-five children. The median number of children in the family was two; thirty-four families (79 percent) had one or two children, four families (9 percent) had three or four children, and five families (12 percent) had five children or more. Of the ninety-five children in the sample, twenty-eight (29 percent) are the biological children of one or both parents in the family and sixty-seven (71 percent) were adopted. Of the sixty-seven adopted children in the sample, eleven children (16 percent) were adopted from China, six children (9 percent) were adopted from Russia, six children (9 percent) were adopted from Guatemala, and twenty-five children (37 percent) were adopted from Ethiopia. Additional children in the sample were adopted from Nepal (three), Brazil (two), the Democratic Republic of the Congo (two), Colombia (one), Haiti (one), Kazakhstan (one), South Korea (one), Mongolia (one), Rwanda (one), and Vietnam (one). One child in the sample was adopted through a private domestic adoption, and four were adopted through state-run foster care systems. Of the sixty-seven adopted children in the sample, parents categorized six (9 percent, all adopted from Russia) as "white," thirty-two (48 percent) as "black," eighteen (27 percent) as "Asian," "Eurasian," or "Asian American," and eleven (16 percent) as "Latino/a" or "Hispanic."

Of the twenty-eight nonadopted children in the sample, only two were conceived using reproductive technologies, both of those children having been born to single mothers through anonymous sperm donation and intrauterine insemination. One single mother in the sample had a biological child from a previous relationship prior to adopting a second child as a single mother. Nine out of the twenty-five married heterosexual couples in the sample were raising full biological children born prior to the adoption of a younger sibling. An additional four families (9 percent of the total sample and 15 percent of the married couples in the sample) included mothers raising their partner's biological children. Only about a third (32 percent) of the married heterosexual couples in the sample pursued international adoption as first-time parents. Of the twenty-six total married couples in the sample, three included one nonwhite partner (two of East Asian ethnicity and one Hispanic, though none of those partners participated in the interview process). Other than those three partners, every adult in the sample was white.

In terms of socioeconomic status, the sample was decidedly upper-middle class. The sample was well-educated: of the sixty-nine parents in the sample, sixty-six (96 percent) had a four-year college degree or higher, and thirty-two

(46 percent) had a terminal degree (JD, MBA, MD, or PhD). Family incomes were high: the median annual family income was between $100,000 and $150,000 for single parents and between $150,000 and $250,000 for married couples. Out of all those interviewed, only two single mothers, both unemployed at the time of their interviews, reported an annual income under $50,000. Three married couples reported an annual family income of more than $250,000. The vast majority of families (forty out of forty-three, or 93 percent) owned their homes. When questioned about college and retirement savings, only four families reported that they were falling short of their financial goals, while six out of the forty-three families (14 percent) reported that they had already reached their savings goals for their children's educations and their own retirements.

Each participant also completed the Duke University Religion Index. I included these questions in the demographic survey because of the high-profile involvement of several Evangelical Christian organizations in international adoption and the stated mission of many Evangelical organizations for their members to adopt children from overseas. I did not actively recruit on any religious basis, nor did I exclude participants based on religious affiliation or belief. Of the forty-three families in the sample, thirty-four (79 percent) identified as secular, nonpracticing, or liberal Christians or Jews, or as irreligious all together. Five families (12 percent) identified as Evangelical Christians, and four families (9 percent) identified as "very religious" non-Evangelicals (this included two extremely devout Catholic families and two Orthodox Jewish families). I also asked each participant to identify his or her position on abortion ("pro-choice," "pro-life," or neither) and his or her political affiliation, if any. Of the forty-three families interviewed, thirty-eight (88 percent) identified as pro-choice and five (12 percent) identified as pro-life. Those identifying as pro-life included both of the two "very religious" Catholic families and three of the five "very religious" Protestant Christian families. The mothers of the two Evangelical Christian families who identified as "pro-choice" both emphasized that they were politically in favor of access to abortion despite their strong personal opposition to the procedure. In terms of political orientation, thirty-three (77 percent) of those interviewed identified as "Democrat," "liberal" or "progressive." Four (9 percent) identified as "Republican" or "conservative," and six (14 percent) identified as "Independent" or as unidentified with any political party. One mother identified herself as an Independent and her husband as a Republican, noting, "But he's not here, is he?" Other than that single case, no couple identified differing political or religious beliefs, and no respondent specifically identified as apolitical. The religious and political profile of my sample is on par with the overall demographics of the Northeast, if slightly to the left politically (Pew Research Center for Religion and Public Life 2015a, 2015b).

As noted above, almost a third of the children in the sample were the biological children of one or both parents in their families. Indeed, of the forty-three families in the sample, twenty-six (60 percent) chose to pursue adoption *without* experiencing infertility. Of those twenty-six families, ten (38 percent) included a biological child of one or both parents. Five of the families (19 percent) who did experience infertility had a biological child prior to their experiencing infertility. Of the seventeen families that pursued adoption after experiencing infertility (40 percent of the sample), nine (53 percent) described "giving up" on medical treatments before they had pursued all available medical options. Several mothers described having watched their friends exhaust their savings only to be met with one failed round of in vitro fertilization after another. Two mothers I interviewed, both physicians, explained that their in-depth knowledge of the procedures, risks, and outcomes of various fertility treatments and procedures led them to decide against pursuing a pregnancy. Others described a feeling that, when balanced against the number of children in the world who are living outside of a family, the effort of, in the words of one mother, "making one from scratch" wasn't "worth it." Only eight out of the forty-three families in my sample (19 percent) could be described as adopting as a "last resort" after exhausting all (or even most) available methods of having a child who was genetically related to the parents.

Participant Biographies

Abby is a single white mother in her late fifties with a sixteen-year-old daughter, Alex, whom she adopted from Russia. They live in a middle-income, family-oriented suburb, and Abby is employed full time by the federal government.

_____

Alan is a white gay-identified single father in his early fifties with two teenage sons adopted from Brazil. A social worker, Alan decided to adopt his sons—biological brothers, ages eight and ten at the time—when Brazil changed their laws to allow gay men to adopt.

_____

Alyssa and Keith are a white married couple in their midthirties with a three-year-old daughter, Isabella, whom they adopted from the Democratic Republic of the Congo. They live in a neighborhood full of young families in a rural midsized college town.

_____

Andrea and Matt are a white married couple in their midforties with a seven-year-old daughter, Audrey, whom they adopted from China.

_____

Angela is a divorced white mother in her late forties with an eight-year-old daughter, Olivia, whom she and her ex-husband, Troy, adopted from Colombia. Angela and Olivia live in a single-family home in a suburban town. Troy lives in an apartment nearby and he and Angela parent Olivia jointly. Angela is a physician, employed full time, and Troy is employed part time as a university lecturer.

Anna and Dan are a white married couple in their midforties with a seven-year-old son, Jacob, whom they adopted from Nepal. They live in a single-family home in an affluent suburb and are both employed full time. Anna was born and raised in Europe and retains citizenship in her natal country, but she has lived most of her adult life in the United States.

Arden and Steven are a white married couple with four children: two older sons from Steven's first marriage (he is a widower), a young daughter by birth, and an infant girl whom they were in the process of adopting from the Democratic Republic of the Congo at the time of our interview. The family lives in a large home in an exclusive community.

Barrett is a single white mother of a daughter, Addison, whom she adopted as an infant from Ethiopia.

Beth is a single white mother in her midforties with a twelve-year-old daughter, Rosa, whom she adopted from Russia. Beth is self-employed, and they live in a diverse urban neighborhood.

Betty is a single white mother in her late fifties with a ten-year-old son adopted from Mongolia. They live in a cozy apartment in an affluent suburb of mostly single-family homes. She is employed full time.

Bridget is a single white mother in her early sixties with an eighteen-year-old son by birth and a sixteen-year-old daughter, Alicia, whom she adopted from Guatemala. They live in a single-family home in an affluent suburb.

Catherine is a single white mother in her late fifties with an eight-year-old son, Tucker, whom she adopted from Kazakhstan. They live in a large single-family home in an urban neighborhood with a suburban feel. She is employed full time.

Danielle and Mark are a white married couple in their early fifties. They have a high school-age biological daughter, Rachel, and an eight-year-old daughter, Elianna, whom they adopted from China. They live in a newly renovated single family home in an affluent suburb. Mark is a technology executive and Danielle runs her own small business.

––––––––––

Deirdre and Thomas are a white married couple in their early fifties. Their two sons, who are biological brothers, were adopted from Ethiopia. The family lives in a close-knit neighborhood in a rural New England town.

––––––––––

Donna is a married white mother in her midforties who, as a single woman, adopted her son Hunter from Ethiopia. Soon after Hunter came to the United States, Donna began dating her now-husband, Phil, who immigrated to the United States with his mother from Southeast Asia as a young boy. Donna and Phil are raising Hunter along with Phil's daughter, Candice, who strongly identifies as biracial (with an Asian father and a white biological mother—Phil's ex-wife). They live in a single-family home in a small ethnically diverse working-class city. Donna and Phil are both employed full time.

––––––––––

Emily is a single white mother in her late thirties, with a daughter, Mara, whom she adopted from Ethiopia. Emily and Mara live in a modest home in a suburban neighborhood. Emily left work to devote herself to raising Mara full time, relying on financial support from her parents.

––––––––––

Erin and Scott are a white married couple in their midthirties with a five-year-old son, Dominic, whom they adopted from Ethiopia. They live in a single-family home in an outer suburb and they are both employed full time by the local public school district.

––––––––––

Gabby and Barry are a white married couple in their late forties. Their oldest child, Zach, is adopted from Russia. Gabby and Barry also have three younger children, a sibling group adopted through the state-run foster care system.

––––––––––

Gail is a single white mother of a daughter, Peyton, whom she adopted from Ethiopia as a toddler.

––––––––––

Hannah and Reuben are a white married couple, both employed full time in demanding careers, who live in an affluent inner suburb with their two children,

Zev, whom they adopted from Guatemala, and Dalia, whom they adopted through a private domestic adoption.

Ivy and Paul are a white married couple in their early fifties, with a college-age biological son, Josh, and a twelve-year-old daughter, Becca, whom they adopted from Nepal. Ivy and Paul are both professors and live in a single-family home in a racially and socioeconomically diverse suburban town.

Jackie is a single white mother who lives with her second daughter, Zhara, whom she adopted from Ethiopia. Jackie's first daughter, Ana, died in foster care in Guatemala while waiting for her visa to be processed after her adoption was finalized. Jackie and Zhara live in a restored historic home in the affluent but family-friendly village center of a large New England town. Jackie is employed full time as a physician.

Jane and Tom are a white married couple in their midfifties with a seven-year-old daughter, Julia, whom they adopted from China. They live in a single-family home in an affluent suburban town.

Jen is a single white mother in her midforties with two daughters, Ruby and Eva, whom she adopted from Ethiopia. The family lives in a rural midsized college town where Jen, a big-city transplant, is employed by the local public university.

Joan and David are a white married couple in their midfifties, each with biological children from previous marriages. Together, they adopted biological sisters Hamda and Amina from Ethiopia, followed by Shakira, whom they adopted through the state-run foster care system. With several adult children out of the house and three daughters in high school, Joan and David are both employed full time and live in a vibrant and diverse urban neighborhood.

Karen is a single white mother of twelve-year-old Leora, whom she adopted from Russia. They live in a comfortable apartment in an affluent urban neighborhood. Karen has historically worked full time outside of the home but, at the time of our interview, was freelancing and struggling with underemployment.

Kate is a married white mother in her early forties. She and her husband, Greg, live in a single-family home in an affluent inner suburb with their two children, Jonah, whom they adopted from Ethiopia, and Cecily, whom they adopted from Rwanda. Kate and her husband are both employed full time in the legal field.

Leah is a married white mother in her late thirties. She and her husband, Eli, live in a single-family home in an affluent inner suburb with their two children, Adina, whom they adopted from Ethiopia, and Ezra, whom they adopted from South Korea. Leah's husband is employed full time in finance, while she devotes herself full time to her kids.

Leslie is a married white mother in her early fifties. She and her longtime partner, Amélia, who immigrated to the United States from Latin America as a young woman, live in a single-family home in an affluent suburb and are both self-employed, working primarily from home. They raised Amélia's college-age biological children together and are now mothers to Judy, a five-year-old adopted from Nepal.

Linda and Steve are a white married couple in their late fifties. They raised three biological sons, who are now young adults. As almost–empty nesters, Linda and Steve adopted biological siblings Irina and Nick from Russia. With most of the kids now on their own, Linda, Steve, and sixteen-year-old Nick live in the family's home in a large middle-class suburb. Steve is employed full time and Linda is a homemaker.

Lisa and Nick are a white married couple in their late forties. Lisa is a stay-at-home mother and they live with their five children in a large, open outer suburban home that Nick, a home builder, designed and constructed. Lisa and Nick chose to adopt their two youngest children from Ethiopia after attending a program on international adoption at their church.

Lynne and Mike are a white married couple in their early fifties. They have a high school-age biological daughter, Grace, and an eight-year-old daughter, Peppa, whom they adopted from China.

Marjorie and Andrew are a white married couple in their midfifties with three children adopted from China.

Marty is a single white mother in her early fifties. She lives in a large home in a midsized suburban town with five children, all biological siblings, whom she adopted from Ethiopia. She has another daughter by birth, who lives on her own in a nearby apartment.

Mary is a single white mother in her midfifties with a seven-year-old son, Aiden, whom she adopted from China. They live in a modest apartment in an affluent urban neighborhood. Mary worked in lucrative sales jobs for most of her life but recently stopped working to spend more time with Aiden.

Parker and John are a white married couple in their midthirties with two sons, eight-year-old Gabriel, adopted from Guatemala, and six-year-old John Jr., adopted from China. They live in a modest apartment in an affluent inner suburb. John is employed full time and Parker combines part-time college teaching with a postdoctoral research fellowship.

Pat and Rich are a white married couple in their midfifties with two daughters, Laura and Jessica, whom they adopted from Guatemala. They live in a single-family home in a small ethnically diverse working-class city. Rich is retired and Pat is self-employed.

Phillip and Amy are a white married couple in their midforties with a young son adopted from Ethiopia. Amy works long hours in a very demanding career, and Phillip left part-time college teaching to parent their son full time when he arrived in the United States.

Robin and Bill are a white married couple with two children: Logan, whom they adopted from Vietnam, and Bailey, whom they adopted from China.

Sandra and Craig are a white married couple in their midforties with five children. After giving birth to their first three, the couple adopted Jeremiah from

Ethiopia and Faith from Haiti and, at the time of our interview, had just begun the process of adopting another child from Ethiopia. The family lives in a large but cozy home in a small New England town.

———————

Tracy and Seth are a white married couple in their early fifties. They live in a diverse urban neighborhood with their two children, an older son by birth and a younger daughter adopted from Ethiopia.

———————

Wendy is a married white mother in her late forties. She and her husband have two sons, seven-year-old James, who was conceived shortly after they got married, and five-year-old Preston, whom they adopted from China. They live in a single-family home in an ethnically diverse middle-income urban neighborhood. Wendy has worked as a lawyer but now devotes herself full time to raising her kids and homeschooling James.

———————

Zoe is a single white woman in her midthirties, who, at the time of our interview, was in the early stages of pursuing an international adoption. Zoe was born in Eastern Europe and immigrated to the United States with her parents when she was five years old. She intends to adopt an older child from her country of origin, where she has many relatives, frequently travels, and speaks the language fluently. In preparation to adopt, she is in the process of moving from her small urban apartment to a larger home in a family-oriented suburb with supportive public schools. She is employed full time in the technology sector.

Acknowledgments

First and foremost, I would like to thank the mothers and fathers who took the time to speak with me, tell me their stories of becoming parents, educate me about adoption, and share their struggles with a stranger.

My sincerest gratitude goes to my dissertation advisor, Linda Blum, who has supported me continuously through the ups and downs of graduate school and the process of writing this book. Linda went above and beyond, listened to me patiently, and offered extensive critiques of all my writing. Linda has truly been a role model, and it has been an honor to learn from and work with her. Thank you to the other members of my dissertation committee, who were so generous with their time and thoughtful contributions: Lorraine Bayard de Volo, Jeff Juris, Doreen Lee, and Liza Weinstein. I would also like to thank my good friend Margot Abels as well as Leandra Smollin, Brett Lee, Michael Brown, Alisa Lincoln, and Steve Vallas for many fruitful conversations and their humor and encouragement.

Joy Cauthron, Marti Waters, Kelly Pivik, Russ Davis, and Fred Myers welcomed me to the University of West Alabama with open arms. Their interest in this project has contributed so much, and I would like to thank Joy, in particular, for her insights, suggestions, and logistical support.

Peter Mickulas at Rutgers University Press has been wonderful, and I thank him for his encouragement and guidance. Naomi Gerstel, along with the other Families in Focus editors, provided generous, detailed, and thoughtful feedback on multiple drafts. Their intellectual guidance has been invaluable, and I am truly grateful for their contributions.

My husband, Eli, has been with me every step of the way, and I could not have done this work without him. Thank you so much for all the things you do, big and small. Thanks to our three daughters—Abby, Naomi, and Laila—who teach me new things every day. And thank you to all of our friends who have debated, cried over, gone through, and otherwise thought through being parents with us over the years. Additionally, this book would not have been possible without the help of four amazing young women—Tess Larsson, Jessica Regan, Sarah Klassen, and Roberta Pedrini—who lived with our family and mothered my children while I tried to write about how complicated motherhood is. I only hope that you four have benefitted from the exchange as much as I have.

Finally, I would like to thank my students. This project began the first semester I taught sociology, when I decided to include some material on international adoption in my Sociology of the Family course. I was hooked by the theoretical, ethical, and emotional puzzle that our society's debates about international adoption present. Fortunately, this has interested my students too. Their questions, insights, and personal experiences have deeply enriched my thinking—not only about international adoption but also about the broader struggle for reproductive justice.

Notes

1. There is a vast literature on adoption, including international adoption, in sociology, as well as in anthropology, social work, psychology, and law. The primary themes in the social work and psychology literature address children's adjustment and family dynamics following adoption (Barcons et al. 2014; Brand and Brinich 1999; Grotevant and McDermott 2014), including in transracial adoptive families specifically (DeBerry, Scarr, and Weinberg 1996; Lee 2003; Manzi et al. 2014), as well as best practices, both in terms of adoption processes (Hollingsworth 2008; Siegel 2013) and therapeutic interventions (Schwartzwald et al. 2015; Wrobel and Neil 2009). Additionally, some scholarship has emerged within social work that addresses the macro-level ethical issues involved in international adoption (Gibbons and Rotabi 2012; Rotabi 2010a, 2010b, 2012; Rotabi and Bunkers 2011; Selman 2009a). A substantial body of work in sociology addresses the racial and ethnic identity formation of children adopted into interracial families (Samuels and LaRossa 2009; Shiao and Tuan 2008; Trask 2013), including the work that mothers in particular perform to foster their children's racial and ethnic identities that differ from their own (Jacobson 2008; Johnston et al. 2007; Louie 2015). This project departs from this literature, however, and is grounded in a parallel literature on reproductive marketplaces.

2. Zelizer's designation of modern adoptions as "emotional" signals this shift not only in the economy writ large but also in the precise economic significance of children on a micro level. In a premodern economy, where foster children provided useful labor to their foster parents, there was a preference for boys who were old enough to perform farm labor as well as a readier supply of boys whose birthparents didn't have work for them to do. While girls old enough to perform domestic labor were also valued as foster children, Zelizer suggests that there was a scarcer supply of girls because biological parents were reluctant to give up their own daughters' domestic labor. "Useful" foster children were paid a wage for their labor. Yet mothers often had to pay a fee to orphanages or baby homes to accept "useless" infants and young children. It was within the emergence of an industrial economy, the simultaneous rally of Progressive reformers against child labor, the rise of developmental psychology, and the overall cultural shift toward a "sentimental valuation" of children that U.S. adoptions became emotionally rather than instrumentally driven.

Zelizer (1985) grounds this argument in a dramatic shift in adoptive parents' preferences, from older children to infants and toddlers (see also Guthrie and Grossman 1999).

3. Joshua Gamson (2015) in particular does a beautiful job of describing the ethical complexity of parents' reproductive decision-making and the seriousness with which parents enter into reproductive markets.

4. See Melinda Cooper and Catherine Waldby (2014) for a thorough discussion of how Foucault's concept applies specifically to reproduction.

5. A classic understanding of *compulsory motherhood* sees motherhood as the default, normative, and utterly expected achievement for all women, whose status is defined by patriarchal control over their bodies and reproductive lives.

6. Anthropologist Shellee Colen first defines *stratified reproduction* as the phenomenon by which "physical and social reproductive tasks are accomplished differentially according to inequalities that are based on hierarchies of class, race, ethnicity, gender, place in a global economy, and migration status and that are structured by social, economic, and political forces" (1995: 78). Even outside of an explicitly commercial context, stratified reproduction can be understood as a "power relation by which some categories of people are empowered to nurture and reproduce, while others are disempowered" (Ginsburg and Rapp 1995: 3). It has always been the case in the United States that poor women—and women of color, in particular—have faced very different kinds of reproductive scrutiny and control than white women, from the availability of welfare benefits (Quandango 1996), to the scrutiny of the child welfare system (Reich 2005; Roberts 2002), to portrayals in the media (in particular, Collins 2000; Collins 2004), to ugly histories of forced reproduction and forced sterilization (Collins 2000; Marsh and Ronner 1996; May 1997; Roberts 1997) and ongoing unequal access to reproductive health care (Bridges 2008).

7. Linda Blum describes breastfeeding as an embedded social institution that has historically been manipulated both by commercial interests and the state (through public health). She argues that while breastfeeding can be a way to "revalue our bodies and force a public reevaluation of caregiving," it also functions as "acquiescence to dominant regimes of self-sacrifice, overwork, and surveillance" (1999: 198). Glenda Wall (2001) specifically frames breastfeeding and the accompanying maternal responsibility as an example of our culture's neoliberal obsession with personal responsibility, which is sold—in this case, to mothers—as a promise of individual "choice." Orit Avishai (2007), citing Wall, argues that breastfeeding is indeed a "compulsory choice" and, as such, signifies the expectation of "work and self-discipline" that our society exacts on mothers, in particular. In the same conceptual vein, Claudia Malacrida and Tiffany Boulton (2012) describe women's childbirth preferences as another place, in the realm of motherhood, where mothers' "choices" stand in both for the "selfless[ness] of maternal nurturance" and for neoliberal risk management. Jennifer Reich (2014) makes a similar argument in terms of mothers who oppose vaccinating their children. She argues that for these "anti-vax" mothers, "individual maternal choice" serves as evidence of commitment to their children and to intensive, proper, ideal, and what Blum (1999) calls "exclusive," attached, dyadic mothering. In all of these cases, motherhood and mothering function both as locations of choice and as sites of control.

8. Journalist and adoption advocate Adam Pertman cites an American birth mother who, in terms of domestic adoption, relates, "All things being equal, if I've got a choice of couples who seem secure and loving . . . why wouldn't I pick the one who can give my son the best doctors and toys and schools and the other things money can buy? That's what

everyone wants for their kids . . . and so do I" (2011: 268). Pertman's implication seems to be that if we, in our cultural imagination, allow that mothers want the best for their children, this should extend to birth mothers as well. Similarly, Karen Dubinsky, in a study of Guatemalan adoptions, interviews a Guatemalan social worker who relates a Guatemalan birth mother's feelings of "pride and satisfaction in a photo of her daughter growing up outside the country, posed [in a photo sent to the birth mother] at a piano." The social worker tells Dubinsky, "[The birth mother] showed the photo to all her neighbors. 'Look,' she'd say, 'this is my daughter playing a piano.' No one in her village had even *seen* a piano" (2010: 126). Both Pertman (an adoption advocate) and Dubinsky (a highly critical historian) offer the same kinds of stories about encounters with birth mothers that the adoptive mothers I interviewed shared. The birth mothers' tone in these stories is grateful, redemptive, and ultimately—for the adoptive parents—triumphal. Moreover, these stories depict adoption, first and foremost, as a means of upward socioeconomic mobility for adopted children. Adoptive parents and adoption advocates should not speak for birth mothers but when they do, their accounts clearly point to the ways that a triumphal narrative, as an ideological apparatus, not only promotes American exceptionalism but also directly promotes American capitalism.

CHAPTER 1 — INTERNATIONAL ADOPTION
IN THE TWENTY-FIRST CENTURY

1. As Herman writes, "For Americans, saving the 'children of calamity' infused adoption with the particular patriotism of the cold war era. . . . As with earlier phases in adoption history, displays of American benevolence conveniently dovetailed with pursuit of citizens' desires" (2008: 217).

2. Karen Dubinsky concludes that, ironically, "Americanization included a conversion to anti-aristocratic, egalitarian values—presumably some of the very forces they were fleeing in Cuba. Yet somehow this confirmed the superiority of the life the children would find in the United States" (2010: 40). As Herman likewise notes, the adoption of children "sight unseen" presumes "that childhood in America [is] unquestionably superior to childhood in developing nations" (2010: 222). Ultimately, Dubinsky argues that this sense of inherent superiority fuels the "centrality of children to state building projects. . . . What could be more suited to the benevolent supremacy of Cold War America than the story of thousands of its citizens providing refuge for young victims of communism?" (2010: 55).

3. As U.S. troops began to withdraw from Vietnam, President Ford ordered the evacuation of more than 2,500 orphaned and abandoned Vietnamese children. They were flown to the United States and adopted over several months in a mission termed Operation Babylift, which drew media attention from its humanitarian impulse as well as from the crash of the first Babylift flight (see Martin 2015; Moritz 2015).

CHAPTER 2 — "WE'RE ON THE MARKET AGAIN"

1. In an early stage of this project, I interviewed several international adoption social workers and observed informational meetings for prospective adoptive parents, both in Massachusetts and in Guatemala City, Guatemala. I asked one of the Massachusetts social workers how she thought prospective parents understood the recent changes to

international adoption programs, and she replied that they don't. "They want to know how they can adopt *now*," she said. "They don't care what was possible in the past; they only care about the child they are waiting for now."

2. Within sociology, the literature has classically addressed questions including adoptive parents' motivations for adopting (Bausch 2006; Fisher 2003; Smock and Greenland 2010); their "satisfaction" postadoption, particularly in cases of adopting children with special needs (Nalavny, Glidden, and Ryan 2009); their experiences of open adoptions in a domestic context (Goldberg et al. 2011); adoptive parents' attitudes surrounding biology and the nature of kinship (Hamilton, Cheng, and Powell 2007); and the experiences of single women and GLBT adoptive parents (Battle and Ashley 2008; Bock 2000; Kinkler and Goldberg 2011; Mannis 1999; Berkowitz and Marsiglio 2007; Raleigh 2012).

CHAPTER 3 — PARENTAL ANXIETY AND INTERWOVEN DECISION-MAKING SURROUNDING RACE, HEALTH, AND "FITNESS"

1. While Randall Kennedy (2004) is among the most prominent scholars to advocate interracial adoption as part and parcel of a wider push for racial integration, Dorothy Roberts (1997, 2002) takes the position that adoption and child welfare can be sites of deep racial injustice and that transracial adoption should not be lauded as a remedy to that injustice. The National Association of Black Social Workers has famously argued that the adoption of African American children by white parents robs the black community of its children while robbing African American children of their cultural heritage. Yet as Rothman (2005) points out in her consideration of this argument, the benefits to children of living in permanent families need to be weighed against the very real impact of what some consider cultural "genocide." For Rothman, this tension is deeply personal. As a white mother of a black child, she was accused of participating in "cultural genocide" as she sat on an academic panel about interracial adoption.

2. In 2010, 8 percent of all marriages and 15 percent of new marriages were between partners of a different race or ethnicity. The rate of intermarriage continues to vary widely by race, however. Among those marrying in 2010, only 9 percent of whites and 17 percent of blacks married someone of a different race or ethnicity, while 26 percent of Hispanics and 28 percent of Asians did so (Wang 2012).

3. The example of early twentieth-century Jewish immigrants—the first model minority—illustrates this dialectic. As Karen Brodkin argues, "Model minorities and deficit cultures are like two hands clapping; the Jewish ethnicity that intellectuals claimed for themselves as model minorities . . . characterized by values of hard work, delayed gratification, education, and strong, two-parent families . . . [depended on] the invention of a deficient African American culture that illustrated [the model minority's] exemplariness" (1998: 150–151). Likewise, Steven Steinberg writes, "The same logic that underlies the myth of ethnic success has produced an opposite myth about groups that never escape from poverty. Such groups are said to be encumbered with a set of disabling or dysfunctional cultural values that impede social and economic mobility" (1981: 106).

4. For recent studies on parental anxiety, see, notably, Linda Blum (2015), Marianne Cooper (2014), Annette Lareau (2003), Margaret Nelson (2010), Debora Spar (2013), Glenda Wall (2010), and Joan Wolf (2010). In relation to the shift from treatment to prevention, see Kirsten Bell, Darlene McNaughton, and Amy Salmon (2011) and Norah

Mackendrick (2014) on neoliberal health discourses in the context of childrearing and Adele Clarke et al. (2010) on the concept of "biomedicalization" more generally. On mothers' responsibility for mitigating these risks, see Sara Afflerback (2013), Terry Arendell (2000), Elizabeth Armstrong (2003), Ellie Lee (2008), Darlene McNaughton (2011), Caitlin Myers (2014), and Dorothy Roberts (2009). See also Anita Garey and Margaret Nelson (2011) on the surveillance and "policing" of motherhood more generally.

5. Blum (2015) makes this argument particularly forcefully in the context of mothers raising children with invisible neurological disabilities, such as autism spectrum disorder, bipolar disorder, and attention-deficit/hyperactivity disorder. See also Jennifer Reich (2014) and Wall (2010).

6. Writing about the wave of international adoptions from Romania in the early 1990s, Ortiz and Briggs (2003) explore precisely how we've come to perceive U.S. birth mothers as inherently riskier than poor birth mothers abroad. The Romanian children being adopted by U.S. parents at that time were, on average, the same age as kids in U.S. foster care, and Romanian adoptees presented with the same constellation of behavioral and physical health challenges as the U.S. foster kids. Ortiz and Briggs initially argue that race is key: Romanian children were so much more "adoptable" than African American children in foster care because Romanian children would, upon arrival in the United States, be white. Yet Ortiz and Briggs point out that at the time of the Romanian adoption boom, nearly 40 percent of children in the U.S. foster care system were white. This leads Ortiz and Brigs to conclude that we find children abroad to be more "adoptable" than children in the United States.

CHAPTER 4 — MURKY TRUTHS AND DOUBLE-BINDS

1. Almeling's argument concerns the ways that men understand sperm donation to be a purely economic exchange, whereas women who "donate" eggs see their actions as partially altruistic, despite the money that changes hands.

2. See Blair-Loy (2003), Coltrane (2004), Gerson (2010), Hays (2004), Hochschild (1997), Stone (2007).

3. It is in this vein that Janet Gornick and Marcia Meyers call the contemporary model of the American family a "highly gendered partial specialization between men and women" (2005: 25), arguing that it is the partial nature of this specialization that creates a particularly disproportionate caregiving burden for mothers.

4. In her classic depiction of the "second shift," Arlie Hochschild (1989) finds that most of the women in her sample were simply working two jobs. More recent depictions of the division of family labor describe two parents sharing three jobs rather than a mother working two, but that sharing, of course, remains profoundly unequal—see Kathleen Gerson (2010) Hochschild (1997), Barbara Schneider and Linda Waite (2005)

5. Gerson (1993) clearly argues that the gender revolution must extend to accommodate fathers and create space for fatherhood in workplaces and men's professional lives. Fathers have, indeed, become more involved in childrearing over the past quarter century, yet many men continue to be held back from fuller participation in their children's upbringings in part by inflexibility and unsupportive policies in the workplace. For a review, see William Marsiglio et al. (2000). Further, Joan Williams (2012) argues particularly forcefully that inattention to fathers, both in the scholarly literature and on a policy level, lies at the core of the persistent gender inequality in family arrangements.

6. Coltrane (1996) was one of the first to argue that when mothers care for children, they go to the supermarket and the doctor, whereas when fathers care for children, they go to the park and the zoo.

7. Hochschild (1983) describes these gendered norms as "feeling rules" that circumscribe women's and men's understandings of their own feelings, particularly surrounding gendered forms of work.

CONCLUSION

1. Writing in the *American Sociological Review* in April 2017, Eva Rosen introduces the concept of "narrative rupture" and suggests focusing on the moments in which narratives, as cultural scripts, "break down." She argues that "in these moments, we have a unique window of insight to learn something about how these narratives are created and the function that they serve" (2017: 275).

References

Abu El-Haj, Nadia. 2007. "The Genetic Reinscription of Race." *Annual Review of Anthropology* 36:283–300.

Afflerback, Sara, Shannon Carter, Amanda Koontz Anthony, and Liz Grauerholtz. 2013. "Infant-Feeding Consumerism in the Age of Intensive Mothering and Risk Society." *Consumer Culture* 13 (3): 387–405.

Agencia AFP. 2010. "Guatemala y EE.UU. acuerdan transparentar adopciones de niños." *Prensa Libre*, December 9. Retrieved February 8, 2011. http://www.prensalibre.com/ noticias/Guatemala-EE-UU-transparentar-adopciones_0_386961525.html.

Alba, Richard. 2009. *Blurring the Color Line: The New Chance for a More Integrated America.* Cambridge, Mass.: Harvard University Press.

Alba, Richard, and Victor Nee. 2005. *Remaking the American Mainstream: Assimilation and Contemporary Immigration.* Cambridge, Mass.: Harvard University Press.

Almeling, Rene. 2011. *Sex Cells: The Medical Market for Eggs and Sperm.* Berkeley: University of California Press.

Arendell, Terry. 2000. "Conceiving and Investigating Motherhood: The Decade's Scholarship." *Journal of Marriage and Family* 62 (4): 1192–1207.

Armstrong, Elizabeth. 2003. *Conceiving Risk, Bearing Responsibility: Fetal Alcohol Syndrome and the Diagnosis of Moral Disorder.* Baltimore: Johns Hopkins University Press.

Avishai, Orit. 2007. "Managing the Lactating Body: The Breast-Feeding Project and Privileged Motherhood." *Qualitative Sociology* 30 (2): 135–152.

Bahrampour, Tara. 2014. "A Lost Boy Finds His Calling." *Washington Post*, January 30. Retrieved May 6, 2015. http://www.washingtonpost.com/sf/style/2014/01/30/a-lost-boy -finds-his-calling/.

Barcella, Laura. 2013. "How the Christian Right Perverts Adoption." *Salon*, May 4. Retrieved May 8, 2015. http://www.salon.com/2013/05/04/how_the_christian_right_perverts _adoption/.

Barcons, Natàlia, Neus Abrines, Carme Brun, Claudio Sartini, Victoria Fumadó, and Diana Marre. 2014. "Attachment and Adaptive Skills in Children of International Adoption." *Child and Family Social Work* 19 (1): 89–98.

Bartholet, Elizabeth. 1999. *Family Bonds: Adoption, Infertility, and the New World of Child Production.* Boston: Beacon Press.

———. 2005. "International Adoption." In *Children and Youth in Adoption, Orphanages, and Foster Care,* edited by Lori Askeland, 107–131. Westport, Conn.: Greenwood.

————. 2010a. "International Adoption: The Human Rights Issues." In *Baby Markets: Money and the New Politics of Creating Families*, edited by Michele Bratcher Goodwin, 94–117. New York: Cambridge University Press.

————. 2010b. "International Adoption: A Way Forward." *New York Law School Review* 55 (1): 687–699.

————. 2011. "Ratification by the United States of the Convention on the Rights of the Child: Pros and Cons from a Child's Rights Perspective." *Annals of the American Academy of Political and Social Science* 633 (1): 80–101.

————. 2015a. "The Hague Convention: Pros, Cons, and Potential." In *The Intercountry Adoption Debate: Dialogues across Disciplines*, edited by Robert L. Ballard, Robert F. Cochran, Naomi H. Goodno, and Jay Milbrandt, 239–244. Newcastle upon Tyne, UK: Cambridge Scholars.

————. 2015b. "The International Adoption Cliff: Do Child Human Rights Matter?" In *The Intercountry Adoption Debate: Dialogues across Disciplines*, edited by Robert L. Ballard, Robert F. Cochran, Naomi H. Goodno, and Jay Milbrandt, 193–202. Newcastle upon Tyne, UK: Cambridge Scholars.

Battle, Juan, and Colin Ashley. 2008. "Intersectionality, Heteronormativity, and Black Lesbian, Gay, Bisexual, and Transgender (LGBT) Families." *Black Women, Gender + Families* 2 (1): 1–24.

Bausch, Robert. 2006. "Predicting Willingness to Adopt a Child: A Consideration of Demographic and Attitudinal Factors." *Sociological Perspectives* 49 (1): 47–65.

Beck, Ulrich. 1992. *Risk Society: Towards a New Modernity*. London: Sage.

————. 2008. *World at Risk*. Cambridge: Polity Press.

Becker, Gay. 2000. *The Elusive Embryo: How Women and Men Approach New Reproductive Technologies*. Berkeley: University of California Press.

Bell, Ann. 2009. "'It's Way Out of My League': Low-Income Women's Experiences of Medicalized Infertility." *Gender and Society* 23 (5): 688–709.

————. 2010. "Beyond (Financial) Accessibility: Inequalities within the Medicalization of Infertility." *Sociology of Health and Illness* 32 (4): 631–646.

————. 2014. *Misconception: Social Class and Infertility in America*. New Brunswick, N.J.: Rutgers University Press.

Bell, Kirsten, Darlene McNaughton, and Amy Salmon, eds. 2011. *Alcohol, Tobacco, and Obesity: Morality, Mortality, and the New Public Health*. New York: Routledge.

Berkowitz, Dana, and William Marsiglio. 2007. "Gay Men: Negotiating Procreative, Father, and Family Identities." *Journal of Marriage and Family* 69 (2): 366–381.

Bertolli, Andrea. 2013. "Gendered Divisions of Fertility Work: Socioeconomic Predictors of Female versus Male Sterilization." *Journal of Marriage and Family* 75 (1): 13–25.

Bianchi, Suzanne, John Robinson, and Melissa Milkie. 2007. *Changing Rhythms of American Family Life*. New York: Russel Sage Foundation.

Biblarz, Timothy, and Evren Savci. 2010. "Lesbian, Gay, Bisexual, and Transgendered Families." *Journal of Marriage and Family* 72 (3): 480–497.

Blair-Loy, Mary. 2003. *Competing Devotions: Career and Family among Women Executives*. Cambridge, Mass.: Harvard University Press.

Blum, Linda. 1999. *At the Breast: Ideologies of Breastfeeding and Motherhood in the Contemporary United States*. Boston: Beacon Press.

————. 2015. *Raising Generation Rx: Mothering Kids with Invisible Disabilities in an Age of Inequality*. New York: New York University Press.

Bock, Jane. 2000. "Doing the Right Thing? Single Mothers by Choice and the Struggle for Legitimacy." *Gender and Society* 14 (1): 62–86.

Bonilla-Silva, Eduardo. 2006. *Racism without Racists*. Lanham, Md.: Rowman and Littlefield.

Boudreau, John. 2014. "U.S. to Allow Adoptions from Vietnam after Ban in 2008." *Bloomberg Business*, September 15. Retrieved May 7, 2015. http://www.bloomberg.com/news/articles/2014-09-14/u-s-to-allow-adoptions-from-vietnam-after-ban-in-2008.

Brand, Ann, and Paul Brinich. 1999. "Behavior Problems and Mental Health Contacts in Adopted, Foster, and Nonadopted Children." *Journal of Child Psychology and Psychiatry* 40 (8): 1221–1229.

Bridges, Khiara. 2008. *Reproducing Race: An Ethnography of Pregnancy as a Site of Racialization.* Berkeley: University of California Press.

Briggs, Laura. 2012. *Somebody's Children: The Politics of Transracial and Transnational Adoption.* Durham, N.C.: Duke University Press.

———. 2017. *How All Politics Became Reproductive Politics: From Welfare Reform to Foreclosure to Trump.* Berkeley: University of California Press.

Briggs, Laura, and Diana Marre. 2009. "Introduction: The Circulation of Children." In *International Adoption: Global Inequalities and the Circulation of Children,* edited by Diana Marre and Laura Briggs, 1–28. New York: New York University Press.

Brodkin, Karen. 1998. *How Jews Became White Folks.* New Brunswick, N.J.: Rutgers University Press.

Bureau of Consular Affairs. 2012. "Country Statistics: Ethiopia." United States Department of State. Retrieved December 22, 2012. http://adoption.state.gov/country_information/country_specific_info.php?country-select=ethiopia.

———. 2013a. "Statistics—Intercountry Adoption." United States Department of State. Retrieved March 11, 2013. http://adoption.state.gov/about_us/statistics.php.

———. 2013b. "FY 2012 Annual Report on Intercountry Adoption." United States Department of State. Retrieved March 11, 2013. http://adoption.state.gov/content/pdf/fy2012_annual_report.pdf.

———. 2013c. "Statistics—Intercountry Adoption." United States Department of State. Retrieved March 11, 2013. http://adoption.state.gov/about_us/statistics.php.

———. 2016. "Statistics—Intercountry Adoption." United States Department of State. Retrieved March 17, 2016. https://travel.state.gov/content/adoptionsabroad/en/about-us/statistics.html.

———. 2018. "FY 2017 Annual Report on Intercountry Adoption." United States Department of State, March 23. Retrieved May 13, 2018. https://travel.state.gov/content/travel/en/Intercountry-Adoption/adopt_ref/adoption-publications.html.

Cahn, Naomi. 2009. *Test Tube Families: Why the Fertility Market Needs Legal Regulation.* New York: New York University Press.

———. 2013. *The New Kinship: Constructing Donor-Conceived Families.* New York: New York University Press.

Carp, E. Wayne, ed. 2009. *Adoption in America: Historical Perspectives.* Ann Arbor: University of Michigan Press.

Carter, Julian. 1997. *The Heart of Whiteness: Normal Sexuality and Race in America, 1880–1940.* Durham, N.C.: Duke University Press.

Casper, Lynne M., and Suzanne M. Bianchi. 2002. *Continuity and Change in the American Family.* New York: Sage.

Chiaramonte, Perry. 2014. "U.S. Families, Congolese Orphans in Limbo as African Government Halts Adoptions." Fox News, August 24. Retrieved May 8, 2015. http://www.foxnews.com/world/2014/08/24/american-families-congolese-orphans-in-limbo-as-african-government-halts/.

Chodorow, Nancy. 1978. *The Reproduction of Mothering.* Berkeley: University of California Press.

Choy, Catherine. 2013. *Global Families: A History of Asian International Adoption in America.* New York: New York University Press.

Christopher, Karen. 2012. "Extensive Mothering: Employed Mothers' Constructions of the Good Mother." *Gender and Society* 26 (1): 73–96.

Clarke, Adele E., Laura Mamo, Jennifer Ruth Fosket, Jennifer R. Fishman, and Janet K. Shim, eds. 2010. *Biomedicalization: Technoscience, Health, and Illness in the U.S.* Durham, N.C.: Duke University Press.

Clemetson, Lynette. 2007a. "Working on Overhaul, Russia Halts Adoption Applications." *New York Times*, April 12. Retrieved May 7, 2015. http://www.nytimes.com/2007/04/12/us/12adopt.html?_r=0.

———. 2007b. "Adoptions from Guatemala Face an Uncertain Future." *New York Times*, May 16. Retrieved May 4, 2015. http://www.nytimes.com/2007/05/16/us/16adopt.html.

Cohn, D'Vera, Gretchen Livingston, and Wendy Wang. 2014. *After Decades of Decline, a Rise in Stay-at-Home Mothers*. Pew Research Center Social and Demographic Trends, April. Washington, D.C.: Pew Research Center.

Colen, Shellee. 1995. "'Like a Mother to Them': Stratified Reproduction and West Indian Childcare Workers and Employers in New York." In *Conceiving the New World Order: The Global Politics of Reproduction*, edited by Faye Ginsburg and Rayna Rapp, 78–102. Berkeley: University of California Press.

Collins, Patricia Hill. 2000. *Black Feminist Thought: Knowledge, Consciousness, and the Politics of Empowerment*. New York: Routledge.

———. 2004. *Black Sexual Politics: African Americans, Gender, and the New Racism*. New York: Routledge.

Coltrane, Scott. 1996. *Family Man: Fatherhood, Housework, and Gender Equity*. New York: Oxford University Press.

———. 2004. "Elite Careers and Family Commitment: It's (Still) about Gender." *Annals of the American Academy of Political and Social Science* 596:214–220.

Coontz, Stephanie. 2006. "Having It All." *New York Times*, November 26. Retrieved May 13, 2015. http://www.washingtonpost.com/wp-dyn/content/article/2006/11/22/AR2006112201801.html.

Cooper, Marianne. 2014. *Cut Adrift: Families in Insecure Times*. Berkeley: University of California Press.

Cooper, Melinda, and Catherine Waldby. 2014. *Clinical Labor: Tissue Donors and Research Subjects in the Global Bioeconomy*. Durham, N.C.: Duke University Press.

Corbett, Sara. 2002. "Where Do Babies Come From?" *New York Times Magazine*, June 16. Retrieved May 4, 2015. http://www.nytimes.com/2002/06/16/magazine/where-do-babies-come-from.html.

Cornell, Stephen, and Douglas Hartman. 1998. *Ethnicity and Race: Making Identities in a Changing World*. Thousand Oaks, Calif.: Pine Forge Press.

Crary, David. 2010a. "Adoptions from Ethiopia Rise, Bucking Global Trend." Associated Press, October 12.

———. 2010b. "Ethiopia Provides Hope to U.S. Adopters." *Washington Post*, October 24. Retrieved May 8, 2015. http://www.washingtonpost.com/wp-dyn/content/article/2010/10/23/AR2010102300170.html.

C-SPAN. 2013. "Confirmation Hearing for Senator John Kerry as Secretary of State." C-SPAN, January 24. Retrieved February 4, 2013. http://www.c-span.org/Events/Confirmation-Hearing-for-Sen-John-Kerry-as-Secretary-of-State/10737437516-1/.

Custer, Charlie. 2013. "Kidnapped and Sold: Inside the Dark World of Child Trafficking in China." *Atlantic*, July 25. Retrieved May 7, 2015. http://www.theatlantic.com/china/archive/2013/07/kidnapped-and-sold-inside-the-dark-world-of-child-trafficking-in-china/278107/.

Daar, Judith. 2008. "Accessing Reproductive Technologies: Invisible Barriers, Indelible Harms." *Berkeley Journal of Gender, Law, and Justice* 23 (1): 23–34.

Dao, James. 2013. "Vietnam Legacy: Finding G.I. Fathers, and Children Left Behind." *New York Times*, September 15. Retrieved May 7, 2015. http://www.nytimes.com/2013/09/16/us/vietnam-legacy-finding-gi-fathers-and-children-left-behind.html.

Davis, Angela. 1993. "Outcast Mothers and Surrogates: Racism and Reproductive Rights in the Nineties." In *American Feminist Thought at Century's End: A Reader*, edited by Linda S. Kauffman, 355–366. Cambridge, Mass.: Blackwell.

DeBerry, Kimberly, Sandra Scarr, and Richard Weinberg. 1996. "Family Racial Socialization and Ecological Competence: Longitudinal Assessments of African-American Transracial Adoptees." *Child Development* 67 (5): 2375–2399.

Delva, Joseph Guyler. 2010. "Americans Arrested Taking Children Out of Haiti." Reuters, January 30. Retrieved May 8, 2015. http://www.reuters.com/article/2010/01/30/us-quake-haiti -arrests-idUSTRE60T23I20100130.

Dockterman, Eliana. 2014. "Russia Extends Adoption Ban: Targets Single People of Any Orientation in Countries Where Gay Marriage Is Legal." *Time*, February 13. Retrieved May 8, 2015. http://world.time.com/2014/02/13/russia-bans-adoption-by-singles-in-gay-marriage -legal-countries/.

Dorow, Sara. 2006. *Transnational Adoption: A Cultural Economy of Race, Gender, and Kinship*. New York: New York University Press.

———. 2010. "Producing Kinship through the Marketplaces of Transnational Adoption." In *Baby Markets: Money and the New Politics of Creating Families*, edited by Michelle Bratcher Goodwin, 69–83. New York: Cambridge University Press.

Dubinsky, Karen. 2010. *Babies without Borders: Adoption and Migration across the Americas*. New York: New York University Press.

Fagan, Kevin, Melissa Fletcher Stoeltje, and Aaron Nelson. 2014. "Halt in Guatemalan Adoptions May Be Fueling Border Surge." *San Francisco Gate*, October 5. Retrieved May 4, 2015. http:// www.sfgate.com/nation/article/Halt-in-Guatemalan-adoptions-may-be-fueling-5801663.php.

Fisher, Allen. 2003. "Still 'Not Quite as Good as Having Your Own'? Toward a Sociology of Adoption." *Annual Review of Sociology* 29:335–361.

Fisher, Philip. 2015. "Review: Adoption, Fostering, and the Needs of Looked-After Children." *Child and Adolescent Mental Health* 20 (1): 5–12.

Flintoff, Corey. 2012. "Russia's Putin Signs Controversial Adoption Bill." *Morning Edition*, produced by National Public Radio, December 28. Retrieved February 6, 2013. http://www .npr.org/2012/12/28/168178292/russias-putin-signs-controversial-adoption-bill.

Fourcade, Marion. 2012. "The Moral Sociology of Viviana Zelizer." *Sociological Forum* 27 (4): 1055–1061.

Franklin, Sarah. 1995. "Postmodern Procreation: A Cultural Account of Assisted Reproduction." In *Conceiving the New World Order: The Global Politics of Reproduction*, edited by Faye Ginsburg and Rayna Rapp, 323–345. Berkeley: University of California Press.

Gailey, Christine Ward. 2010. *Blue Ribbon Babies and Labors of Love: Race, Class, and Gender in U.S. Adoption Practice*. Austin: University of Texas Press.

Gaines, Steven. 2009. "Hungry Heart: The Global Celebrity Adoption Didn't Start with Madonna." *New York Magazine*, April 10. Retrieved March 25, 2013. http://nymag.com/ news/intelligencer/56005/.

Gamson, Joshua. 2015. *Modern Families: Stories of Extraordinary Journeys to Kinship*. New York: New York University Press.

Garey, Anita, and Margaret Nelson. 2011. "Policing Motherhood." *International Journal of Sociology of the Family* 37 (1): 1–7.

Gerson, Kathleen. 1993. *No Man's Land: Men's Changing Commitments to Family and Work*. New York: Basic Books.

———. 2010. *The Unfinished Revolution: How a New Generation Is Reshaping Family, Work, and Gender in America*. New York: Oxford University Press.

Gibbons, Judith, and Karen Rotabi, eds. 2012. *Intercountry Adoption: Policies, Practices, and Outcomes*. Surrey, UK: Ashgate.

Giddens, Anthony. 1999. "Risk and Responsibility." *Modern Law Review* 62 (1): 1–10.

Ginsburg, Faye, and Rayna Rapp, eds. 1995. *Conceiving the New World Order: The Global Politics of Reproduction*. Berkeley: University of California Press.

Glassner, Barry. 2010. *The Culture of Fear: Why Americans Are Afraid of the Wrong Things*. New York: Basic Books.

Glenn, Evelyn Nakano. 1992. "From Servitude to Service Work." *Signs* 18:1–43.

———. 2002. *Unequal Freedom: How Race and Gender Shaped American Citizenship and Labor.* Cambridge, Mass.: Harvard University Press.

———. 2010. *Forced to Care: Coercion and Caregiving in America.* Cambridge, Mass.: Harvard University Press.

Goldberg, Abbie, Lori Kinkler, Hannah Richardson, and Jordan Downing. 2011. "Lesbian, Gay, and Heterosexual Couples in Open Adoption Arrangements: A Qualitative Study." *Journal of Marriage and Family* 72 (2): 502–518.

Good Morning America. 2005. "Angelina Jolie Inspires International Adoptions." ABC News, October 1. Retrieved March 25, 2013. http://abcnews.go.com/GMA/story?id=1175428& page=1.

Goodwin, Michele. 2005. "Assisted Reproductive Technology and the Double-Bind: The Illusory Choice of Motherhood." *Journal of Gender, Race, and Justice* 9 (1): 1–54.

Goodwin, Michele, ed. 2010. *Baby Markets: Money and the New Politics of Creating Families.* New York: Oxford University Press.

Gornick, Janet, and Marcia Meyers. 2005. *Families That Work.* New York: Sage.

Gowen, Annie. 2015. "Legacies of War: Forty Years after the Fall of Saigon, Soldiers' Children Are Still Left Behind." *Washington Post*, April 17. Retrieved May 7, 2015. http://www.washingtonpost.com/graphics/world/vietnam/.

Graf, Heather. 2015. "Sammamish Family Shares Its First Thanksgiving after Adoption Delays." KING 5 News, November 27. Retrieved December 7, 2015. http://www.king5.com/story/news/local/2015/11/27/family-shares-first-thanksgiving-together-after-adoption-delays/76439520/.

Graff, E. J. 2008. "The Lie We Love." *Foreign Policy*, November/December, 58–66.

———. 2010a. "The Baby Business." *Democracy*, Summer 2010. Retrieved May 7, 2015. http://www.democracyjournal.org/17/6757.php?page=all.

———. 2010b. "Anatomy of an Adoption Crisis." *Foreign Policy*, September 12. Retrieved May 7, 2015. http://foreignpolicy.com/2010/09/12/anatomy-of-an-adoption-crisis/.

———. 2012a. "International Adoption or Child Trafficking?" *American Prospect*, January 6. Retrieved October 2, 2014. http://prospect.org/article/international-adoption-or-child-trafficking.

———. 2012b. "Don't Adopt from Ethiopia." *American Prospect*, May 3. Retrieved May 8, 2015. http://prospect.org/article/dont-adopt-ethiopia.

———. 2014. "They Steal Babies, Don't They?" *Pacific Standard*, November 24. Retrieved May 7, 2015. http://www.psmag.com/politics-and-law/they-steal-babies-dont-they-international-adoption-schuster-institute-95027.

Grainger, Sarah. 2009. "Guatemala Pushes for DNA Tests of Kids Adopted in U.S." Reuters, December 8.

Gross, Jane. 2007. "U.S. Joins Overseas Adoption Overhaul Plan." *New York Times*, December 11. Retrieved May 4, 2015. http://www.nytimes.com/2007/12/11/washington/11hague.html.

Gross, Jane, and Will Connors. 2007. "Surge in Adoptions Raises Concern in Ethiopia." *New York Times*, June 4. Retrieved May 8, 2015. http://www.nytimes.com/2007/06/04/us/04adopt.html.

Grotevant, Harold, and Jennifer McDermott. 2014. "Adoption: Biological and Social Processes Linked to Adaptation." *Annual Review of Psychology* 65:235–265.

Guthrie, Chris, and Joanna Grossman. 1999. "Adoption in the Progressive Era: Preserving, Creating, and Recreating Families." *American Journal of Legal History* 43:235–253.

Hague Conference on Private International Law. 1993. "Convention of 29 May 1993 on Protection of Children and Co-operation in Respect of Intercountry Adoption." Retrieved January 30, 2019. https://www.hcch.net/en/instruments/conventions/full-text/?cid=69.

Hamilton, Jon. 2014. "Orphans' Lonely Beginnings Reveal How Parents Shape a Child's Brain." *Morning Edition*, produced by National Public Radio, February 24. Retrieved May 6, 2015. http://www.npr.org/blogs/health/2014/02/20/280237833/orphans-lonely -beginnings-reveal-how-parents-shape-a-childs-brain.

Hamilton, Laura, Simon Cheng, and Brian Powell. 2007. "Adoptive Parents, Adaptive Parents: Evaluating the Importance of Biological Ties for Parental Investment." *American Sociological Review* 72 (1): 95–116.

Harwood, Karey. 2007. *The Infertility Treadmill: Feminist Ethics, Personal Choice, and the Use of Reproductive Technologies*. Chapel Hill: University of North Carolina Press.

Hays, Sharon. 1996. *The Cultural Contradictions of Motherhood*. New Haven: Yale University Press.

———. 2011. "The Mommy Wars: Ambivalence, Ideological Work, and the Cultural Contradictions of Motherhood." In *Family in Transition*, edited by Arlene Skolnick and Jerome Skolnick, 16th ed., 41–59. Boston: Allyn and Bacon.

Herman, Ellen. 2008. *Kinship by Design: A History of Adoption in the Modern United States*. Chicago: University of Chicago Press.

Herszenhorn, David, and Erik Eckholm. 2012. "Putin Signs Bill That Bars U.S. Adoptions, Upends Families." *New York Times*, December 27. Retrieved May 7, 2015. http://www .nytimes.com/2012/12/28/world/europe/putin-to-sign-ban-on-us-adoptions-of-russian -children.html.

Hertz, Rosanna. 2004. "The Contemporary Myth of Choice." *Annals of the American Academy of Political and Social Science* 596:232–244.

———. 2006. *Single by Chance, Mothers by Choice: How Women Are Choosing Parenthood without Marriage and Creating the New American Family*. New York: Oxford University Press.

Hochschild, Arlie. 1983. *The Managed Heart: Commercialization of Human Feeling*. Berkeley: University of California Press.

———. 1989. *The Second Shift*. New York: Viking.

———. 1997. *The Time Bind*. New York: Metropolitan Books.

———. 2003. *The Commercialization of Intimate Life: Notes from Home and Work*. Berkeley: University of California Press.

Hollingsworth, Leslie. 2008. "Does the Hague Convention on Intercountry Adoption Address the Protection of Adoptees' Cultural Identity? Should It?" *Social Work* 53 (4): 377–379.

Hondagneu-Sotelo, Pierette. 2007. *Doméstica: Immigrant Workers Cleaning and Caring in the Shadows of Affluence*. Berkeley: University of California Press.

Howell, Signe. 2006. *The Kinning of Foreigners: Transnational Adoption in Global Perspective*. New York: Bergham Books.

Ignatieff, Noel. 1995. *How the Irish Became White*. New York: Routledge.

Inskeep, Steve. 2013. "NPR Host Steve Inskeep on His Two Adoptions." *Newsweek*, February 19. Retrieved May 10, 2018. http://www.newsweek.com/npr-host-steve-inskeep-his -two-adoptions-63337.

Jacobs, Jerry, and Kathleen Gerson. 2004. *The Time Divide*. Cambridge, Mass.: Harvard University Press.

Jacobson, Heather. 2008. *Culture Keeping: White Mothers, International Adoption, and the Negotiation of Family Difference*. Nashville: Vanderbilt University Press.

———. 2013. "Framing Adoption: The Media and Parental Decision Making." *Journal of Family Issues* 35 (5): 654–676.

———. 2016. *Labor of Love: Gestational Surrogacy and the Work of Making Babies*. New Brunswick, N.J.: Rutgers University Press.

Johnson, Kay Ann. 2016. *China's Hidden Children: Abandonment, Adoption, and the Human Costs of the One-Child Policy*. Chicago: University of Chicago Press.

Johnston, John. 2004. "With 22 Children, the Ingles and the Wallises Share a Blended Bounty of Love and Work." *Cincinnati Enquirer*, June 8. Retrieved May 10, 2018. http://www.enquirer.com/editions/2004/06/08/tem_tueledeo8.html.

Johnston, Kristen, Janet Swim, Brian Saltsman, Kirby Deater-Deckard, and Stephen Petrill. 2007. "Mothers' Racial, Ethnic, and Cultural Socialization of Transracially Adopted Asian Children." *Family Relations* 56 (4): 390–402.

Jones, Maggie. 2007. "Looking for Their Children's Birth Mothers." *New York Times Magazine*, October 28. Retrieved May 4, 2015. http://www.nytimes.com/2007/10/28/magazine/28biological-t.html.

Jordan, Miriam. 2012. "Inside Ethiopia's Adoption Boom." *Wall Street Journal*, April 28. Retrieved May 8, 2015. http://www.wsj.com/articles/SB10001424052702304811304577368243366708110.

Joyce, Katherine. 2011. "How Ethiopia's Adoption Industry Dupes Families and Bullies Activists." *Atlantic*, December 21. Retrieved May 8, 2015. http://www.theatlantic.com/international/archive/2011/12/how-ethiopias-adoption-industry-dupes-families-and-bullies-activists/250296/.

———. 2013a. "Orphan Fever: The Evangelical Movement's Adoption Obsession." *Mother Jones*, May/June. Retrieved April 24, 2013. http://www.motherjones.com/politics/2013/04/christian-evangelical-adoption-liberia.

———. 2013b. "The Problem with the Christian Adoption Movement." *Huffington Post*, June 2. Retrieved May 8, 2015. http://www.huffingtonpost.com/kathryn-joyce/christian-adoption-movement-problems_b_3367223.html.

———. 2013c. "The Evangelical Orphan Boom." *New York Times*, September 21. Retrieved May 8, 2015. http://www.nytimes.com/2013/09/22/opinion/sunday/the-evangelical-orphan-boom.html.

———. 2013d. *The Child Catchers: Rescue, Trafficking, and the New Gospel of Adoption*. New York: Public Affairs Press.

———. 2015. "Arkansas Adoption Preys on Cultural Misunderstanding with Marshallese." *New Republic*, April 21. Retrieved May 8, 2015. http://www.newrepublic.com/article/121556/arkansas-adoption-preys-cultural-misunderstanding-marshallese.

Kapstein, Ethan. 2003. "The Baby Trade." *Foreign Affairs*, November/December. Retrieved May 4, 2015. https://www.foreignaffairs.com/articles/2003-11-01/baby-trade.

Kasinitz, Philip, Mary Waters, John Mollenkopf, and Jennifer Holdaway. 2009. *Inheriting the City: The Children of Immigrants Come of Age*. New York: Russel Sage Foundation.

Katz, David. 2006. "China Restricts Adoption Policies." ABC News, December 21. Retrieved May 7, 2015. http://abcnews.go.com/Health/story?id=2743016.

Kaufman, Gayle. 2013. *Superdads: How Fathers Balance Work and Family in the 21st Century*. New York: New York University Press.

Kaw, Eugenia. 1993. "Medicalization of Racial Features: Asian American Women and Cosmetic Surgery." *Medical Anthropology Quarterly* 17 (1): 74–89.

Kaye, Randi, and Wayne Drash. 2017. "Kids for Sale." CNN. Retrieved May 10, 2018. https://www.cnn.com/specials/kids-for-sale.

Kennedy, Randall. 2003. *Interracial Intimacies: Sex, Marriage, Identity, and Adoption*. New York: Vintage.

Keteyian, Armen. 2010. "Child: U.S. Adoption Agency Bought Me." CBS News, February 15. Retrieved May 8, 2015. http://www.cbsnews.com/news/child-us-adoption-agency-bought-me/.

Khabibullina, Lilia. 2009. "International Adoption in Russia: 'Market,' 'Children for Organs,' and 'Precious' or 'Bad' Genes." In *International Adoption: Global Inequalities and the Circulation of Children*, edited by Diana Marre and Laura Briggs, 174–189. New York: New York University Press.

Khanna, Nikki, and Caitlin Killian. 2015. "'We Didn't Even Think about Adopting Domestically': The Role of Race and Other Factors in Shaping Parents' Decisions to Adopt Abroad." *Sociological Perspectives* 58 (4): 570–594.

Kim, Katherin. 2008. "Out of Sorts: Adoption and (Un)Desirable Children." In *Mapping the Social Landscape*, edited by Susan Ferguson, 393–406. Boston: McGraw-Hill.

King, Shani. 2012. "Owning Laura Silsby's Shame: How the Haitian Child Trafficking Scheme Embodies the Western Disregard for the Integrity of Poor Families." *Harvard Human Rights Journal* 25 (1): 1–47.

Kinkler, Lori, and Abbie Goldberg. 2011. "Working with What We've Got: Perceptions of Barriers and Supports Among Small-Metropolitan Area Same-Sex Adopting Couples." *Family Relations* 60 (4): 387–403.

Kirpalani, Reshma, and Christina Ng. 2011. "Missouri Couple Silent on Order to Return Adopted Daughter to Guatemala." ABC News, August 5. Retrieved May 4, 2015. http://abcnews.go.com/US/missouri-couple-silent-order-return-adopted-daughter-guatemala/story?id=14234379.

Klein, Naomi. 2007. *The Shock Doctrine: The Rise of Disaster Capitalism*. New York: Picador.

Koenig, Harold, and Arndt Büssing. 2010. "The Duke University Religion Index (DUREL): A Five-Item Measure for Use in Epidemiological Studies." *Religions* 1:78–85.

Kuruvilla, Carol. 2014. "Five American Families Stuck in Congo, Fighting to Bring Adopted Children Home." *New York Daily News*, January 2. Retrieved May 8, 2015. http://www.nydailynews.com/news/national/americans-stuck-congo-fighting-bring-adopted-children-home-article-1.1564496.

Lacey, Mark. 2007a. "Guatemala: U.S. Cautions on Adoptions." *New York Times*, February 28. Retrieved May 4, 2015. http://www.nytimes.com/2007/02/28/world/americas/28briefs-adoptions.html?_r=0.

———. 2007b. "Guatemala: Adoption Protocol Endorsed." *New York Times*, May 23. Retrieved May 4, 2015. http://www.nytimes.com/2007/05/23/world/americas/23briefs-guatemalaadoption.html.

———. 2007c. "Guatemala: U.S. Adoptions to Go Through." *New York Times*, December 12. Retrieved May 4, 2015. http://www.nytimes.com/2007/12/12/world/americas/12briefs-adopt.html.

———. 2008. "Guatemala: Hiatus in Foreign Adoptions Is Ordered." *New York Times*, May 7. Retrieved May 4, 2015. http://www.nytimes.com/2008/05/07/world/americas/07wbriefs-HIATUSINFORE_BRF.html.

Lamont, Michèle, and Marcel Fournier, eds. 1993. *Cultivating Differences: Symbolic Boundaries and the Making of Inequality*. Chicago: University of Chicago Press.

Lareau, Annette. 2003. *Unequal Childhoods: Class, Race, and Family Life*. Berkeley: University of California Press.

Larsen, Elizabeth. 2007. "Did I Steal My Daughter?" *Mother Jones*, November/December. Retrieved May 4, 2015. http://www.motherjones.com/politics/2007/10/did-i-steal-my-daughter-tribulations-global-adoption.

Lee, Ellie. 2008. "Living with Risk in the Age of 'Intensive Motherhood': Maternal Identity and Infant Feeding." *Health, Risk, and Society* 10 (5): 467–477.

Lee, Jennifer, and Frank Bean. 2012. *The Diversity Paradox: Immigration and the Color Line in Twenty-First Century America*. New York: Russel Sage Foundation.

Lee, Richard. 2003. "The Transracial Adoption Paradox: History, Research, and Counseling Implications of Cultural Socialization." *Counseling Psychology* 31 (6): 711–744.

Leinaweaver, Jessaca. 2008. *The Circulation of Children: Kinship, Adoption, and Morality in Andean Peru*. Durham, N.C.: Duke University Press.

Ligtvoet, Frank. 2014. "Democratic Republic of Congo, Christianity, and International Adoption." *Huffington Post*, April 14. Retrieved December 7, 2015. http://www.huffingtonpost.com/frank-ligtvoet/congo-christianity-and-in_b_5134492.html.

Lim, Louisa. 2009. "Widespread Alcohol Abuse Clouds Mongolia's Future." *Morning Edition*, produced by National Public Radio, September 9. Retrieved December 16, 2013. http://www.npr.org/templates/story/story.php?storyId=112485545.

Lipman, Masha. 2012. "What's behind the Russian Adoption Ban?" *New Yorker*, December 21. Retrieved May 7, 2015. http://www.newyorker.com/news/news-desk/whats-behind-the-russian-adoption-ban.

Llorca, Juan Carlos. 2006. "Hague Treaty Likely to Slow Guatemala Adoptions." Associated Press, July 29.

———. 2008. "To Save Adopted Daughter, Calif. Couple Gives Her Up." Associated Press, November 23.

———. 2009a. "Guatemala: Dirty War Orphans Put Up for Adoption." Associated Press, March 23.

———. 2009b. "U.S. Couple Almost Adopted Stolen Guatemalan Baby." Associated Press, December 31.

Louie, Andrea. 2015. *How Chinese Are You? Adopted Chinese Youth and Their Families Negotiate Identity and Culture*. New York: New York University Press.

Mackendrick, Norah. 2014. "More Work for Mother: Chemical Body Burdens as a Maternal Responsibility." *Gender and Society* 28 (5): 705–728.

Malacrida, Claudia, and Tiffany Boulton. 2012. "Women's Perceptions of Childbirth 'Choices': Competing Discourses of Motherhood, Sexuality, and Selflessness." *Gender and Society* 26 (5): 748–772.

Mannis, Valerie. 1999. "Single Mothers by Choice." *Family Relations* 48 (2): 121–128.

Manzi, Claudia, Laura Ferrari, Rosa Rosnati, and Veronica Benet-Martinez. 2014. "Bicultural Identity Integration of Transracial Adolescent Adoptees." *Journal of Cross-Cultural Psychology* 45 (6): 888–904.

Markens, Susan. 2007. *Surrogate Motherhood and the Politics of Reproduction*. Berkeley: University of California Press.

Marsh, Margaret, and Wanda Ronner. 1996. *Empty Cradle: Infertility in America from Colonial Times to the Present*. Baltimore: Johns Hopkins University Press.

Marsiglio, William, Paul Amato, Randal Day, and Michael Lamb. 2000. "Scholarship on Fatherhood in the 1990s and Beyond." *Journal of Marriage and Family* 62 (4): 1173–1191.

Martin, Lauren Jade. 2010. "Anticipating Infertility: Egg Freezing, Genetic Preservation, and Risk." *Gender and Society* 24 (4): 526–545.

Martin, Rachel. 2015. "Remembering the Doomed First Flight of Operation Babylift." *Weekend Edition Sunday*, produced by National Public Radio, April 26. Retrieved May 7, 2015. http://www.npr.org/2015/04/26/402208267/remembering-the-doomed-first-flight-of-operation-babylift.

Matthews, Bill. 2009. "Brad and Angelina Set to Adopt Two More Black Children." *Huffington Post*, June 11. Retrieved March 25, 2013. http://www.huffingtonpost.com/bill-matthews/brad-and-angelina-set-to_b_214350.html.

May, Elaine Tyler. 1997. *Barren in the Promised Land: Childless Americans and the Pursuit of Happiness*. Cambridge, Mass.: Harvard University Press.

———. 2008. *Homeward Bound: American Families in the Cold War Era*. New York: Basic Books.

McClintock, Anne. 1995. *Imperial Leather: Race, Gender, and Sexuality in the Colonial Contest*. New York: Routledge.

McNaughton, Darlene. 2011. "From the Womb to the Tomb: Obesity and Maternal Responsibility." In *Alcohol, Tobacco, and Obesity: Morality, Mortality, and the New Public Health*, edited by Kirsten Bell, Darlene McNaughton, and Amy Salmon, 163–176. New York: Routledge.

Melosh, Barbara. 2002. *Strangers and Kin: The American Way of Adoption*. Cambridge, Mass.: Harvard University Press.

Mintz, Steven. 2006. *Huck's Raft: A History of American Childhood*. New York: Belknap Press.

Misca, Gabriela. 2014. "The 'Quiet Migration': Is Intercountry Adoption a Successful Intervention in the Lives of Vulnerable Children?" *Family Court Review* 52 (1): 60–68.

Modell, Judith. 1994. *Kinship with Strangers: Adoption and Interpretations of Kinship in American Culture.* Berkeley: University of California Press.

Moore, Mignon, and Michael Stambolis-Ruhstorfer. 2013. "LGBT Sexuality and Families at the Start of the Twenty-First Century." *Annual Review of Sociology* 39 (1): 491–507.

Moritz, John. 2015. "'Operation Babylift' Kids, Soldiers Reunite 40 Years Later." Associated Press, April 25.

Mydans, Seth. 2001. "U.S. Interrupts Cambodian Adoptions." *New York Times*, November 5. Retrieved May 7, 2015. http://www.nytimes.com/2001/11/05/world/us-interrupts-cambodian-adoptions.html.

Myers, Caitlin. 2014. "Colonizing the (Reproductive) Future: The Discursive Construction of ARTs as Technologies of Self." *Frontiers: A Journal of Women's Studies* 35 (1): 73–106.

Nalavny, Blace, Laraine Glidden, and Scott Ryan. 2009. "Parental Satisfaction in the Adoption of Children with Learning Disorders: The Role of Behavior Problems." *Family Relations* 58 (5): 621–633.

Nash, Meredith. 2014. *Reframing Reproduction: Conceiving Gendered Experiences.* New York: Palgrave Macmillan.

National Indian Child Welfare Association. 2015. "Adoptive Couple vs. Baby Girl: Information and Resources." National Indian Child Welfare Association. Retrieved April 24, 2015. http://www.nicwa.org/babyveronica/.

Navarro, Mireya. 2008. "To Adopt, Please Press Hold." *New York Times*, June 5. Retrieved May 4, 2015. http://www.nytimes.com/2008/06/05/fashion/05adopt.html.

Nazworth, Napp. 2013. "Why Is Guatemala Blocking Americans from Adopting Its Orphans?" *Christian Post*, November 18. Retrieved May 4, 2015. http://www.christianpost.com/news/why-is-guatemala-blocking-americans-from-adopting-its-orphans-109006/.

Nelson, Diane. 1999. *A Finger in the Wound: Body Politics in Quincentennial Guatemala.* Berkeley: University of California Press.

Nelson, Margaret. 2010. *Parenting Out of Control: Anxious Parents in Uncertain Times.* New York: New York University Press.

Noonan, Emily. 2007. "Adoption and the Guatemalan Journey to American Parenthood." *Childhood* 14 (3): 301–391.

Ochs, Elinor, and Tamar Kremer-Sadlik, eds. 2013. *Fast-Forward Family: Home, Work, and Relationships in Middle-Class America.* Berkeley: University of California Press.

Office of Children's Issues. 2013. "FY 2012 Annual Report on Intercountry Adoption." Bureau of Consular Affairs, United States Department of State. Retrieved March 11, 2013. http://adoption.state.gov/content/pdf/fy2012_annual_report.pdf.

Office of Congresswoman Michelle Bachmann. 2013. "Bachmann, Bass Introduce Bipartisan Resolution Condemning Russian Ban on American Adoptions." Press release, January 15. Retrieved February 4, 2013. https://bachmann.house.gov/press-release/bachmann-bass-introduce-bipartisan-resolution-condemning-russian-ban-american.

O'Grady, Mary. 2014. "Guatemala's Stranded Orphans: UNICEF's Pressure to Stop International Adoptions Has Tragic Results." *Wall Street Journal*, January 26. Retrieved October 2, 2014. http://online.wsj.com/news/articles/SB10001424052702303947904579340613770603296.

Okie, Susan. 2009. "The Epidemic That Wasn't." *New York Times*, January 26. Retrieved April 26, 2015. http://www.nytimes.com/2009/01/27/health/27coca.html?pagewanted=all.

Omi, Michael, and Howard Winant. 1994. *Racial Formation in the United States from the 1960s to the 1990s.* New York: Routledge.

Ortiz, Ana, and Laura Briggs. 2003. "The Culture of Poverty, Crack Babies, and Welfare Cheats: The Making of the 'Healthy White Baby Crisis.'" *Social Text* 21 (3): 39–57.

Parreñas, Rhacel Salazar. 2001. *Servants of Globalization: Women, Migration, and Domestic Work.* Stanford, Calif.: Stanford University Press.

Patton-Imani, Sandra. 2002. "Redefining the Ethics of Adoption, Race, Gender, and Class." *Law and Society Review* 36 (4): 813–862.

Pertman, Adam. 2010. *Adoption Nation: How the Adoption Revolution Is Transforming Our Families—and America*. Cambridge, Mass.: Harvard Common Press.

Pew Research Center for Religion and Public Life. 2015. "America's Changing Religious Landscape." Pew Research Center. Retrieved January 27, 2019. http://www.pewforum.org/2015/05/12/americas-changing-religious-landscape/.

Pham, J. Peter. 2015. "No Exit: Congolese President Joseph Kabila Is Shamefully Preventing Adopted Children from Leaving the Country." *U.S. News and World Report*, September 4. Retrieved December 7, 2015. http://www.usnews.com/opinion/blogs/world-report/2015/09/04/congo-president-joseph-kabila-uses-adopted-children-as-pawns.

Pitts-Taylor, Victoria. 2010. "The Plastic Brain: Neoliberalism and the Neuronal Self." *Health* 14 (6): 635–652.

Quandango, Jill. 1996. *The Color of Welfare: How Racism Undermined the War on Poverty*. New York: Oxford University Press.

Quiroz, Pamela Anne. 2008. "From Race Matching to Transracial Adoption: Race and the Changing Discourse of U.S. Adoption." *Critical Discourse Studies* 5 (3): 249–264.

Raleigh, Elizabeth. 2012. "Are Same-Sex Couples and Single Adoptive Parents More Likely to Adopt Transracially? A National Analysis of Race, Family Structure, and the Adoption Marketplace." *Sociological Perspectives* 55 (3): 449–471.

Reich, Jennifer. 2005. *Fixing Families: Parents, Power, and the Child Welfare System*. New York: Routledge.

———. 2014. "Neoliberal Mothering and Vaccine Refusal: Imagined Gated Communities and the Privilege of Choice." *Gender and Society* 28 (5): 679–704.

Riben, Mirah. 2007. *The Stork Market: America's Multi-billion Dollar Unregulated Adoption Industry*. Dayton, N.J.: Advocate Publications.

———. 2015. "Adoption Criminality and Corruption." *Huffington Post*, January 14. Retrieved May 8, 2015. http://www.huffingtonpost.com/mirah-riben/adoption-crimes-and-corru_b_6467540.html.

Roberts, Dorothy. 1997. *Killing the Black Body: Race, Reproduction, and the Meaning of Liberty*. New York: Vintage.

———. 2002. *Shattered Bonds: The Color of Child Welfare*. New York: Basic Books.

———. 2009. "Race, Gender, and Genetic Technologies: A New Reproductive Dystopia?" *Signs* 34 (4): 783–804.

———. 2012. *Fatal Invention: How Science, Politics, and Big Business Re-create Race in the Twenty-First Century*. New York: New Press.

Roediger, David. 2007. *The Wages of Whiteness: Race and the Making of the American Working Class*. Rev. ed. New York: Verso.

Romo, Rafael. 2011. "Guatemalan Mother Says Daughter Kidnapped, Adopted in the U.S." CNN, August 16. Retrieved May 4, 2015. http://www.cnn.com/2011/WORLD/americas/08/15/guatemala.kidnapping.adoption/index.html.

Rosen, Eva. 2017. "Horizontal Immobility: How Narratives of Neighborhood Violence Shape Housing Decisions." *American Sociological Review* 82 (2): 270–296.

Rotabi, Karen. 2010a. "Vulnerable Children in the Aftermath of Haiti's Earthquake." *Journal of Global Social Work Practice* 3 (1). https://doi.org/10.1177/030857591103500405.

———. 2010b. "Commentary on Russian Child Adoption Incidents: Implications for Global Policy and Practice." *Journal of Global Social Work Practice* 3 (2). https://doi.org/10.1177/2158244011428160.

———. 2012. "Fraud in Intercountry Adoption: Child Sales and Abduction in Vietnam, Cambodia, and Guatemala." In *Intercountry Adoption: Policies, Practices, and Outcomes*, edited by J. L. Gibbons and Karen Rotabi, 67–76. Surrey, UK: Ashgate.

Rotabi, Karen, Lucy Armistead, and Carmen Mónico. 2015. "Sanctioned Government Intervention, 'Misguided Kindness,' and Child Abduction Activities of U.S. Citizens in the Midst of Disaster: Haiti's Past and Its Future as a Nation Subscribed to the Hague

Convention on Intercountry Adoption." In *The Intercountry Adoption Debate: Dialogues across Disciplines*, edited by Robert L. Ballard, Robert F. Cochran, Naomi H. Goodno, and Jay Milbrandt, 629–650. Newcastle upon Tyne, UK: Cambridge Scholars.

Rotabi, Karen, and Kelley McCreery Bunkers. 2011. "In an Era of Reform: A Review of Social Work Literature on Intercountry Adoption." *SAGE Open* 1 (3): 1–16.

Rothman, Barbara Katz. 1989. *Recreating Motherhood*. New Brunswick, N.J.: Rutgers University Press.

———. 2005. *Weaving a Family: Untangling Race and Adoption*. Boston: Beacon Press.

Ruddick, Sara. 1995. *Maternal Thinking: Towards a Politics of Peace*. Boston: Beacon Press.

Samuels, Gina, and Ralph LaRossa. 2009. "'Being Raised by White People': Navigating Racial Difference among Adopted Multiracial Adults." *Journal of Marriage and Family* 71 (1): 80–94.

Scheper-Hughes, Nancy. 2004. "Parts Unknown: Undercover Ethnography of the Organs-Trafficking Underworld." *Ethnography* 5 (1): 29–73.

Scheper-Hughes, Nancy, and Loïc Wacquant, eds. 2002. *Commodifying Bodies*. London: Sage.

Schneider, Barbara, and Linda Waite. 2005. "Why Study Working Families?" In *Being Together, Working Apart: Dual-Career Families and the Work-Life Balance*, edited by Barbara Schneider and Linda Waite, 3–17. New York: Cambridge University Press.

Schwartzchild, Todd. 2013. "Red Flags Wave over Uganda's Adoption Boom." CNN, March 2. Retrieved May 8, 2015. http://www.cnn.com/2013/02/27/world/africa/wus-uganda-adoptions/.

Schwartzwald, Heidi, Elizabeth Montgomery Collins, Susan Gillespie, and Adiaha Spinks-Franklin. 2015. *International Adoption and Clinical Practice*. New York: Springer.

Seligman, Linda. 2013. *Broken Links: Enduring Ties: American Adoption across Race, Class, and Nation*. Stanford, Calif.: Stanford University Press.

Selman, Peter. 2007. "The Diaper Diaspora." *Foreign Policy*, January/February, 32–40.

———. 2009a. "The Movement of Children for International Adoption." In *International Adoption: Global Inequalities and the Circulation of Children*, edited by Diana Marre and Laura Briggs, 32–51. New York: New York University Press.

———. 2009b. "The Rise and Fall of Intercountry Adoption in the 21st Century." *International Social Work* 52 (5): 575–594.

Shiao, Jiannbin, and Mia Tuan. 2008. "Korean Adoptees and the Social Context of Ethnic Exploration." *American Journal of Sociology* 113 (4): 1023–1066.

Siegel, Deborah. 2013. "Adoption Competency in Clinical Social Work." *Social Work Today* 13 (6): 16–20.

Smock, Pamela, and Fiona Greenland. 2010. "Diversity in Pathways to Parenthood: Patterns, Implications, and Emerging Research Directions." *Journal of Marriage and Family* 72 (3): 576–593.

Smolin, David. 2005. "Intercountry Adoption as Child Trafficking." *Valparaiso Law Review* 39 (2): 281–325.

———. 2006. "Child Laundering: How the Intercountry Adoption System Legitimizes and Incentivizes the Practices of Buying, Trafficking, Kidnapping, and Stealing Children." *Wayne Law Review* 52 (1): 113–200.

———. 2010. "Child Laundering and the Hague Convention on Intercountry Adoption: The Future and Past of Intercountry Adoption." *University of Louisville Law Review* 48 (3): 441–498.

———. 2013. "The Corrupting Influence of the United States on a Vulnerable Intercountry Adoption System: A Guide for Stakeholders, Hague and Non-Hague Nations, NGOs, and Concerned Parties." *Journal of Law & Family Studies* 15 (4): 1065–1135.

———. 2015. "Can the Center Hold? The Vulnerabilities of the Official Legal Regimen for Intercountry Adoption." In *The Intercountry Adoption Debate: Dialogues across Disciplines*, edited by Robert L. Ballard, Robert F. Cochran, Naomi H. Goodno, and Jay Milbrandt, 245–276. Newcastle upon Tyne, UK: Cambridge Scholars.

Solinger, Rickie. 2002. *Beggars and Choosers: How the Politics of Choice Affects Adoption, Abortion, and Welfare in the United States*. New York: Hill and Wang.

Spar, Debora. 2006. *The Baby Business: How Money, Science, and Politics Drive the Commerce of Conception*. Boston: Harvard Business School Press.

———. 2013. *Wonder Woman: Sex, Power, and the Quest for Perfection*. New York: Sarah Crichton Books.

Spar, Debora, and Anna Harrington. 2009. "Building a Better Baby Business." *Minnesota Journal of Law, Science, and Technology* 10 (1): 41–69.

Stacey, Judith. 1996. *Brave New Families: Stories of Domestic Upheaval in Late-Twentieth-Century America*. Berkeley: University of California Press.

———. 2006. "Gay Parenthood and the Decline of Paternity as We Knew It." *Sexualities* 9 (1): 27–55.

Stein, Arlene. 1997. *Sex and Sensibility: Stories of a Lesbian Generation*. Berkeley: University of California Press.

Steinberg, Stephen. 1981. *The Ethnic Myth: Race, Ethnicity, and Class in America*. Boston: Beacon Press.

Stone, Pamela. 2007. *Opting Out? Why Women Really Quit Careers and Head Home*. Berkeley: University of California Press.

Sullivan, Meghan. 2012. "For Romania's Orphans, Adoption Is Still a Rarity." National Public Radio, August 19. Retrieved May 6, 2015. http://www.npr.org/2012/08/19/158924764/for -romanias-orphans-adoption-is-still-a-rarity.

———. 2013. "Painful Lessons from Romania's Decade-Old Adoption Ban." *Time*, March 15. Retrieved May 6, 2015. http://world.time.com/2013/03/15/painful-lessons-from-romanias -decade-old-adoption-ban/.

Sweeny, Kathryn. 2013. "Race-Conscious Adoption Choices, Multiraciality, and Color-Blind Racial Ideology." *Family Relations* 62:42–57.

Tenney, Garrett. 2013. "Missouri Family Takes in Orphaned Peruvian Siblings after Learning Email Was No Scam." Fox News, January 27. Retrieved February 6, 2013. http://www .foxnews.com/us/2013/01/'27/missouri-family-takes-in-orphaned-siblings-from-peru -after-learning-email-was/.

Thompson, Ginger. 2010. "After Haiti Quake, the Chaos of U.S. Adoptions." *New York Times*, August 3. Retrieved May 8, 2015. http://www.nytimes.com/2010/08/04/world/americas/ 04adoption.html.

Tran, My-Thuan. 2008. "Children of Vietnam War Servicemen Seek U.S. Citizenship." *Los Angeles Times*, October 10. Retrieved May 7, 2015. http://www.latimes.com/local/la-me -amerasians10-2008oct10-story.html#page=1.

Trask, Bahira. 2013. "Locating Multiethnic Families in a Globalizing World." *Family Relations* 62 (1): 17–29.

Twine, France Winddance. 2011. *Outsourcing the Womb: Race, Class, and Gestational Surrogacy in a Global Market*. New York: Routledge.

Twohey, Megan. 2013. "The Child Exchange: Inside America's Underground Market for Adopted Children." Reuters, September 9. Retrieved May 8, 2015. http://www.reuters.com/ investigates/adoption/#article/part1.

Under Secretary for Public Diplomacy and Public Affairs. 2010a. "Secretary Clinton Designates Special Advisor for International Children's Issues." United States Department of State, July 1. Retrieved May 4, 2015. http://www.state.gov/r/pa/prs/ps/2010/07/143892.htm.

———. 2010b. "Special Advisor for Children's Issues Ambassador Susan Jacobs to Travel to Guatemala." United States Department of State, December 6. Retrieved February 8, 2011. http://www.state.gov/r/pa/prs/ps/2010/12/152441.htm.

UNICEF, UNAIDS, and USAID. 2004. "Children on the Brink: A Joint Report of New Orphan Estimates and a Framework for Action." USAID. Retrieved May 26, 2015. www .unicef.org/publications/index_22212.html.

United States Citizenship and Immigration Services. 2015. "Adoption Information: Democratic Republic of Congo." United States Department of Homeland Security. Retrieved December 7, 2015. http://www.uscis.gov/adoption/country-information/adoption-information-democratic-republic-congo-drc.

Valdez, S., R. González, and G. Contreras. 2011. "Senadora sugiere abrir procesos de adopción externa." *Prensa Libre*, April 26. Retrieved April 28, 2011. http://www.prensalibre.com/noticias/Senadora-sugiere-procesos-adopcion-externa_0_469753053.html.

Vincent, Carol, and Steven J. Ball. 2007. "'Making Up' the Middle-Class Child: Families, Activities, and Class Dispositions." *Sociology* 41 (6): 1061–1077.

Voigt, Kevin. 2013. "International Adoption: Saving Orphans or Child Trafficking?" CNN, September 18. Retrieved October 2, 2014. http://www.cnn.com/2013/09/16/world/international-adoption-saving-orphans-child-trafficking/.

Voigt, Kevin, and Sophie Brown. 2013. "International Adoptions in Decline as Number of Orphans Grows." CNN, September 17. Retrieved May 7, 2015. http://www.cnn.com/2013/09/16/world/international-adoption-main-story-decline/.

Wall, Glenda. 2001. "Moral Constructions of Motherhood in Breastfeeding Discourse." *Gender and Society* 15 (4): 592–610.

———. 2010. "Mothers' Experience with Intensive Parenting and Brain Development Discourse." *Women's Studies International Forum* 33 (3): 253–263.

Wall, Glenda, and Stephanie Arnold. 2007. "How Involved Is Involved Fathering? An Exploration of the Contemporary Culture of Fatherhood." *Gender and Society* 21 (4): 508–527.

Wang, Wendy. 2012. *The Rise of Intermarriage: Rates, Characteristics Vary by Race and Gender.* Pew Research Center Social and Demographic Trends, February. Washington, D.C.: Pew Research Center.

Waters, Mary. 1999. *Black Identities: West Indian Immigrant Dreams and American Realities.* Cambridge, Mass.: Harvard University Press.

Wexler, Martha. 2012. "In Contentious System, Hope for a Russian Orphan." *Weekend Edition Sunday*, produced by National Public Radio, March 25. Retrieved March 22, 2013. http://www.npr.org/2012/03/25/149319484/incontentious-system-hope-for-a-russian-orphan.

Williams, Joan. 2012. *Reshaping the Work-Family Debate: Why Men and Class Matter.* Cambridge, Mass.: Harvard University Press.

Wilson, Kristin. 2014. *Not Trying: Infertility, Childlessness, and Ambivalence.* Nashville: Vanderbilt University Press.

Wolf, Joan. 2010. *Is Breast Best? Taking on the Breastfeeding Experts and the New High Stakes of Motherhood.* New York: New York University Press.

Wrobel, Gretchen, and Elisabeth Neil, eds. 2009. *International Advances in Adoption Research for Practice.* Malden, Mass.: Wiley-Blackwell.

Yancey, George. 2003. *Who Is White? Latinos, Asians, and the New Black/Nonblack Divide.* Boulder: Lynne Rienner.

Zelizer, Viviana. 1985. *Pricing the Priceless Child: The Changing Social Value of Children.* Princeton, N.J.: Princeton University Press.

———. 2007. *The Purchase of Intimacy.* Princeton, N.J.: Princeton University Press.

———. 2010. "Risky Exchanges." In *Baby Markets: Money and the New Politics of Creating Families*, edited by Michele Bratcher Goodwin, 267–277. New York: Cambridge University Press.

———. 2013. *Economic Lives: How Culture Shapes the Economy.* Princeton, N.J.: Princeton University Press.

Zerubavel, Eviatar. 2012. *Ancestors and Relatives: Genealogy, Identity, and Community.* New York: Oxford University Press.

Zhang, Yuanting, and Gary R. Lee. 2011. "Intercountry versus Transracial Adoption: Analysis of Adoptive Parents' Motivations and Preferences in Adoption." *Journal of Family Issues* 32 (1): 75–98.

Index

About the Author

ESTYE FENTON is an assistant professor of sociology at the University of West Alabama.